the sensation of being somebody

Books by this author —

the sensation of being somebody

BUILDING AN ADEQUATE SELF-CONCEPT

Maurice E. Wagner

ZONDERVAN PUBLISHING HOUSE

OF THE ZONDERVAN CORPORATION
GRAND RAPIDS, MICHIGAN 49506

THE SENSATION OF BEING SOMEBODY

Copyright © 1975 by Maurice E. Wagner
Published by The Zondervan Corporation
Grand Rapids, Michigan

LIBRARY OF CONGRESS CATALOG CARD NUMBER: 74-25350

The *King James Version* of the Bible is used except when another version is indicated. The *Revised Standard Version* is copyright © 1946, 1952 by the Division of Christian Education of the National Council of Churches of Christ in the United States of America.

PRINTED IN THE UNITED STATES OF AMERICA

83 84 85 86 87 88 / 16 15 14 13 12

*This book is dedicated
to my three children and
six grandchildren who each
in turn has made unwittingly
a living contribution to my
understanding of the developmental
factors in the unfolding of self-concept.*

contents

PART TWO — HOW WE BECAME WHAT WE ARE

Self-concept factors in the development of a child from conception to adulthood; Environmental influences upon emotional development; False security factors within self-concept structure.

*problem; Faith in God provides elements needed
for development; Faith is fundamental to hope and
love; How faith in God closes the separation gap.*

*A. In our perception of the situation: The heart
cries for the absolute; True security available by
accepting the absolute; God's one great frustration; Faith in God permeates the relative with the
absolute.
B. In the functioning of the inner self: Man has a
privilege of choice with responsibility.*

*Spiritual premise gives new equation to self-
identity; Relate to God the Father, validate belongingness; Relate to God the Son, validate
worthiness; Relate to God the Holy Spirit, validate competence; Reorient by obeying the first
great commandment.*

*God's design for relationships; Relationships can
be peer in quality; Basic fear of people abated by
love; Relationships are triangular, but seem
linear; Relationships provide an island of security.*

*The tendency to treat people as things; The ten-
dency to resent unpleasant circumstances; The
tendency to resent loss of control; The tendency to
resent humiliating happenings; The tendency to
give up when proven wrong; The tendency to be
paralyzed when fearful; The tendency to dread
problems; The tendency to be unforgiving.*

*Natural origins of selfism; A few telltales to self-
ism; Dynamic factor in selfism; Selfism in the*

foreword

As I had the opportunity to read *The Sensation of Being Somebody,* my reaction of both delight and relief came because of discovering a work that would speak to the specific needs of so many with whom I counsel. At the heart of many individual and marital problems is an inadequate self-concept, and the resources available to solve this need have not been abundant. Laymen, ministers, and professional counselors will find this volume a practical resource that will minister directly and practically to one of today's greatest needs.

Maurice Wagner is a man whose ministry centers in the healing of lives spiritually and psychologically by moving to the source of individuals' difficulties with the only lasting answer available. This book is an outgrowth of his experience and sensitivity to the lives of people within his pastorates and private practice and reflects deep insights and capabilities.

It is rare that one can discover a book with an adequate blending of Scripture, theology, and psychology, but Dr. Wagner has developed that unique talent of doing so and remaining true and accurate to all areas. A reader cannot help but grasp the simple yet complete discussion of the development of self-concept as developed here, but Dr. Wagner goes further in illustrating thoroughly how the three elements of belongingness, worthiness, and competence form the three pillars of self-concept.

A relationship to Jesus Christ and a life of faith are paramount to a healthy self-concept, and these thoughts are not just presented, but are developed practically.

I count it a privilege to have read this second of Dr. Wagner's works, and as I have been blessed and encouraged I trust that you, the reader, will be enriched as you read and apply these thoughts.

H. Norman Wright
Associate Professor of Psychology
Biola College, La Mirada, Calif.

preface

An adequate self-concept is a precious possession. It is the premise upon which a person can devote himself wholeheartedly to living a useful and productive life. It prepares the mind to think clearly so that a person can be at his best, enables him to concentrate upon definite goals, and motivates him to a complete commitment to the task at hand.

An inadequate self-concept is a handicap. It affords no premise upon which a person can give himself completely to what he wants to do. It provides no cohesive for the various forces of the mind so that an inner wholeness can be realized, and it binds a person under the tyranny of having to measure up in some way in order to feel accepted.

Persons with an inadequate self-concept spend much attention, time, and energy trying to establish a secure premise of self-identity in each situation instead of being able to function because they already have such a premise. Some people are so completely preoccupied with feelings of being a nobody, in a world of people who seem to them to be more or less stable somebodies, that they can scarcely apply themselves to any certain task. Anxiety over possible failures and rejections and humiliations allows them no place to rest from their labors or to take pleasure from their efforts and accomplishments or to build an abiding confidence in the goodness of life.

My concern in writing this book is to explain the dynamics of self-concept with both a degree of simplicity and a practical thoroughness. It is my hope that those who feel they are deficient in self-concept may realize more accurately why they feel as they do about themselves and what they might do to improve their own sense of being somebody.

The early chapters discuss the development of self-concept from infancy. Toward the middle of the book the discussion points up various illusive devices of self-deception we all tend to practice in some degree to obtain inner security. It seems necessary to me to elaborate upon the natural inclinations of our thinking and the various life styles which develop in order to point up with clarity the need for a spiritual dimension in our thinking.

After explaining in some detail the human dilemma regarding self-concept, I introduce the biblical concepts regarding the subject. The spiritual dimension of relating to God in childlike faith, added to the quest for a more adequate self-concept, brings to the person a true sense of being somebody. This self-concept is based upon objective truths and principles as well as upon the subjective aspects of faith and relationship with God whom we do not see. The latter part of the book offers many practical applications of the gospel of saving grace to problems of inner security and a stable self-concept.

Before the book is used as a reference, it should be read through to obtain the overall message. If this is done, the practical applications of the insights suggested are more likely to be meaningful.

Illustrations are given of real experiences of various people, but the names and identifying facts have been slightly altered to protect the identity of the persons involved.

Parents who read the earlier chapters may be encouraged to love each other and their children more as they realize the crippling effects of unloving relationships. They will probably find suggestions in the later chapters on how this might be accomplished. Young people who are looking forward to marriage and establishing their own homes may be inspired to establish ideals and priorities that will insure happiness. Students of psychology will observe insights helpful to their understanding of the nature of man and how faith in God and the Bible can have a most helpful influence upon mental health. Pastors and others who counsel people in distress should find this and its companion volume, *Put It All Together – Developing Inner Security,* of practical value.

We are aware that there are definite limitations to the therapeutic value an emotionally disturbed person can derive from reading a book, yet experience has proven that a discussion of insights leading to self-understanding can be very helpful. This is especially true when those insights direct the person to the Word of God to find there the divine truth which applies to his particular deficiency. I trust many who are unable to find in their community someone with whom they can counsel on a professional level, as well as many who are in a program of psychotherapy, will find the pages here both encouraging and informative.

Part 1

What We Are

A brief look at our present way of thinking about ourselves. What our basic self-identity needs actually are. Outline of mental processes for accomplishing an adequate self-concept.

1

The Illusive Image Called Self

Marlene peered intently at her oval mirror. She turned her head to the right and to the left, held the mirror at arm's length and then up close. She couldn't find what she was looking for. She laid the hand mirror down and went to the wall mirror. Finally she tried both mirrors.

I watched her for several minutes. She noticed I was watching, but didn't seem to mind. At length I interrupted her concentration. "What are you trying to find?" I asked.

"I'm trying to see myself" was her matter-of-fact reply, scarcely looking toward me as she talked.

"Trying to see yourself," I echoed flatly, pondering what she actually meant.

"Yes, I'm trying to see myself. No matter how I hold these mirrors, I can't be sure how I really look. I just can't make it work!" She turned toward me with distress in her face.

"Can't make it work?" I echoed again, hoping she would tell me more.

"I want to be the person in the mirror I see looking at me, but I can't make it work," she explained.

"If you were the person in the mirror and you were looking at yourself, what would you see?" I asked.

"Don't you know?" she inquired a little puzzled. "I'd

see what others see when they look at me."

"Then you could tell who you really are," I added.

"Yes, of course!" she declared as though I should have known what she was trying to do. "But I can't get inside the mirror! If only I could be the person I see looking at me, I know I could find who I am."

Marlene was a patient in a neuropsychiatric hospital where I was a chaplain. Her intense need to feel like a person of value contributed to her mental illness. She was trying to use mirrors to discover some tangible evidence that she was an acceptable person. Instead of verifying herself in wholesome relationships with people, she was looking for herself in a mirror.

Many people who have never been treated for mental illness — and probably never will be — also have difficulty sensing their value as persons. Being troubled about one's identity does not imply mental illness, but it does indicate the possibility of emotional insecurity.

In the conceptual matrix of our minds is a fog-shrouded image of self. We want to know that self, and we keep brushing the mists away to define the lines of that image. Now and then the sense of self emerges, but usually it completely eludes definition.

Three Questions Define Awareness of Self

Three questions frequent our thinking: "Who am I?" "What am I?" "Why am I?" These questions define our awareness of self.

The "Who am I?" question points to marks of identification which distinguish us from other people. Our name is a mark of identification. When asked who we are, we usually give our name. Our height, size, weight, sex, coloring, nationality, skills, and accomplishments all serve to identify us. These factors define our sense of being an individual.

The "What am I?" question points to our label among people. Sometimes the answer is "I am a husband," "I am a wife," "I am single." Other times we answer, "I am a teacher," "I am a businessman," "I am an attorney." The question also can draw attention to how we rate: good or bad, average or poor, valuable or worthless, superior or inferior.

The "Why am I?" question points to our reason for living. We are thinking of goals and motives when we ask this kind of question. "I cannot function unless I have a goal or a reason for doing it," Jean said.

We all are so constituted that we need to be assured our

lives count for something worthwhile. We ask such questions as "Why am I here?" "Why am I doing this?" "Why was I born?" "Why did it happen to me?" We want to know that we count, that our effort and discipline and sacrifice have value. Otherwise we have foolishly spent ourselves for nothing, and this implies failure and uselessness.

The answer to these Who, What, and Why questions seems always to lack a feeling of specific conclusiveness. We grope at times for a better answer. We want to know ourselves more definitely.

Gary was obese. He had applied at three medical schools and was turned down at each. He was a good student, and he passed his qualifying exams with high scores. When he corresponded with the schools, he felt encouraged; but when he went for a personal interview, he was turned down. One examiner was kind enough to explain, "When you've lost a hundred pounds, you might have a good chance of getting accepted."

Gary had tried to reduce before, but now he had to. He knew *who* he was — no question about that. He knew *what* he was — a good student, but "too fat!" He couldn't be completely sure of *why* it all had to happen. Was it only for a better health and longer life? Or was it so he could identify with obese people? Or perhaps was it an indicator he should someday specialize in weight reduction?

If we are thinking straight, we usually are fairly clear about *who* we are. We have more trouble being completely satisfied with our answer to the *what* question. We have achieved many skills and we can give labels, such as "student" or "worker" or "boss" or "the owner"; no single label really says it all. The *why* question is usually most difficult. We have immediate goals and long-range goals. Then there is the possibility of the unknown goal that may seem superimposed upon our plans by God. We are especially aware of this unknown reason for living when we are suddenly faced with some overwhelming situation over which we have no immediate control.

Everyone Has Some Opinion of Himself

We occasionally hear in conversation, "That's the way I am." This kind of remark is used to explain a style of behavior, or it is used in a defensive way to avoid responsibility. As an illustration of the former, we will listen to Leonard describe his garage workshop: "I keep everything in place. I have hooks on the wall with painted outlines for all my tools; nothing lays around. When I use something, I always put it back in its place. That's the way I am."

To illustrate how this remark is used to avoid responsibility, we speak of Elsie. She declared, "When someone crosses me, I go into a blind rage and start pounding on someone. That's the way I am."

The point is, we may not believe we have a clear opinion of ourselves, but usually we are acquainted well enough with ourselves to explain how we do things or how we usually feel about things.

Self-concept is that image we all have of ourselves. It is a mental picture of our self-identity. Self-identity is the "I am" feeling of being a person. Self-concept is fabricated through the years by an assortment of experiences. Some of these experiences have been forgotten long ago; nevertheless, they still influence our thinking and feeling regarding ourselves. Self-concept is the sense of being somebody.

Self-Concept Is Constituted by Many Memories

It is probably accurate to assume that the unconscious mind never forgets an experience. The mind may not have the capacity for immediate recall, but the memory is still there. With a different context of associations, we are surprised by how clearly we can recall incidents we thought we had completely forgotten.

Almost everyone has many memories of situations in which he rated highly as a valuable person. Perhaps he was somewhat the hero. There are other memories not so pleasant to recall of occasions when he was painfully humiliated and emotionally crushed. Memories, good and bad, congregate in the mind to influence one's present self-concept.

Alma seldom recalled anything but bad memories. She worked hard as a student at the local university. She dressed neatly in colorful clothes appropriate for the occasion, but Alma didn't seem to feel comfortable in her clothes. She frequently made adjustments, pinching some inside garment now and then to make her clothes feel better. For her, walking seemed to be a continual choice between long and short steps. Sitting presented a restless crossing and un-crossing of legs, a tucking-in to cover possible exposure, an uneasiness that didn't fit the occasion. Naturally Alma was vulnerable to comments others made about her appearance. Compliments embarrassed her; criticism debased her.

"I always wonder what people really think," she told me. "I don't expect people to like me." When Alma became sufficiently acquainted with me to share more of her true feelings, she said, "I'm never sure if I am acceptable or not. When I was small, my mother criticized me and compared me with other girls, always in a bad way. I never could please her. She'd surely find something wrong with my clothes or my looks. My older sister also chimed in with her big mouth. She was so caustic and cruel. I could never dress right!''

''What about your father?'' I inquired. ''Did he ever reassure you?''

''No. Dad was too busy to notice things at home. He came home only to eat and to sleep. I never got to know my dad. He died last year from a heart attack. I don't think he ever talked to me personally about anything. He just wanted us kids to stay out of his way. I guess he was doing his part earning our living, but I often wish he'd had time to notice me.''

Alma's self-concept was like a big question mark, most of the time pointing toward zero or a minus quantity. She did what she could to feel proper and presentable, but she seldom felt sure of herself. She had nothing in her library of memories to reassure her or make her feel comfortable about herself. Instead she had a host of memories telling her she might not be right.

Sometimes people with a poor self-concept prefer to write out their feelings so that their counselor can understand more clearly the inner turmoil they are experiencing. One attractive young lady wrote me the following about how she regards herself and her body. She titled it, ''The Little Girl in the Pretty House.''

''Someone paused today to tell me that I should get to know that little girl who lives in my pretty house.

''Little girl — very immature and obscure at this time! Obscure because I must not look for a face — she has none; immature because she hasn't had the chance to venture outside into the sunshine of acceptance. She was forced into absentia long ago. The identity she holds is the pretty house in which she lives. Looking closely, you will see her pretty face and body from the yard. Her soul and reason for being lives behind the bolted door. I should like to get to know her, but the door is tightly bolted. I am afraid to know this little girl because I know her only by her house. She would be strange to me and frightening. People who love her say that this child should be known and exposed!

''I enjoy keeping the house painted and trim. People walk by and look her way — we must keep our house lovely. This is safety for us.

''Don't call me naive, for I know I must! Given twenty years, the paint will not cover the wrinkles and cracks, and the building will sag a bit. Lord! What shall I do then? What would remain that would be attractive? The girl inside? She may have died by then.

''God in heaven, no one is as frightened as I. Who will

provide the key? What will I find? Will I accept her and love her? No, no one is more afraid than I — for I am her caretaker. Others may reject this exposed child; some may love her, some may hate her, but I must live with her forever!''

Self-Concept Can Be Improved

Even though self-concept is an illusive image of self, and probably not so adequate as we would like it to be, we can improve it as we gain new insights and work to overcome self-defeating patterns of thinking. The bad memories which influence us to think poorly of ourselves can be disarmed of their controlling power. Our fundamental interpretation of how we rate as a person can be changed.

The book is devoted to a general understanding of self-concept. It discusses certain basic, but relatively simple, principles of life which affect self-concept. The concluding chapters offer practical suggestions for putting this knowledge into practice. Suggestions are also made for maintaining the growth in self-concept after a person has sensed an improvement.

2

More Biased Than We Think

Self-concept exerts a controlling influence on the mind. People think unrealistically about themselves because self-concept is malformed. A person's opinion of himself seriously biases his interpretation of what is happening. All people want the admiration of others, but because of a malformed self-concept they will rigidly contradict the opinions others express about them.

"I'm not pretty"

Gloria's husband delighted in his wife's petite figure. He enjoyed buying her stylish and attractive clothes. Often he spoke of her beauty in honeyed words. Gloria tried to accept his loving admiration, but she felt only flattered. Occasionally she rebuked him by saying, "What you say sounds nice, but I don't believe a word."

This attitude frustrated her husband. Everyone knew how pretty she was, and he knew how attractive she was to him. He often wondered why she could not just accept his feelings at face value. He became especially frustrated when she would accuse him, "You're just flattering me! I know how I look. I have a mirror. Why can't you just love me for me?"

Gloria had a preconceived opinion of how she looked. No amount of sweet talk from her husband could change her mind. She liked his admiration, and she liked to believe she was attractive to him, but she could not accept his sincere compliments. Her self-concept wouldn't let her.

"Beauty is as beauty does"

Delphia told me that flattering compliments bothered her because she knew they weren't so. "My mother told me," she reported, "that 'beauty is as beauty does' whenever anyone would tell me I was pretty. She never told me I did nicely. I know I make mistakes. So I can't feel pretty."

"I am fat"

Mabel was 5'11", unusually slender, with fleshless limbs. She told me she hated mirrors, for they only reminded her of how fat she had become. "You fat!" I exclaimed in surprise. "I find that hard to believe."

"There's only one part of me I think is halfway acceptable, and that is my hair — when it is fixed," she explained. "Otherwise I feel bulgy and fat."

Mabel was not a mental patient — and probably will never become one — but she has spent many years viewing herself in this most unrealistic manner. Regardless of what others tell her, she insists on believing the same about herself. She has an "I am fat" self-concept.

"I am stupid"

Phillip was an electrical engineer with unusual capabilities. He told me, "I've always got to show the other fellows up to prove to myself that I am not stupid. It makes some people mighty mad at me. I know they'd like to kill me. I enjoy showing up other so-called engineers for their stupidities and getting them fired."

Phillip succeeded in embarrassing and humiliating many colleagues, for his mental skills were phenomenal. He told me he was rated "dumb" and "stupid" during his first four grades. His mother, he said, always called him stupid. His father and mother were divorced.

His fifth-grade teacher scolded his mother for rating Phillip stupid, but it didn't change his mother's attitude. "He's a very bright boy," the teacher assured his mother. From that time on, the teacher took personal interest in him. She discovered that Phillip was totally bored with school; the work seemed elementary to him. With a little encouragement he was reading seventh- and eighth-grade material with comprehension. He never did go beyond high school, but in his vocation he competed with college graduates who had advanced degrees.

Phillip's critical and competitive attitude cost him many jobs, but he always seemed to find another. One employer required an intelligence test of all applicants. He could not believe Phillip's score, so he asked him to take it again. It was 168 at the first testing and 170 at the second! Phillip measured a genius quality of intelligence.

Why did Phillip feel he was stupid? His mother had told him he was, when he was young and impressionable. Why did he have to show other engineers how stupid they were? He was unconsciously putting down his mother and vindicating his own sense of intelligence. Even though Phillip knew he was not stupid, his self-concept told him he was, and this conflict kept him fighting with people.

"I'm no good"

Gerald was a good worker: prompt, reliable, and productive. His employer was happy to have him on the job. But Gerald felt he could be replaced at any time by anybody. He could not accept praise for his efforts.

"My father was supercritical of me when I was a child," he recalled. "I could never please him, though I never ceased to try. If I ever did do anything he approved of, he'd only say, 'You can do better than that,' or say nothing at all. When I was eight or ten, I begged dad for just one compliment. He'd reply, 'I don't want you to get the big head. I don't care how well you do something, you can do it better next time. Now stop bothering me.'

"Now that I am older," Gerald continued, "I try to do better. I can't stop feeling like a failure and as if I am no good. Do you suppose it's because my dad always criticized me?"

"I am defective"

Few of Beatrice's friends knew she had had polio when she was a child. Though one limb was slightly smaller than the other, few noticed her trivial limp. But the limp was not trivial to Beatrice. She felt defective because of her misfortune. She liked to hear how nice she looked, but secretly she believed it was probably said because people were being sympathetic. She hated people's sympathy, for that only emphasized that she was defective. Beatrice was an attractive person, but she could not accept the truth about herself. She unrealistically felt defensive over the possibility of appearing deformed or defective.

"I always fail"

Ben was a hard worker, but he usually failed at whatever he attempted to do. He spent three years trying to pass his freshman subjects in college. He never tackled a project expecting to succeed as people normally do. Ben seldom started anything he was not familiar with, for he knew as he started he would chalk up another failure — and he usually did! His self-concept pictured to his mind that he would fail whenever he did something. For most people, their minds visualize their completing a project with success, and this helps them to succeed.

This man was bound like a slave to his self-concept of failure. The thought of succeeding actually frightened him, for he said he would not know how to act.

Ben recalled remarks his parents made about him when he was a child: "Ben can't do anything." "Ben never finishes anything he starts." "Ben's going to be a failure when he grows up. He'll never amount to anything." Ben could not recall that his parents ever instructed him about how to do a job correctly. He said he only felt criticized for failing to get the job done.

I am happy that Ben worked through his problem and developed a much better self-concept. He finally finished college, received his master's degree, and is now succeeding in a professional vocation.

"I can't stand to fail"

Art would not enter into a game where he had to compete with others. He usually tried to capture the attention of his friends by some new joke or a shocking bit of news. He felt threatened by competition. "In my mind, I think I'm better than everyone else. If I should enter a game, I would surely win," he explained. "But when I actually try to play, I get anxious and confused and lose. I can't stand to feel a failure. I guess I'd rather not play and just believe I could win if I did." Art had a "never failing" self-concept, but he had to think unrealistically to maintain his grandiose opinion of himself.

What About Your *Self-Concept?*

Do people frequently seem to contradict your opinion of yourself? Do they tell you you are better looking than you feel you are? Do they seem not to notice you when you feel more attractive than others present? Can you accept your appearance as it is and not fuss about it?

What about your performance? Do you drive yourself, meticulously watching for every flaw so you can become more nearly perfect? Do you have a secret feeling of superiority? When you talk to people, do you customarily talk down to them or up to them or enjoy the feeling of equality?

These are a few of the questions that relate to an inadequate self-concept. This list is not complete, but it should stimulate some introspective thinking.

3

Take A Good Look at Yourself

Imagine for a minute holding a snapshot in your hand. The picture you see is two-dimensional because it is on a flat surface. The idea of a third dimension of depth is implied by the shading and by the way objects vary in size according to their distance from the camera. A snapshot is a representation of some real object that has length and width and height. As we look at the snapshot, we form a mental image of the object that has been photographed.

A snapshot freezes a situation into a fixed representation, a still picture. A mental image is not a still picture; in many ways it is not like a snapshot. A mental picture, or concept, can depict motion, the passing of time, relative values, feelings, relationships, direction, and moods. Mental pictures are subjective impressions of the mind, and they are very much a part of our thinking processes.

A snapshot is a picture that represents an object having three dimensions. Self-concept is a mental picture that represents a person's opinion of himself. This image in the mind has three distinct functional aspects which might be considered like dimensions or sides. Each of these aspects represents a fundamental concern about self in life situations.

The three functional aspects of self-concept are *appearance, performance,* and *status.*

The Aspect of Appearance

"How do I look?" is a question we all ask of others, either

directly or by implication, every day we live. Whether or not we are immediately aware of it, the question of appearance underlies much of our thinking and conversation. It is so much a part of us that we scarcely consider its importance until someone volunteers either to compliment or to criticize us.

Appearance can affect success in our vocation. A nurse must exemplify cleanliness in her dress. A salesman needs to appear both spruce and prosperous. A doctor or a professor must appear professional. When a person applies for a job, he tries to look his best.

Romance often begins on the level of appearance. How a person looks can influence the relationship of marriage.

"My husband looks so sloppy, I'm ashamed to be seen with him," explained one wife.

"My wife is a sight to come home to. The only time she fixes herself up is when we go out. I'm embarrassed when company drops in," declared one upset husband.

Notice how easily we can hear a remark of personal praise or criticism. "You look nice." "You are a handsome man." "I'd like to know where you bought that attractive jacket." Or, "You've gained a little weight, haven't you?" "You seem to be showing your age." Such remarks catch our attention immediately, and they are not easily forgotten. We are naturally more or less vulnerable to what others think of our personal appearance.

In short, *appearance* is a functional aspect of self-concept that relates to how we view our bodies, our dress, and our personal grooming.

The Aspect of Performance

"How am I doing?" is a question that weaves its way into many conversations. The quality of our performance is on our minds most of the time even when we are not immediately aware of it.

From childhood we were trained to do our best, to excel, to try for perfection in whatever we did. Most of us have been brought up to believe that regardless of how well we do a task, we could possibly do better if we tried again.

In the process of developing our abilities we have been rated by performance. In school we received grades and report cards. At home we were criticized and punished for bad conduct and sometimes praised for honest effort. We had duties, chores, and responsibilities, and how we discharged these tasks gave us an evaluative sense of our performance.

In our present vocation we must meet the competition and

continue to do our best. How we succeed may depend somewhat on being opportunistic, but the strength of our success is dependent upon our ability to perform. Performance is a vital aspect of self-concept.

Briefly, *performance* is a functional aspect of self-concept that relates to how we view our abilities, our skills, our knowledge, and our sense of responsibility.

The Aspect of Status

The question "How important am I?" concerns each of us personally. Feeling respected and admired by others is an underlying desire of everyone. We easily feel slighted when someone ignores us, forgets who we are, or makes fun of us.

Our social structure has many status labels, some complimentary and some derogatory. A few we frequently hear are "He's the president of the company." "She's the owner of the store." "She's the black sheep of my family." "He's the school principal." "He's a millionaire." "He's from the ghetto."

Thus *status* is the functional aspect of self-concept which relates to how we view our relative importance among people — our family name, wealth, education, position, or social rating.

Appearance, performance, and status values all combine in the mind to describe self-concept in a functional sense. They serve much like dimensions in our self-image picture to give a sense of reality to our feeling of identity, of being somebody.

Notice that these dimensions are derived from how we feel rated by others. When we think of our appearance or performance or status, we imagine we are standing off and looking at ourselves. What we see is the composite of many memories accumulated chiefly during our childhood when we were most impressionable.

Other self-concept feelings are also derived from childhood experiences. These are not based primarily upon a sense of being rated, but upon emotional reactions to relationships with members of our family and especially with our parents. These are essential elements of self-concept and are discussed in the next chapter.

Self-Concept Reveals Emotional Maturity

A good sense of emotional well-being starts with a good self-concept. If our self-concept is adequate, we feel comfortable with ourselves and have an abiding peace of mind. When problems come, we can put ourselves totally to the task of solving them. We may momentarily become upset, anxious, fearful, guilty, hostile, as anyone might, but with a good self-concept we have inner resources of recovery which return us to a state of peaceful equilibrium. Everyone has crises in his life, but the emotionally secure person, one with an adequate self-concept, copes better and more constructively with them.

The person with a good self-concept can occupy his mind with whatever is happening. His mind is not divided between trying to cope with his own anxieties and coping with the happening. He functions from an inner island of self-confidence. The person with an inadequate self-concept has anxiety and uncertainty that compel him to try to keep his island of inner security above water while he is at the same time trying to launch an attack upon the problem at hand.

He who has a good self-concept can accept his body without feeling uneasy about its distinctive features. He can enjoy his accomplishments without being conceited. He can relax when relaxation is appropriate. He can view his shortcomings as problems to be overcome, rather than rate himself as a bad person because he is unable to meet his standard of perfection. He can honestly take an optimistic view of his own mistakes by saying, "I can do better next time." He is able to accept responsibility for matters over which he has a specific measure of control.

Ideally, the person with a good self-concept functions because he knows he *is*. He is not always trying to *become*.

4

Three Feelings
Blend Together

If we reached into our storehouse of assorted memories to recall various experiences in which we were aware of being an effective person, we eventually would discover three kinds of feelings that have peculiar significance. These three feelings integrate to form the essential elements of self-concept. They not only constitute the mental structure of self-concept, but give it support and stability.

This triad of feelings is *belongingness, worthiness,* and *competence.*

These three feelings blend together in the formation of self-concept like three tones of a musical chord. At times each can be considered separately, but usually it is impossible to distinguish one from the other. As in a musical chord, the first note, or root, is fundamental; so with self-concept, the sense of belongingness is primary and fundamental to the development of the other two elements.

The three feelings also work together like legs of a tripod to support and stabilize self-concept. If any one of the three feelings is weak, the self-concept totters like a camera on a tripod when one leg is slipping.

Each of these feelings is developed on a fundamental level in early childhood during the impressionable years. As one approaches adulthood and the state of responsible independence, he functions from this fundamental base of self-concept feelings.

Feelings of Belongingness

Belongingness is an awareness of being wanted and accepted, of being cared for and enjoyed. It is the "part of," or "we," feeling experienced when we sense we are wanted or desired by some person or a group of people.

It is natural to want to be "in" with the people we admire. We tend to maneuver and manipulate to feel accepted by them. We watch for evidence of their personal interest in us. We may work to capture their attention. In the final analysis, however, they must take the initiative to make us feel accepted, or we doubt if they *really* wanted us.

One complaint often heard is, "I feel on the outside looking in. I seldom feel accepted by others." It's a cold, isolated feeling to admit you are on the outside and not "in."

Judy described this feeling colorfully when I talked to her about becoming a Christian. I asked if she had ever known a Christian. Her impulsive reply was, "Yes. My sister is a Christian. I love to visit her house. She has many Christian friends, and they occasionally gather around the piano and sing. I was there the other evening when they were singing. I don't know their songs; they are all so strange. But I like to sit like a bird in the corner and watch the wholesome, sincere expressions on their faces. They're surely different from the gang I run with!"

"Have you wanted to become a Christian?" I asked.

"Yes, I have! Many, many times," she said longingly. "But, you know, Christianity to me is something like candy in a showcase. I can see it, but I can't get to it!"

We all have a basic need to feel "in with" and "part of" someone, someone who truly cares for us personally. Many who cannot find satisfaction in relating closely to people become preoccupied with the value of things. In their materialism they go beyond frugality to being tight, stingy, and ungiving of time or money.

Some people relate to things affectionately. Larry, a one-man demolition crew with a bulldozer, told me, "I love my big Cat! It works with me and for me. When I'm finished with the day's work, I affectionately slap it on the steel lugs with my gloves. It never answers back angrily or makes me feel less than a man. . . . But," he added, "it's cold and it's steel! It could kill me if I didn't handle it right."

Certain people find satisfaction by turning to animals for affection. They surround themselves with pets of various kinds and treat them as though they were human.

Our sense of belongingness is fundamentally established in infancy. Children develop feelings of belongingness when loving parents anticipate their discomforts and affectionately provide for their needs. A tiny infant is sensitive to being loved. When he is loved in his first year, he develops an essential trust in the goodness of life and the dependability of people. This prepares him for better adjustment in future childhood years and for a happier life.

Feelings of Worthiness

Worthiness is a feeling of "I am good" or "I count" or "I am right." We feel worthy when we do as we should. We verify that sense of worthiness when we sense others' positive attitudes toward us and their hearty endorsement of our actions. When others do not approve, but criticize us, we feel a loss of worthiness. This usually makes us defensive or angry. We will probably attempt to justify ourselves to recover our lost sense of worthiness and self-esteem.

Worthiness is related to a sense of not only being right but doing right. Self-control is important to worthiness.

Worthiness relates to belongingness, for we feel good about ourselves when we are accepted by others. Worthiness is a function of our sense of self-esteem.

We like to believe we are capable of good decisions. In defense of our sense of personal worth, we quickly blurt out, "You don't understand." Then we proceed to set the accuser or the adviser straight. If we have no immediate explanation, we might in exasperation try to recover our worth with "Why don't you mind your own business!"

Some people would rather comply with their critics than risk a confrontation. In being agreeable they presume to have a sense of worth by maintaining the good will of the other person.

Donald had the money to buy the car he had picked out. He knew he could meet the payments. When his older brother, who has the habit of interfering, heard of his plan to buy the car, he instantly said, "You don't want *that* car. You can't afford it." Donald felt helpless to defend himself, though he had carefully worked out a plan of payment and he liked the car. To keep the good will of his brother, he canceled his plans to buy the car and felt depressed. By complying, he lost self-respect, but he maintained the illusion of being important to his brother.

We all tend to preserve a sense of personal worth if we can. Some do it by attacking others, telling them where they are wrong. Some give advice, whether or not they have been asked for it. In their sense of mastery over others, they verify for themselves a peculiar sense of worthiness. Donald's older brother might be an illustration of this.

Some comply, like Donald, to preserve their sense of worthiness. They are afraid of losing more by confronting and defending than by giving in.

Still others are so intimidated by the positive attitude and critical approach of certain people that they try to preserve their sense of worthiness by making practically no decisions at all. They continually ask for the opinions of others, even on simple matters. These people never developed a good sense of worthiness through making good decisions for themselves, and they are very dependent upon others. They have a deficient sense of worthiness by conforming.

The underlying sense of worthiness developed in childhood does not seem to change because one is criticized or praised. When a person receives criticism he deems unfair, he has certain ways of dismissing the feelings of lost worth. For instance, he thinks, "He doesn't understand the situation" or "He never has a good word to say." If, on the other hand, he receives praise he doesn't feel he deserves, he may think, "He doesn't really mean it" or "He's just trying to get something from me."

If we receive more praise than we feel we deserve, we feel hypocritical to accept it. The opinion of others has some influence upon our sense of worthiness, but the heart of worthiness lies within ourselves.

If we have violated our conscience by something we have done, we can scarcely appreciate the admiration of others fully. We know they would think differently of us if they knew the facts.

It is easy to become confused about worthiness. It is difficult always to define our own sense of goodness. This confusion arises from the fact that we do not always accept responsibility for our actions. We are not always honest with ourselves. We project the blame to others or excuse ourselves. "He made me do it" is a projection. "I couldn't help it" is an excuse. Or, there are times we deny we did it; we pretend it did not happen. We then try to conduct ourselves as though we were never involved. This denial can happen consciously or unconsciously.

We never really deceive ourselves. We merely play mental games to maintain the sense of worth we desire. We feel confused because we are trying to specify something we don't want to think about responsibly for fear of facing certain memories which are not complimentary.

Violating conscience by indulging in something immoral

illustrates the point. "I did it in an unguarded moment," we may reason. The mind tries various devices to avoid the guilt. One may project the blame, excuse himself, deny it happened, or rationalize that others also do it. By these mental devices he is merely trying to hold the matter out of awareness. He may succeed in keeping from thinking about the incident, but should someone at any later date compliment him for his morality, he will tend to display a mock humility and reject the praise. He might think, "Am I really that good? I don't know. I really don't want to think about it."

The fine line between deserving praise or criticism becomes blurred by our desire for the approval of others and our refusal to be honest with ourselves. There is a way out of this dilemma which we will discuss in a later chapter.

Feelings of Competence

A third element of self-concept is the feeling of competence. This is a feeling of adequacy, of courage, or hopefulness, of strength enough to carry out the tasks of daily life-situations. It is the "I can" feeling of being able to face life and cope with its complexities.

At first thought, one might imagine that competence is a function of physical health, but this is not true. Though there is a definite relationship between physical and emotional well-being, the feelings of competence transcend physical limitations. If someone has a physical handicap, he can still have a sense of competence. True competence acknowledges one's abilities as well as one's weaknesses. It maintains a realistic balance in the demand one makes upon himself.

An immediate sense of competence derives from what is now happening, but there is also a general sense of competence that reflects the memories of accomplishments and failures of past experiences. Competence begins to develop in preadolescent years, but it grows on to a more fixed attitude as a person finishes his teens. Competence is affected positively by successes, negatively by failures.

Competence is intricately involved in a person's sex-role feelings of adequacy. A man needs to feel adequate as a male, and a woman needs to feel completely satisfactory as a female. When a person feels adequate in his sex-role, he has a richer sense of competence, regardless of what other accomplishments he may have to his credit.

Competence is somewhat related to the service we render

society. If we achieve our goals and approach some of our ideals of perfection, we increase our sense of competence.

Interplay of the Triad of Self-Concept Feelings

Belongingness is fundamental. Worthiness somewhat depends on belongingness, for one must feel accepted by others to value their confirming attitudes concerning how good a person he is. Competence depends partially on belongingness and upon worthiness. We need to feel accepted by others in order to value their approval or profit by their helpful criticism. We also must approve of ourselves to have the incentive to keep trying after we have failed. We tend to become listless and apathetic when we lose our sense of worthiness and feel like a non-person, depressed.

Reviewing the essential nature of these three feelings, we observe these facts: Belongingness rests on the voluntary attitude of others as they display their acceptance. Worthiness rests on the introspective attitude of self-approval. Competence rests on the evaluations received in past relationships and on one's present sense of success.

Note that belongingness positions a person with respect to other people. Belongingness gives an orientation in society as "one of them." One has the underlying feeling of being either "in" or "out" with people.

Worthiness positions a person with respect to his own ideals and conduct. It gives him an orientation with respect to the appropriateness of his behavior. He is aware of being either good or bad, worth something or nothing.

Competence positions a person with respect to life situations. It is related to how he copes with life. Competence orients a person to circumstances, to time, to responsibility, to usefulness, and to fulfillment in his role in life.

These three feelings work together to give a person a sense of identity, a self-orientation to living. Belongingness, worthiness, and competence are essential elements of self-concept and together they affirm to a person that he is somebody.

5

Important Abilities and Reactions

Abilities That Build Emotional Security

People are endowed with three natural abilities — *empathy, identification,* and *love* — that make the development of self-concept possible. We sense the feelings of others because we empathize; we identify with those feelings. In loving relationships with our parents we develop inner security that manifests itself in an adequate self-concept.

Empathy

Empathy is a fundamental talent that makes it possible to relate to others emotionally. Every person is born with the ability to empathize. Empathy is the capacity to sense the other person's feelings by his body gestures and the intonations of his voice. Most of the empathic message comes through the sense of hearing. The ability to empathize by sight is less definite, and the ability to empathize through the sense of touch is less definite than the other two.

We all seem to understand the general mood of another person simply by hearing his voice and seeing his facial expressions. Emotional feelings are communicated from one person to another by empathy as well as by words. This intangible connection between two human beings is called empathic communication.

Alex said, "I don't trust James. I can't tell you why.

Maybe it's the expression on his face, but I don't trust him.'' Alex felt something empathically which warned him about James's character.

Gus entered the restaurant for his morning cup of coffee and didn't say a word. ''You seem upset today, Gus,'' the waiter remarked. ''Is something wrong?''

''Yes, something is wrong, very wrong!'' Gus explained. ''My father is in the hospital. I don't believe he's going to make it. Went in yesterday in an ambulance.'' The waiter sensed Gus's concern empathically.

Empathy begins to manifest itself in the infant's behavior soon after he is born. It becomes the basis of nonverbal communication all through his life. Before the child is able to understand the language of his household, he senses the emotions of the people speaking to him. We see his responses and sense empathically that he understands. How much he understands is open to question. We know he enjoys being liked.

Identification

Identification results from being able to empathize and to remember. The word *identification* comes from the idea of two things being the same. By empathy we sense another person's feelings; those feelings remind us of similar feelings we once had. We instantly feel we are like the other person, for we have feelings that are similar about the same kind of situation. Generalization also takes place; we do not think of being like the other person in one specific aspect, rather we usually generalize our feelings and assume we are like him in many ways.

Little Larry felt bad because every time he piled up his blocks, they fell down before he had them six high. His older brother laughed at him and called him stupid. Larry began to cry. Louise, Larry's playmate from next door, tried to comfort him. ''I know just how you feel,'' she said. Apparently Louise felt as though she had traded places with Larry and shared his frustration and humiliation, and probably his anger as well, for she also said, ''I'd like to hit your big brother for being so mean, but he's too big.''

When we identify, we unconsciously project ourselves into the other person's feelings that we sense empathically, and for a moment we feel we are the other person in his experience. Without thinking, we may behave in a similar way, for we feel as though we are somewhat like him.

Dirk told a funny story and everyone laughed. Vic joined the group and asked, ''Why am I laughing? I didn't hear the story, but it sounds like it was a good one.'' Vic empathically felt the humorous mood of the group and, before he knew what he was doing, joined in.

It is impossible to identify when we lack experience that is similar, though we may empathize and feel sympathetic.

Erma's husband was killed in an auto accident on his way home from work. She was stricken with grief. Susan, a close friend, felt helpless to say anything of comfort. Her husband was still living, and she had never lost anyone close to her by death.

A strange coincidence happened about three years later. Susan's husband was seriously injured on his job, and in a few days he died. Erma consoled Susan at her husband's funeral. Susan spoke up through her tears, "Thanks, Erma, for being here. You know the grief I feel. I wish I could have helped you more when you lost your man. I felt so helpless. It means so much to me to know you understand."

Identification creates the illusion of being identical to the other person. These feelings of being the same, coupled with the special importance given the person we identify with, leave a memory that makes the other person an influential part of our thinking and feeling. In other words, identification brings attributes of other people into ourselves.

Elvin, a five-year-old bundle of energy, liked to watch cowboy movies on television. He always dressed for the occasion — belt, holster, gun, hat, boots, and chaps. During the show and for an hour or so afterward, Elvin was the greatest cowboy in the neighborhood. He identified with the cowboys on the television screen.

When a child identifies with a parent or another authority figure, he has a memory of the experience that becomes an internal image, and this image controls his impulses as though the authoritative person were actually present internally. We hear the voice of conscience, and at times that voice is accompanied by the memory of the person who spoke.

Little Denton was hungry and reached into the cookie jar for something to eat. "No!" commanded his mother. "I said no cookies before dinner." Denton persisted. His mother reminded him, "I said, 'No!' and I mean it. No cookies before dinner. Besides, you ask *before* you reach into the jar for cookies, you understand?" Denton learned to obey finally, both by command and by identifying with his mother's forbidding attitude.

Sometime later, a neighbor lady happened in to borrow something just before dinner. Denton grew impatient with all the talking and interrupted his mother with, "Mother, may I have a cookie?" The neighbor was astonished. "You mean," she said, "that your little three-year-old asks for a cookie when he's hungry? I can't believe it! My five-year-old wouldn't think of asking; he'd have half the jar eaten by now.''

Identification brings the other person's attitudes into ourselves and they become part of us. We learn to do things or not to do things by identification. This is especially true of children who are in a dependent relationship with their parents.

Love

Love is an emotion that gives meaning and helpful purpose to relationships. It is a function of empathy and identification. We sense another person's feelings by empathy; as we identify with those feelings, we care about what is happening to that person as though it were happening to us. Love desires the same benefit for the other person as one would wish for himself. Love is an emotion whose dominant feeling is affection. The goal of love is the close association of another person with oneself.[1]

Thus love shares in the other person's pleasures and is sincerely glad for his happiness. Love also shares in his distresses and miseries and is sincerely sorry for his situation. Love motivates one to be helpful in promoting the other person's welfare. Sympathy and compassion are feelings of caring and are attributes of love.

The Bible says, ''Let love be genuine; . . . Rejoice with those who rejoice, weep with those who weep'' (Rom. 12:9,15 RSV).

Empathy and identification cause one to feel somewhat identical to another person, so identification makes us mimic one another unconsciously. Love adds to this mimicry elements of wishful thinking and idealization of the other person. Hence, love binds people together in a sense of oneness and belongingness.

It is not uncommon to observe an elderly couple who have lived together in love for many years manifesting similar personality traits. In love they have grown to be like each other.

Love is usually directed toward a person who arouses some admiration or delight. When we express love, we commonly convey a complimentary attitude. Love expresses tenderness, understanding, and sympathetic interest; love is kind.

It is important to bear in mind this timeless truth. *Love is consonant with our emotional nature.* All effects of loving relationships are beneficial and become a permanent part of the psyche. In other words, feelings of love cannot be externalized so that one feels less loving because he has expressed love. On the contrary, expressing love tends to increase and enrich the love that is felt.

Self-concept evolves during childhood as a result of loving

relationships with parents and other members of the family. After a person grows to adulthood, self-concept is verified and strengthened in loving relationships with peers. Loving relationships bring meaning and purpose and fulfillment into living regardless of one's age.

Reactions That Contribute to Emotional Insecurity

Three types of emotional reactions block the ability to empathize. These emotions relate to anxiety and are *hostility, guilt,* and *fear.* When empathy is handicapped or inoperative, the ability to perceive love in relationships is considerably limited. A person must resort to other resources for a sense of being somebody, and there are none which give any emotional security.

Empathy can occur only when a person is at ease within himself. No one can be aware of more than one feeling at a time. When a person is absorbed with feelings concerning himself — as he is with hostility, guilt, or fear — he cannot at the same time be sensitive to the feelings of other people.

Hostility

The hostile person is projecting bad feelings toward others and blaming them in some way. He is in no mood to be sensitive to the feelings of others. No one can receive while projecting out, any more than one can swallow and spit at the same time.

The general attitude of the public toward someone convicted of a crime illustrates how empathy is blocked by hostility. The fact of a conviction opinionates the public against the wrongdoer. They are hostile because he violated a law and probably injured some innocent person. The rage the public feels about the crime blocks all possible feelings of empathy they might have had for the man who was convicted. He could be equal to an animal as far as they are concerned.

We observe how empathy is blocked when two people argue. Dean and Eva were arguing about taking a vacation. "You never stop to think that I need a vacation," Eva declared. "You never think of how hard I work to keep things going around the house. You don't care that I want to get away for a while. Whenever you think of a vacation, you always go by yourself and leave us behind. You and your buddies get all the fun!"

"You think I'm made of money, don't you!" Dean denounced sarcastically. "You always want something we can't afford."

"Can't afford!" declared Eva. "Do you realize that the most vacation we have had together as a family in over five years is a half-dozen overnight trips? Labor Day is coming. Then school starts, and all possible vacation times will be over. Can't you take a week off? We'd love to go to the beach.''

Dean looked sheepish and started to say something, then hesitated. Eva stared at Dean in silence, but soon exploded with emotion. ''You've already planned something for Labor Day with your buddies, haven't you?''

''That's all I hear,'' raged Dean. '' 'Take a week off!' Do you realize what a week off costs me? I don't have paid vacations, you know. I pay through the nose when I don't work. If I go anywhere, it will be with my 'buddies,' as you call them; I wouldn't take a week off with a nagging woman like you. Never!''

Obviously Dean was too hostile to hear the yearnings of his wife for his companionship and attention.

Hostility not only makes people insensitive to the feelings of others, but drives them apart; it disunites them. Hostility breeds hostility, for the emotion attacks the other person's self-identity, and he reacts defensively. Hostility holds people in uncaring relationships that compete for supremacy.

Interestingly, hostility originates when a loss of self-identity occurs. A person is threatened with rejection or is actually rejected; this indicates a loss in his fundamental sense of belongingness. Frustration also incites hostility, for it implies a loss of control in a situation; one is disappointed that his plan or idea does not work. Humiliation is another source of hostility, for it indicates a loss in one's feelings of adequacy; he feels depreciated and inferior.

Hostility is a reaction incited by a loss of self-identity. One is struggling while hostile to establish some sense of being somebody. But every effort he makes while hostile isolates him from others and increases his loss of belongingness. Hostility can also affect his sense of worthiness if in it he violates his conscience in the way he acts out his feelings. It can give him a false sense of competence because of the sense of strength a person has while hostile; but there is no security in such feelings of competence. A hostile person is more or less insensitive to the loving acceptance others may be showing him.

Guilt

When a person feels guilty, he is busy feeling bad about himself. His feelings of chagrin and possibly of remorse prevent him from being sensitive to the feelings of others.

It was Edgar and Olive's twelfth wedding anniversary, and they had been talking about celebrating by eating out, then going to the Music Center for a special program. At noon Edgar phoned Olive: "Honey, I'm sorry, but I can't go tonight. I just remembered my income tax is due tomorrow. I've got to do it tonight. It's got to be in by midnight."

"Tonight!" exclaimed Olive in surprise. "Tonight you have to make out income tax forms? You haven't done that yet? I thought you did that last week when you said you would. But tonight on our anniversary, you have to do income tax! I give up!"

"I know, Honey," Edgar tried to explain apologetically. "I feel bad about it. I started last week, but something got my mind off it. Maybe we can go out to celebrate next week. OK?" Edgar had a bad habit of putting things off until the last minute, and this time it really hurt him. He felt guilty for his negligence.

Olive was sick with disappointment and furiously angry with him for procrastinating again. She was especially upset because he had given their special day such low priority.

Edgar tried to compromise the situation by deciding to do the income tax later and paying the penalty. He knew this would be wasting money they could not afford. Moreover, he was in such a double bind with his feelings of guilt that he could not enjoy the anniversary celebration. His guilt prevented him from enjoying his wife's pleasures and sharing with her in their special evening.

While hostility blames others, guilt blames self. Guilt punishes self about as much as if the feelings were hostile and directed at someone else for the same offense. Hostility contradicts feelings of belongingness; guilt cancels feelings of worthiness. Hostility says, in effect, "You are bad, I don't like you." Guilt says, "I am bad, you could not like me. I loathe myself." Thus both hostility and guilt contribute to emotional insecurity. Each contradicts an element of self-concept.

Fear

A fearful person, or one who is inappropriately anxious, has his attention focused upon himself. He is so preoccupied with various threatening situations and his feelings about them that he cannot sense the feelings of others unless they are also afraid.

"I wonder what the doctor will find wrong tomorrow?" Janis pondered out loud in the middle of the night as she shook her husband, Max. She had been troubled with some abdominal pains and was scheduled to undergo an extensive medical examination the next day. "Max, I don't feel good. I'm scared!"

Max grunted sleepily.

"Max! Max! Don't you care what happens to me? I'm

afraid I've got something terribly wrong with me! I might have cancer or something.''

By this time Max was awakening. ''For crying out loud!'' he muttered. ''Can't a guy get any sleep around here? I'm beat!''

''You don't care what happens to me!'' Janis retorted. ''You wouldn't care if I were dying! Maybe I'll die and then you can get another wife!''

''Janis, listen to me,'' Max said softly, trying to be patient. ''I know you are afraid of the examination tomorrow. I wish you didn't have to go, but it must be done. It's only routine to determine why you are having such pains. Please try to wait until the doctor finds what's wrong before you get all worried. It probably isn't anything serious at all.

''Now, Honey,'' Max pleaded, ''I've got to get some sleep. I have a terribly hard day ahead of me tomorrow on the job. Take a Valium or something and try to relax.''

Janis's fears and anxieties blocked all caring about her husband's feelings. She was frightened and could not empathize. Moreover, her fear made her unrealistic and unreasonable in her thinking.

Fear tends to paralyze the mind and cause it to function inadequately. Fear and its close associate, anxiety, cancel the ''I can'' feelings of competence so that a person is inclined to think ''I can't'' about many things.

Hostility, guilt, and fear — each is a defensive attempt to correct a problem. In the way these emotions are usually experienced, they increase emotional insecurity instead of resolving it. Hostility attempts to force the situation to change, but belongingness is lost. Guilt attempts to force the self to change, but worthiness is lost. Fear and anxiety attempt to protect the self from impending dangers, but competence is lost. Elements of self-concept are weakened under the influence of these three negative reactions, and thus one's feelings of emotional insecurity are heightened.

The problem is further complicated in that each of these reactions blocks empathy. Thus we cannot discern or sense the love others show us in our relationships while we are under the influence of these three negative emotions. We are caught in a dilemma. When we are faced with a situation that threatens our sense of being somebody, we inherently react negatively with hostility, guilt, or fear. We want to be wanted or regarded as good or competent, but our reaction increases our anxiety and interferes with the remedy.

Repression

Repression is a mechanism of the mind for removing unwanted ideas from awareness and hiding them in the unconscious. The process happens unconsciously. If a person is conscious of trying to subdue an emotion, he is suppressing it, not repressing it. In repression, after the idea has been banished from the realm of conscious thinking, the mind sets up a barrier to prevent its return to awareness. The barrier is maintained by what is called the *censor*, a force in the mind that controls impulses and behavior.

Whenever situations occur that threaten to reawaken repressed ideas, a person feels anxiety and tension. The mind will attempt all kinds of evasive strategies to maintain the idea in the unconscious. Under certain circumstances, repressed ideas can be revived and dealt with constructively so they will not return to the unconscious. When this occurs, the person experiences some sense of relief, for the energy he dedicated to maintaining the censor is now free to be used generally in other ways. It is possible to dedicate so much energy to repressed ideas that one has little ambition for the normal functions of daily living.

When the mind represses an idea, the idea is barred from awareness. We do not know we have had the idea, but the idea has symbolic representation in our thinking. For example, a person may repress anger. He is not aware of being angry, but his behavior manifests an attitude that is representative of the anger.

Keith, along with three other selected students, was called upon by his teacher to go to the blackboard and demonstrate for the class how to do certain algebra problems. One problem seemed to him to be unsolvable. He struggled with it, trying this and that strategy to obtain the solution that he could see out of the corner of his eye the others had derived. Finally the teacher asked the class to help Keith: "Can anyone show Keith his mistake?"

Annette, a girl in the class he was secretly in love with, volunteered! "Keith should have factored in the second step," she explained. Keith was so embarrassed to be corrected by Annette he could not find his error. The teacher asked Annette to go to the board and correct his work. Two or three in the class snickered. Keith was mortified as she easily did the factoring and derived the proper answer. That ruined his day. He was grumpy and irritable, feeling as though everyone was against him.

On the way home from school he tried to be pleasant and forget anything had happened, but he found himself sarcastic and critical. He wondered why. Then Annette's path crossed his. Usually he would have joined her for several blocks, but he avoided the confrontation. At home Keith could not eat all his dinner, and that was unusual. He felt restless all evening and went to bed early.

Keith had little or no awareness of being angry with the teacher for the humiliation he felt about Annette and the class. To be angry would have been an inappropriate and embarrassing reaction, for he knew he should have done the problem without hesitation. The representatives of his repressed anger were manifested in his day's being spoiled, his grumpy and irritable attitude, his unintentional sarcasm and critical attitude, his avoidance of Annette whom he liked, his loss of appetite, and his restlessness. Actually the effects of the anger were far more destructive being repressed than if he had burst out in a rage in the class. But at the time he could not think of doing otherwise.

Usually when we repress emotions, we need to do something of an opposite nature to keep the matter out of awareness. For instance, when guilt is repressed, the person finds an unusual sense of virtue in doing good, in being generous, or in praising others. He himself may be extremely vulnerable to flattery. Or, he may invert the idea because of repressed guilt and find a sense of virtue out of suffering, in being a martyr, forbidding himself pleasures he rightly deserves.

When fear is repressed, a person may appear fearless and inappropriately courageous. He seems to be defending against the sense of weakness in fear, so he dares to do things that are dangerous as though he had to prove to himself that he is not afraid.

Repression, therefore, brings into our thinking many unrealistic ideas and attitudes. While repression is a device of the mind to protect oneself from unwanted ideas and feelings, it often creates many new problems which are more destructive than the original trauma.

Repression can happen to a variety of ideas and feelings, but we are presently discussing repression as it applies to hostility, guilt, and fear. These are emotions that specifically interfere with the development of self-concept and also introduce unreality factors into the sense of self.

Part 2

How We Became What We Are

Self-concept factors in the development of a child from conception to adulthood. Environmental influences upon emotional development. False security factors within self-concept structure.

First Feelings of
Self-Awareness

Whatever we are, we have been becoming for a long time. If we have a good self-concept, it is because we have experienced certain beneficial influences in our early years that made it so. If we have a poor and inadequate self-concept, it is because critical emotional needs were not met when we were young and that condition seems to have persisted until now.

To understand our feelings about ourselves, we need to turn our attention to the most impressionable years of life, even to the very beginnings of our existence and personality. Making such an inquiry should point out many of our basic emotional needs, perhaps suggest whether those needs were met or not, and further our understanding of present feelings about ourselves.

The general design of emotional development needs to be understood. We will begin to unravel the mysterious processes of life from our prenatal condition through birth and on through the impressionable years of childhood.

Growth of self-concept occurs by building one sensation of awareness upon another. Each experience is recorded in the memory, where it affects spontaneous responses in new situations that are continually happening. This accumulation of memories organizes in the unconscious aspects of the mind to form the bulwark of impulsive interests, initiatives, and responses that shape all thinking.

For example, if a child has been frightened in the dark by some unexpected noise, he may as a result expect darkness to be dangerous and be afraid. He has had an experience that sponsors feelings of fear and guardedness in the dark. The child may need to be reassured several times before he has accumulated enough experience feeling safe in the dark to forget most of his caution when there is no light.

The Prenatal Situation

We assume an unborn infant to be living in a state of unconscious tranquillity. He is a part of his mother enclosed snugly and safely within her. He is surrounded by a watery fluid that absorbs shocks, cushions all movements, and provides a constant temperature with maximum protection. Nourishment is supplied intravenously as needed. All conditions seem to be about as peaceful as can be imagined. The child's little compartment is lined with delicate security. His residence is a veritable Garden of Eden!

No one can actually recall those first feelings of life, but we can reasonably imagine their sponsoring certain aspects of our yearnings as we grow older. For instance, people of all ages tend to seek a state of security in life that is lined with contentment and tranquillity. Furthermore, we not only desire instinctively to live blissfully, but also manifest an innate appreciation for perfection. We have a tendency to idealize and to generalize in a way that makes things seem more perfect than they actually are. We long for peace of mind, a sense of inner unity, and we try to avoid difficulties. It is as though we were unwittingly drawn toward some state of being that we had lost and were trying to reclaim.

Also, we have an intrinsic need to be a part of, to feel united to, others in some bond of relationship. We do not feel complete within ourselves, and we must have a sense of belongingness to survive. While we know that most of these feelings of need are derived from early childhood experiences, we are also aware of an underlying need for a feeling of acceptance and togetherness which makes us feel like whole persons. We can safely assume that this fundamental yearning must somehow be related to the time when we were actually a part of our mother before birth. At least, the idea is consistent with the state of being of an unborn child as we know it.

Before a child is born, he can lie quietly or move a little as he is able. He is provided with everything necessary for healthy growth. This ideal living situation was our continuous experience for about nine months. Every phase of our prenatal development was naturally affected by the state of existence. Thus our unappeasable craving for peace, tranquillity, and security, as well as the need to feel "a part of," points to archaic memories of having experienced such a blissful condition at one time.

Our First Identity Crisis

Whatever peacefulness we enjoyed during the prenatal period ended when we were born. The importance of this fact is that life began in pleasure and blissfulness, not in pain. We lost that undisturbed peacefulness when we experienced birth, and ever since we seem to try persistently to recapture some of it.

Like a person placidly bathing above Niagara Falls only to discover the turbulence ahead, the infant naively finds himself in a physical crisis and an emotional trauma when he is born. Time marches him into an inescapable identity crisis.

Through no fault of his own, except that he has outgrown his quarters and lost his lease, the infant is emphatically expelled from his Eden and forced into the turbulent world of recurring problems. He no longer possesses an abundant supply of his needs by which he is cared for automatically. He must do something to keep himself alive and to maintain some of his own sense of security.

The infant's instinctive drive to live will take him from one crisis to another. If he continues living, he must face problems and overcome them, and in doing so he will grow. Overcoming simple problems today will prepare him for tackling more difficult problems tomorrow. Life is of such a nature that we are again and again faced with problems that increase in intensity as we grow in our ability to cope with them.

The birth itself is about all the trauma a tiny baby can stand. When we speak of childbirth, we usually think of the mother's painful experiences. In this book we must turn our attention to the birth experience from the child's point of view.

Birth for an infant is indeed a revolutionary happening, the first momentous event in his life. He is forced by relentless contractions of the mother's abdominal muscles through a narrow passageway that is too small for his head and body. He must get through somehow! Finally he does.

Immediately upon leaving his prenatal world, he feels the sudden chill of air, sees the brightness of light, and is handled and usually spanked. He hears himself cry as he gasps for his first breath of air.

For an infant who has never before experienced any serious discomfort, all this process of being born is an intense ordeal. He is totally vulnerable to whatever takes place.

When he is born, he is severed from his mother. He can never return to his comfortable, prenatal cradle, He is too young and inexperienced to anticipate or to be concerned. He only reacts passively to things as they happen to him. He is not old enough to realize that he is separated from his mother, but experiences will eventually impress this realization upon his mind.

Meaning of Hunger and Eating

After the infant has been born, bathed, weighed, and measured, he begins to settle down in his downy, soft clothing and cozy, warm blankets. The infant begins to resume his sleepy, paradisiac state of prenatal bliss when another crisis occurs: He begins to feel irritated by a feeling he has never experienced before. The irritation becomes more and more intense until it is painful. He cries, but the misery only becomes greater. This certain distress will become a familiar sensation, and it will gnaw at him every day of his life at regular intervals. The infant is hungry!

We must remember that for an undeveloped infant, hunger is singly the most significant problem he has to overcome.

The infant is on his own now. He cries to let the world know he is in need. While crying and sucking are instinctive, these activities are actually work for him. He is doing something to take care of himself. He is investing himself, as much as he is able, in solving his own problems.

This suggests a life principle: *We must at any age do what we can to take care of ourselves.* We are individuals and responsible to a large extent for our own welfare.

Hunger is an infant's continuing problem. He usually is successful in overcoming his devastating problem; he eats and then sleeps. This gives him the sense of awakening to new problems. He invests himself as much as he knows how in overcoming his problems. He feels successful in his efforts before returning to his restful sleep.

It is interesting that at the roots of our thinking is an expectation of being successful in whatever we attempt. Our first experience in life in tackling problems was a successful experience, and it was repeated over and over again in the cycle of waking and sleeping. We naturally, therefore, expect somehow to overcome whatever problem we encounter all through life. It is not natural for a person to undertake a problem and expect himself to fail.

Another life principle exists here in embryo: *The situation in life that seems most overpowering usually contains the greatest potential for growth if we can expect success and attempt to overcome it.*

Hunger was our first problem. We conquered that problem successfully until we no longer felt devastated by the sensation, but learned to take the feeling simply as a sign that we needed nourishment, and then we set about getting it. Because we tackled this problem, we grew physically, and we grew emotionally to feel capable of attacking future problems.

Other problems were overwhelming in our childhood — such as having to wait for service, being restricted, and competing — and we were threatened by many situations involving these kinds of problems. We attempted to cope with these, and how we faced the threats involved had definite effects on the shaping of our personality. Each identity crisis conquered produced growth; each one avoided or mishandled caused a hangup. The hangups remain as an aspect of emotional immaturity until something happens to force us to deal with the issues courageously and constructively once again.

Early Beginnings of Awareness

Birth changes the infant's whole structure of living. Before birth he was a part of his mother physically and was totally involved with her life. At birth the infant is separated from his mother. In a very real sense, he is on his own to establish the fact of his individuality to himself and to the world. Before birth the infant had significance only because of his mother; after his birth he becomes a total person in miniature, though undeveloped. He is no longer a part of his mother; he has become apart from her.

The important aspect of this change to keep in mind is the separation of the infant from his mother and how that fact continually impinges a problem upon the growing child. As he attempts courageously to cope with separation, he will grow emotionally, developing a self-concept. The vital condition for emotional growth is similar to physical growth. Parents must provide a resource for loving relationship within the home for a healthy emotional growth, just as they must provide a resource for nourishing food for physical growth.

The infant does not arrive at the feeling of being separated from his mother all at once. His hunger is probably the most significant experience in this regard. When he is hungry, he becomes aware of an irritation that mounts to painful proportions. He cries out in his misery, and his mother normally comes with relief. He eats, and the hunger vanishes. This cycle is repeated several times every day.

As the infant repeatedly deals with his hunger, he eventually senses a separation from his mother during the time he is appealing for help. His mind begins to associate discomfort, pain, and hunger pangs with being alone and in need of mother. He also begins to associate pleasure, comfort, and the satisfaction of having a full stomach with being with mother and united to her.

Thus, as far as the infant is aware, when he is in need of food he feels empty and alone. When he eats he feels full and together with his mother. At this age, eating is equal in effect to taking mother inside himself. By eating, he closes the separation gap completely. He is able to solve his problems of aloneness with his mouth by crying and by eating his fill.

It is interesting in this connection to note how we as adults may feel sort of hungry and loiter at the refrigerator when we are lonely or a little anxious. We may not associate our interest in eating with returning to our first source of inner security when we look for something to put into our mouth in times of boredom, depression, or unrest, but we are doing just that.

In the base of our thinking are two polarities of emotion: one set of memories is categorized as pleasant and contentable; the other is categorized as unpleasant and painful. Each category sponsors its own impulsive emotional reactions. Our innate reaction to pleasure is quietness and peace of mind. Our impulsive reaction to pain is tension and an appeal for help.

The infant's spontaneous reaction to pleasure is delight, perhaps manifested in a smile. His impulsive reaction to discomfort is tension, which he may manifest by crying. The tiny infant's scope of needs is so narrow at this time in his life that eating erases almost all his miseries. By crying for help and eating, he is able to reestablish his state of contentment and sense of security.

Apparently this leaves an indelible memory trace, for all through life we tend to think of putting something into our mouth — like food or drink or some pill to relieve tension — when we feel upset. Without thinking, we seem to assume that putting something into our mouth will restore our lost contentment.

It is appropriate to notice how the mother's instinctive attention to her newborn infant simulates the prenatal state. She wraps him snugly in cozy blankets and dresses him in soft garments. She attempts to keep her baby warm in a fairly constant temperature that is about the same as her own body. She does her best to protect the infant from shocking experiences, overheatedness, sudden noises, falling, and getting hurt.

Mother rocks her baby — the prenatal motion is a rocking, swaying motion. She hums to him — research reveals that sounds are heard by the unborn infant, and they are all humming sounds.[2] The mother seems instinctively to know that rocking and humming are quieting agents for her child; they have a tranquilizing effect because they correspond to a former state of being for the child when all was well.

Whether or not the mother knows the meaning of all she does, she is helping her baby bridge the separation gap by the way she cares for him. She is helping her baby to minimize his feelings of aloneness when she is not present.

Growth Brings a New Identity Crisis

The tiny infant normally begins to settle down in a few weeks after birth to a routine of living. He has adjusted to his new surroundings and the recurring pain of hunger; his body has accepted his daily diet fairly well. The infant cries when in misery, and mother comes consistently as needed. He eats until satisfied, feels the warm comfort of having mother, and returns to blissful slumber. This happens daily and with regularity.

Whenever the infant loses his blissful contentment because of a need for attention, he begins to be threatened with the idea of being alone and away from his mother. He cries; she comes. If he is hungry, he eats and is filled. He has his mother again and feels united with her. Because his needs are so few and simple, he feels in complete command of his own comfort and security.

For a brief period of time, an infant in his first month or so of life enjoys an unmolested sense of omnipotence. When he feels a loss of mother, which occurs whenever he is irritated and tense, he simply cries, she comes, and his bliss is soon restored. This happens so consistently that his memory of being satisfied and united with mother is no longer absolute in the sense of total loss as it was at first. The idea of mother not being with him at any moment becomes only a threat to his underlying tranquillity. He can cry and his bliss is restored, for his mother quickly attends to his needs.

This sense of unchallenged control of every factor that would threaten the infant's essential tranquillity continues long enough to leave an indelible memory trace. The infant grows. As he grows, his awareness of the world about him also grows, and his scope of pleasurable experiences enlarges. Crying and eating do not resolve all issues which cause him discomfort. His idealistic throne crumbles from under him. He discovers that he cannot command his world to be pleasant and make it happen. He is not self-sufficient or in total command. He must depend upon mother, and this immediately begins to give mother a peculiar value. He has lost his sense of self-determination and is becoming aware that he needs his mother, that he is very dependent upon her. This causes him to set up a new goal to compensate for his lost utopia. He attempts with increasing forcefulness to control mother.

From within, because of his grandiose experience of being in a command position of self-sovereignty, he expects himself to be omnipotent in his world. From without, he is reminded by his inability to enforce his commands that he is dependent. The dilemma of life is reawakened, and the old sense of separation from mother begins to dog him.

All through life we seem fundamentally to expect to be the center of our world and somehow able to command our environment to change to make us comfortable and bring us pleasure. Nevertheless, whenever our life situations do become exceedingly pleasant and we begin to feel in such an omnipotent position, we tend to fear that soon we will lose our happiness. We habitually tell ourselves whenever things go well, "This is too good to be true. It can't last." Some people go as far as to say, "I don't deserve all this luxury of happiness; I will pay for it somehow."

Apparently we are affected by both the memory of having at one time a total command of life and the trauma of losing that grandiose position. We are constantly seeking a state of sovereign control in situations wherein we can maintain our sense of satisfaction. As soon as circumstances begin to be pleasant consistently, we also begin to be anxious about the possibility of losing it all and being miserable.

Waiting for Service Magnifies the Crisis

That the infant often has to wait for mother's attention is perhaps the influence most threatening to destroy his assumed sense of omnipotent dominion. As the weeks pass, mother is not always so available to her baby as she was when he was first born. A variety of family duties crowd in and take priority over her need to be immediately at her baby's side when he is in need.

We need to interject here the idea that anyone who cares for the infant at this time is regarded as mother. The infant is many weeks old before he is able to perceive differences in the people who attend to him. They all serve him in a maternal role.

Having to wait for service heightens his miseries. He is unable to cope with this problem by anything he knows to do. Waiting makes the infant impulsively angry, for he has lost control of mother. Anger is his insistence that he be served immediately. He is doing all in his power to force his environment to serve his needs and restore his lost contentment. All through life, anger often serves the purpose of trying to force the environment to make things comfortable, and we are usually angry when we know of ·nothing else to do.

When his mother comes, the infant eats greedily while he is angry. Not only is he hungry, but he seems to be trying to eat enough never to be hungry again — and if never hungry, he will never feel separated from mother. If hunger makes the infant feel separated from mother, having to wait for service makes him feel isolated from her. These feelings create a terrifying identity crisis for the infant.

A new development begins to occur because of this identity crisis, due to the loss of being in control of his own securities. This growth occurs because the mother is consistent in supplying his needs, though he does have to wait at times for service. The infant begins to anticipate his mother's coming when he cries. After crying, he will listen. If he does not hear anyone moving toward him, he will begin crying again.

This is the beginning of the formation of a mental bridge which closes the separation gap caused by birth. The memories of his mother's coming cause him to fantasize her arrival with all the food and relief he desires. Instead of the infant's depending upon his own ability to call and get his own relief in an omnipotent way, he begins to depend upon his mother's faithfulness. The fantasy of her coming lays the foundation for a sense of trust in the goodness of life.

With the emergence of his ability to fantasize, the infant has made a major step in development. He had a trust in his own efforts to bring the supply of his needs, but he had a traumatic failure trusting only in himself. Now he is beginning to trust in the idea that his mother is reliable as well as in his own efforts to get her attention.

The mental picture the infant has of his mother's coming with the supply of his needs is idealistic. Our ability to idealize is derived from a very ordinary experience — having had to wait for our food when we were tiny infants! The infant's ability to anticipate the ideal satisfaction based upon trust in the reliability of his source of supply lays the basis for an important aspect of thinking that reaches a more complete development later in childhood. The trait is called *hope*.

Early Beginnings of Relationship Feelings

We have previously indicated that empathy is an infant's instinctive talent for communication with other people which provides him as he grows with the ability to identify and to experience love.

An infant is only a few weeks old when he manifests his ability to empathize. We smile at the baby and he smiles back.

Someone in the home may be frightened by something the baby knows nothing about, but he cries out in fear.

Empathy brings a new factor into the accumulation of experiences for the growing child. Eating and feeling satisfied have a tentative effect upon the feelings of separation from mother. But while mother is attending to his needs, she talks to her baby and affectionately holds him. His ability to empathize with her feelings makes him feel as if he is somebody. This interaction lays the fundamental idea of being a person in the infant's mind. His mother and others who attend to him, when love is present, treat him with respect and dignity as a little person of importance with feelings. He empathically senses these attitudes and values himself accordingly.

When the infant is hungry and waiting for his food, he not only imagines his mother coming with what he wants, but he naturally thinks of her pleasant attitude and affectionate love. In fantasy he hears her exclamations of delight. In this way satisfaction and pleasure become associated in the unconscious with ideas of being somebody, a person of importance. Also, discomfort and irritation begin to associate with feelings of unimportance and ideas of being nobody. If a child has to wait excessively long, or is scolded angrily for the inconvenience he causes his parents, a terrifying sense of aloneness and abandonment periodically dominates the infant's mind. He has no way of relieving this sense of isolation except by seeking excessive sensual gratification; but even this gives him no lasting security.

In this early period of life, the feelings of being somebody that begin to occur through the empathic sense of mother's love cause the infant to want to be close to his mother whether he is hungry or not. In her affectionate presence he feels accepted, secure, and quite at home. It is a traumatic adjustment for an infant to discover his mother's absence when he needs her. When she does arrive, his extreme delight with her presence is apparent.

All through life a person needs to feel acceptable. When one loses his fundamental sense of being somebody, he feels depressed. If the condition continues for any lengthy period of time, he loses interest in continuing to live. We must feel like somebody in order to want to continue living and to feel enthusiastic about circumstances.

Research indicates that infants who are cared for only in a perfunctory manner — by several persons acting as mother, without the affectionate care usually given to infants — soon become sickly and seldom live beyond their first year. Infants who receive the same attention to all their physical needs, but with the usual loving affection of a mother, thrive and are healthy and happy.[3]

The infant's ability to empathize with his mother's loving affection begins to show its effects before he is four months old. From this time on, the infant manifests an attachment for his mother that is technically known as a *symbiotic* relationship. He feels a part of her when he is near her and comforted.

The ability to respond empathically to mother also leads the infant to recognize that he can control his mother's reactions to himself and cause her to feel pleasured. This interaction between infant and mother pleasuring each other enhances the symbiotic relationship, and it also is employed by the infant as he grows into greater awareness. He learns that he can execute some control of his mother by his own attitudes.

The child keeps growing. His needs for feeling like somebody grow as he grows. His resources for self-identity also grow because his awareness is enlarging and experiences are accumulating. Just having a full stomach and being comforted by a loving mother are not his only resources for pleasure. He finds pleasure in touching his own body and looking at himself. He finds pleasure in putting objects into his mouth for examination. He finds pleasure in certain simple toys and in interacting with other members of his family. By this variety of contacts with his environment, he develops an inner world of memories which congregate in his mind to supply him with feelings of being somebody.

It is important to note that a world of experience is growing for the infant that supplants the need to have sensual contentment at all times in order to feel secure. This inner world is primarily related to people, and it becomes the beginning of a healthy, positive self-concept if the child is truly loved. If his environment is not loving, he cannot built this positive world of interaction, but must hold on to the proven security of being sensually gratified.

The contrasting feelings of being pleasured and ''in'' with others and being miserable and ''out'' with others form the polarities of emotional growth for strength or for weakness in self-concept. The environment has the power to build either inner security or insecurity with the infant. The first year is fundamental to developing a sense of being somebody or of being nobody, and these basic feelings can last a lifetime.

7

Early Beginnings of Self-Concept

A child experiences the beginning of many important aspects of his personality during the first year of his life. The most significant of these is the sense of belongingness, the first element of his self-concept. Belongingness is an island of emotional security within the psyche that develops in loving relationships because the child is able to empathize and to identify.

Empathy and Identification at Work

Grandpa and Grandma came from the East to visit Luke, their first grandchild. It was indeed an exciting moment when they got off the plane and arrived at the house. Three-month-old Luke joined in the celebration as though he knew just what was happening. He smiled and effervesced joyously as his grandparents delighted themselves in him. Luke was able to communicate because of his ability to empathize.

Carla, Luke's mother, had become friends with Coleen while they were roommates in the maternity ward at the hospital. They promised to keep in touch with each other after they went home. One day, when their babies were about four months old, they got together. The two babies were placed side by side. Both mothers were surprised at the way their babies tried to entertain each other. It was obvious the infants felt they had much in common. Later, when one baby cried, the other baby cried also. This indicated that the babies were not only empathizing, but beginning to identify with each other.

When an infant is only a few months old, he seems to distinguish between being complimented, being just spoken to, or being scolded. He not only perceives the mood of his parents, but also identifies with their feelings. The words they use that describe their thoughts and feelings form memory patterns of sound in the mind which associate with the feelings being expressed. This becomes the basis of the child's learning to speak.

The child apparently senses his own importance when he receives distinguished attention. He perceives a loss of value when he is not pleasing or is reprimanded. He identifies with how his parents feel about him, and this forms the basis of his self-concept.

As a child's ability to identify grows — and it does as his variety of experiences increases — he regards himself as being a person in about the same degree as others regard him. Either he identifies with their love and develops positive feelings about himself, or he identifies with their disapproval and develops negative feelings about himself.

A problem fundamental to emotional insecurity is that a child identifies with both attitudes manifested by his parents, and he grows up to feel unsure of himself. Sometimes he feels positive about himself and sometimes he feels negative. Sometimes he seems able to get what he wants, and sometimes he doesn't.

The infant's first sense of emotional security is associated with being made to feel comfortable. When he is satisfied, he feels contented — he is somebody; when he is hungry, in pain, or miserable and alone, he is threatened by feelings of being nobody. As the child grows toward his first birthday, he increases in his ability to identify; this ability sponsors the development of a mental structure that transcends the child's earlier need to be comforted in order to have a sense of security. The child feels good about himself when he is comfortable, when he seems able to get what he wants, but he also feels good about himself when others show they like him.

Thus, identification and love sponsor the development of a mental structure called a self-concept which provides a child with a sense of his own integrity. This structure in the mind takes the place of having to feel contented and comfortable, perhaps pampered, in order to have a sense of being somebody.

Two Ways of Feeling Like Somebody

The infant has two ways of feeling like somebody, and these two means of self-identity remain with him all his life. One is by being made to feel comfortable and contented — that is, getting his way — and the other is by feeling loved. Both resources meet at the same point when the child is comforted by loving parents. As the child grows a little older, even in his second year, these two may diverge and become separate.

Obviously, the first is narcissistic and as unstable as the very pleasure that created the sense of security. As long as the child is comfortable, he is somebody; but as soon as he is uncomfortable, he tends to lose that sense of self-approval. He feels like a nobody.

The infant compensates for the unconscious loss of self-approval by projecting the irritation to some other object. In anger he blames whatever is "not I" and this maintains the illusion of self-approvel. Moreover, this pattern follows a person all his life; he reacts to displeasure by becoming angry. An angry person never views himself as being wrong, for being responsible for what he does not like, or for how he is reacting. His anger maintains a sense of self-approval for whatever he does, because he projects all badness to some "not I" object.

The other resource for feeling like somebody is in the accumulated unconscious memories of identification when the infant, on various occasions, has felt loved by his parents. In this structure of memories, he retains a sense of self-approval whether or not he is immediately pleased. Displeasure does not result in feeling insecure, only miserable. Thus self-concept gives an inner stability to withstand the vicissitudes of pain and pleasure in the daily life situations.

In early infancy, the evidences of this stabilizing memory structure are not apparent, for they are just beginning to form in the unconscious. By the time the child begins his teenage years, and sometimes before that, he manifests the stabilizing values of self-concept. If he has been reared in a home with loving relationships, he can trust his parents' promises, depend upon his parents' goodness in truly being interested in his welfare. He may not like unpleasant situations, for no one does, but he is not liable to question his own integrity because of the situation. He has a resilience in coping with distressing situations. The child who has not felt so loved will be more likely to experience an identity crisis because of the distress.

The child who has not been sufficiently loved is more dependent upon being comforted and in getting his own way for his sense of self-identity. He tends to manifest a high level of hostility in his thinking. When we say this, we must remember that hostility is, in the general sense of the term, a negative, unaccepting, distrusting attitude toward people and situations. Hostility is not only a reaction to feeling unloved, but a way of maintaining a sense of self-approval through projecting irritation and responsibility for displeasure to anything that is "not I."

Effects of Unloving Parental Attitudes

When an infant in his first year of life does not feel loved, he has no resource for a sense of being somebody. His only means of bridging the separation gap caused by his birth is the sensual pleasure of eating and his ability to force his mother or others to attend to his needs by his angry demands expressed usually in a tantrum. When he is inconsistently attended to and neglected, he has no way of determining a reliable sense of contentment, a condition that simulates his prenatal state, in which at one time he felt secure.

Physical growth involves eating nourishing food and getting proper exercise. In doing this, a person overcomes the silent forces of death within himself. But he must have some consistency in eating and exercising. He cannot feast at one meal and then not eat again for several days. He cannot be healthy if he nibbles at food and never eats a full meal. Good health relies upon some regularity in one's habits of exercise and eating.

Emotional growth and emotional health also depend upon needs being met regularly and dependably. "The development of emotional security in the child is dependent upon the gratification of three specific needs: according to Preston's formulation, security rests upon three pillars of affection, approval, and consistency."[4]

Emotional growth for a child occurs naturally in the usual stress and rest cycle of daily events when the parents provide stable, reliable, consistent input to the child's awareness of being a person who is loved and cared for tenderly. When physical trauma or discomfort comes to the child, he is threatened with feelings of being isolated from mother. Isolation feelings are associated in the child's thinking with loss of security and with being nobody. The mother's loving care creates the illusion for the child that he is not separate, but united to her and a part of her. This sense of symbiotic relationship overcomes for the child his devastating sense of aloneness.

A child has a natural anger when he feels deprived and has to wait for service. When parents do not love their child, they either reject his appeals or punish him for bothering them with his needs. This forces the child to live with his anger feelings. Anger feelings are separation feelings: "I don't like you, for you are bad." When these negative feelings persist at this very young age, they interfere with the child's developing any primary love-object relationships. As many people know, the inability to form love-object relationships is a root cause for serious forms of emotional disturbance and mental illness.

The First Way Love Is Felt

Because of empathy and identification, the infant is continually affected by the attitudes of the people who attend to his needs, and especially by those who attempt to socialize with him. An infant reacts with relief to having a physical need met. His natural reactions are much more pronounced if he also is responding to love feelings being expressed by the person caring for him.

When a child is loved, he receives the message that he is accepted, desirable, lovable, important, and all right. The infant naturally associates the message he feels empathically with the pleasure feelings of being comforted that the mother provides as she cares for his necessities. Thus, at the roots of feeling loved lies the association of physical pleasure with emotional acceptance and approval.

If the infant were able to explain his first feelings of being loved, he might say, "I feel loved when mother lovingly makes me comfortable. I do not feel loved if she neglects me, makes me wait, or cares for me just because it is her duty." Since love is consonant with our nature, whatever feels like love at one period of life will always feel like love. All through life we tend to feel loved when someone cares enough about our feelings to take the initiative to make us feel comfortable. We do not feel loved if the same comfort is administered in a perfunctory manner or unwillingly.

The baby, as he grows toward his first birthday, begins to accept himself in the same degree that he feels accepted by his parents. If their love regards him as a little person with tender feelings, their compassion reflects within him a feeling of being a person who is dear to them. If he were able to talk, he might say, "I know I am a person because I belong to my parents; I feel loved because I am their child."

A Child Wants to Be Included

Feeling included in the family's affairs helps to develop a sense of belongingness. Belongingness is the first stable "somebody" feeling.

As soon as a baby is old enough to identify with his parents' feelings, he begins to show signs of wanting to be included in whatever is happening. He does not like to be an observer from the vantage point of a highchair or playpen; he wants to be a participant. He usually does not like his parents to leave him alone or with a baby-sitter; he has a natural desire to be with them. Babies often object rather strongly to being left, until they get used to the parting.

A baby is pleased when others notice him and speak to him. He identifies with his family continually as they relate to him as a person of value. He identifies with his family and learns to talk because they talk, and to walk because they walk. He learns to feed himself and to have table manners, to dress himself, and to express himself because of the influence of his family.

A child learns to regard himself as a person because others accept him and relate lovingly to him. By the process of identification, the infant becomes related to his family emotionally. As he feels included, he develops a sense of belongingness. Feelings of belongingness erase the dreaded feelings of separation and aloneness even when he may be apart from his family for a short period of time.

The child is still somewhat threatened by feelings of separation when he gets hungry or tired or has to wait very long for something he wants, but as the months of his first year of life come and go, these feelings become less threatening. Yet unpleasant feelings that are painful tend to reinforce feelings of separateness when the parent is not compassionate or concerned.

Love Must Be Voluntary

Parental love is voluntary if it is genuine. The child needs to do nothing to earn it or qualify for feeling loved. Love must not be conditional. Whether the child is a boy or a girl, beautiful or homely, healthy or crippled, he must feel loved because he is a person. True love is voluntary on the part of the lover and unconditional. A child can tell if love is true or not. Adults also know when someone is, with good intentions, only *trying* to love or to be loving.

This is a most important truth. At the heart of personality is the need to feel a sense of being lovable without having to qualify for that acceptance.

Beginnings of Hope Feelings

A baby is only a few weeks old when he cries for attention and then listens for his mother's coming. His crying and listening indicates he has developed a memory of his mother's consistent concern and care. He is beginning to depend upon her coming when he cries. This is a rudimentary beginning of faith in the reliability of people and in the goodness of life. It is fundamental to the sense of expecting help when one appeals for it. Later in life this aspect of thinking becomes what we call anticipation and hope.

It is interesting to note the early beginnings of three positive reactions. They are most important to emotional growth and a healthy maturation. These three positive reactions are faith, hope, and love.

Observe that the mother's consistent care leads the child to have faith. The mother's delight in being able to care for her child and to satisfy his needs leads him to have hope. All of this happens because of her unconditional love. Her love teaches him to love.

The Bible says, concerning these three pillars of an abundant life, "Faith, hope, love abide, these three; but the greatest of these is love" (1 Cor. 13:13 RSV). Love is a positive emotion of relationship that is satisfying.

When the infant begins to manifest an expectation of his mother's attention, he is exercising the very earliest feelings of belongingness. Though they are exceedingly fragmentary, they are sufficient for his momentary infantile needs. He is beginning to bridge the separation gap which he experienced emotionally when he was born and cut off from her. He keeps reexperiencing this gap whenever he feels in distress. This gap between mother and child is magnified when he has to wait for service. Nevertheless, because of the distress and its continual recurrence with each physical discomfort or misery, the mother continually manifests her love in the care she gives. The distress reveals to the child his mother's love, and this strengthens his sense of emotional oneness with her.

Thus the very distress which threatens to annihilate the infant with feelings of separation and a loss of identity becomes, in the contest of feeling loved, the very agent for developing emotional security. At this point in the child's life, the security is felt as a sense of belongingness; later, as he grows and has other needs, worthiness and competence will be experienced in the context of being loved when threatened with separation and isolation and aloneness.

Coping With an Infant's Anger

The natural anger of the infant which occurs because he must at times wait for service is a force to be considered. Anger is an emotion that contradicts whatever feelings of belongingness the infant may be developing. The loving care of the mother in these first weeks of life, and all through the impressionable years, is crucial in preventing this anger from becoming a strong deterrent to emotional growth.

Mother's love and care do more than just relieve a child's distress about which he is complaining. Her love gives him a sense of being somebody that is apart from and transcendent to any self-identity he may be able to enforce by his anger feelings. The value of his mother's love is a gift offered to him; the value he is trying to enforce by his anger requires effort. Because the mind always follows the line of least effort and greatest pleasure, the child readily gives up trying to enforce a self-identity and receives his mother's love and her feelings that he is someone important. In her love his anger is erased.

A loving mother attends to her child's needs as soon as it is practically possible. She does not neglect him, nor does she overindulge him with immediate service every time. When he becomes angry, she speaks affectionately to him, and he gets over it. For instance, the infant may be too angry to nurse after he has waited for a while. She caresses him, touches a little milk to his lips, speaks kindly and coaxingly, and he tastes the good flavor. In his anger, his world became all bad; the good flavor of milk makes him realize that all is not so bad. Soon, in her loving appeal, he loses his anger and begins eating. His mother has restored his island of inner security.

The importance of this little maneuver in overcoming the infant's anger in the early beginnings of life cannot be overestimated. If the mother performs her duties to her child without the love factor, perhaps scolding him for being angry, she can unconsciously give him a sense of value for his anger. The infant may feel she is coming to him in answer to his rage, or because she is afraid of him, not because she wants to be helpful. If he were able to think cognitively, he might say, "Mother helps me because I *make* her do it."

If this impression gets started in the child's first year, he will have a most difficult time learning to obey after that. He will tend to feel he is more in control of his mother than controlled by her. Her normal instructions may seem to him to be domination.

The child may interpret also that he has to wait because his anger keeps his mother from coming. He may think either that she resents him for being angry at her and is punishing him, or that she is actually afraid of his anger. He may view his own anger as omnipotent and fearful, just as he feels afraid of his parents' anger. For this reason, the infant may be inclined as he grows to try to contain his anger so as not to frighten his parents or to irritate them and make them angry at him. His need to contain his anger in order to please his parents has a beginning in this very early period of a child's life.[5]

When a child expresses his anger, he may obtain what he wants from his parents. When a child contains his anger, he may also obtain what he wants from his parents. Some children obtain more reward from the first behavior; some obtain more from the second. Either way, the child knows he is *doing* something to get what he wants from his parents, and many of these wants may also be needs that the parents want to fulfill because they love him. He may feel he either has to overpower his parents, or has to submit to them and please them.

In either frame of mind, he may not perceive that they love

him and want to give him what he really needs. The child will have begun to perceive love as a relationship he must do something to obtain. He will begin to feel he has to qualify for his love. If he is good, he is loved; if he is bad, he is not. This idea keeps invading the child's mind naturally because of his reaction to discipline, but parents need to be careful not to reinforce it by their own attitudes. In the parental love, a child can resolve this feeling of being either "in" or "out" with his parents because they do not reject him for disobedience.

The problem of having to qualify for love has its origin in the child's needing to contain his own hostile feelings to get what he wants. We theorize that if the parents were always able to deal with their child's anger objectively and lovingly, he would not be so prone to try to qualify for the love he wants and needs.

The parent's own anger is the offender here most of the time. The parent may be aggravated at his child's behavior, but he must not allow himself to resent the child. Parents need to keep child and behavior separate in their thinking. Reject the behavior, not the child. In other words, *hold tenderly the child's self-esteem with gentle respect while you are reproving him of his inappropriate and wrong behavior.*

This issue is very important to the emotional welfare of the child. It cannot be overemphasized. Having to qualify in some way for love is the quicksand upon which emotional insecurity is built!

If parents consider seriously their very first reactions to their tiny child's first display of anger, they can develop a healthy habit of coping with these negative reactions. Then they will be more successful in coping with the child's anger feelings as he grows up. The unfortunate fact remains that parents often wait until their child is in his second or third year, and sometimes later, before they begin to deal with his anger feelings and his willfulness. This is most unfortunate, for the child then has his habits formed, and to change is a traumatic adjustment. The parents seem to him to change. He has had a chance to develop the habit of accepting his anger as a proper emotion, a manipulative weapon. As parents realize the value of the little displays of anger in the very first year of a child's life, and cope lovingly with the negative feelings, they reduce the growth of the weeds of anger from the garden of the child's emotions before they become unmanageable.

Three Types of Negative Feelings in Infants

A tiny infant manifests negative feelings in three ways. First, he cries and thrashes about in his crib, signaling to all that he has a need. He is attempting to project out his irritation to get rid of it.

Second, the child often becomes angry because of delay. His irritation is not reduced by his projecting it out, and he begins to feel overcome by irritation. His increased efforts to project it out become his anger. In this state of mind, the child is sensing his aloneness. He is separated from his mother, and this awakens ideas of being cut off, isolated, and feeling like a nothing. This loss of security also intensifies his anger, for the child feels rejected.

Third, when his anger brings no results, he feels overwhelmed by his own irritation. Being overwhelmed, he starts feeling sorry for himself. His fantasy of expectation has collapsed, and he feels helpless and hopeless. Self-pity projects blame to ''it,'' the mother, for being absent when he needs her. Unwittingly the child is trying to hold onto a sense of self-identity in the midst of his irritation by being the innocent victim.

The infant may progress through the first two feelings rapidly and arrive at the third very soon, or he may remain in either of the first two and not assume the self-pity position. But any one of the three negative feelings is quickly canceled and erased empathically from the infant's mind by the mother when she brings relief. It is the attitude of the mother as well as the relief she brings that corrects the infant's emotional problem related to his identity. If she identifies with the child's feelings, the child feels accepted in his bad state of mind; if she is provoked by his bad feelings, he feels rejected for his bad state of mind.

Fathers also take pride in their babies and often share in the intimate care. At this point in the baby's life, father is sensed as an extension of mother. Father serves in a mother role to the child in the first two years or so of the child's life, though the infant may be able to recognize that one is ''daddy,'' and the other is ''mommy.''

First Awareness of Self-Concept

At about eight months to one year, a baby has experienced enough in relationships with his mother to regard her as a total person. To this time, he has identified with her only in a fragmentary way.

During this time, observing parents also note that their child is beginning to show signs of regarding himself as an individual. His thinking and responses are not all simple reactions to stimuli as they have been. He starts to reveal a character to his thinking that shows he regards himself as a person and a part of his family. When he is able to view his mother as a total person, he is also able to begin to view himself as a total person.

The child in a home where he has felt loved will identify with how his parents feel about him. This shapes his self-identity. Loving relationships in the home give the child a sense of belongingness. He feels "a part of" and begins to think "we" in his ideas. As he identifies with good feelings about himself, he develops a bank of memories that sustain him with self-identity feelings of belongingness while under the stress of unpleasant happenings and of situations that make him angry.

If parents do not love their baby, and no one else consistently shows him love either, he has no way to discover a sense of self-identity apart from his first feelings of security — that is, through being gratified in some sensual way. He will, indeed, suffer severe emotional deprivation. All his life he will strive to be comforted, indulged, and pampered, for this is his emotional security. He may be inclined to pamper himself in many ways for the same reason. Also, he will deeply resent every inconvenience, every disappointment, and every painful experience, for he will not have developed the resources in love to resolve his feelings of loss of self-identity. He will continue to associate discomforts with separation, isolation, and aloneness that say to him he is nobody.

Though he may seek earnestly to find love from many friends, he will secretly believe he can never be loved, for he has so much unresolved rage within himself. If his parents could not take his anger when he was an infant, how can he expect a friend to accept him with his rage when he is an adult? Without an essential sense of belongingness, a person is seriously handicapped in all his relationships.

Such a problem need not be regarded as unresolvable. It is obvious, however, that it requires some very special relationships to reach into those very primitive feelings of being unwanted to overcome the hostility problem that has blighted life for many years.

It must be emphasized that the love-starved child will seek to be loved in life because his emotional needs were not met earlier. He will also resist anyone who does love him, because his self-concept indicates he is unlovable and unwanted. He sincerely believes that if he trusts others and accepts their love, he will only be rejected again and feel more devastated than ever. To accept love means to believe oneself lovable. That idea to the unloved child is so idealistic he is afraid of it.

This may explain the shallowness of many relationships. We want to be close, but not too close. We keep a distance, but are careful not to get too far away. The person who is secure enough in himself to love unconditionally and persistently with patience can usually win with the person who is afraid of love, but not easily.

The First Birthday

As the baby approaches his first birthday, he imaginatively begins to project himself into his parents. They become for him a living illustration of what he will be like when he grows up. When he learns to talk, he may say, "When I grow up, I'm going to be *you*." He may say this to either parent; sexual differences are not important to a child of this age.

One factor that has stimulated the child's growth toward identifying with his mother as a total person and viewing himself as an individual who belongs in his family is the experience of cutting teeth. Until the time when teeth begin to erupt through the gums, the baby invests most of his good feelings in his mouth. But when he teethes, his mouth becomes very sore and thus is a bad object. He must find another object. The sympathy of his family, and especially his mother, during this period of suffering helps him to turn from sensual pleasure to love as a source of his own security. As his mother expresses sympathy and attempts to make his mouth feel better during this painful experience, he is encouraged to identify with her as a total person and be reaffirmed in his relationship with her.

The awareness of belonging to his family and to his parents in particular is just beginning to become established at the opening of the child's second year. Belongingness will be taxed again and again with the stresses that the various growth factors initiate into the child's thinking.

Belongingness is the first and primary element in the development of self-concept, and its development overlaps the evolution of both worthiness and competence. All three elements of self-concept become then about what they will be by the time the child has reached adulthood.

8

Parental Discipline Critically Affects Self-Concept

.   About the time a child blows out the candle on his first birthday cake, he faces a new threat to his germinating sense of being somebody. At this period the child is growing and changing very rapidly from being dependent and helpless to being an active investigator and a threat to the tranquillity of the home. The whole household marshals into a defensive unit to protect the child from injury and valuable properties from irreparable damage.

The irksome restrictions enforced upon the child and the painful consequences of his own willfulness reactivate the old feelings of being separated, isolated, and alone. He usually has lost most of the parental indulgence he formerly enjoyed and is faced with firm discipline and its immanent possibility of dreaded punishment.

The Change Created by Growth

In his second year the child usually begins to walk. This achievement makes him mobile and capable of getting into various areas of the house without assistance or permission. Not long after he learns to walk, he experiments with climbing and standing on precarious edges totally unaware of impending dangers. He also explores the effects of various sounds — loud sounds and soft sounds — but his family scarcely appreciate his investigations. He puts almost everything into his mouth for examination whether or not it is clean. He enjoys cracking raw eggs, playing in his food, and seeing what a mess he can make at the table by spilling milk and dropping food and utensils on the floor.

As the child learns to talk and to express himself more clearly, he naturally attempts to make his wishes and dislikes profoundly understood. Since he was in the habit of getting what he wanted during his first year, and since being made comfortable is associated in his mind with feeling secure, he now has an insatiable demand for getting his own way in whatever suggests itself to his inquisitive mind.

His parents must limit his activities and control his behavior. They know from observation that if they do not begin early to discipline their child, he will grow up to become the tyrannical monarch of the household with no compassion or consideration for the rights and feelings of others. They know he will feel he has an innate prerogative to anything he wishes and that he will consider everyone obligated to come to his service instantly upon demand.

Thus parental discipline is a necessity, brought upon the child by the nature of his own growth and the environmental situation in which he lives. From the child's point of view, his parents — especially his mother, because she usually is with him the most — seem to have drastically changed. Once mother humored his every wish; now she forbids and punishes much of the time. Little does the child realize that he is the cause of the apparent change or that the resolution to his confusing dilemma is to learn to obey.

When the parents feel they must punish him for disobedience, the child's first inclination is to feel rejected, separated, and cut off from them. They have never treated him this way before. They scold and administer pain. As the parents consistently enforce their regulations, the child begins to learn to surrender his desired object to them and yield to their commands. When he does so, he is restored to their good graces and his separation anxiety is healed. He is again at peace with them. This is the essence of child training and emotional development.

In the parents' loving forgiveness is restoration. Belongingness that was threatened is reaffirmed when correction is appropriate and fair. As belongingness is again and again restored and verified in parental discipline, a new sense of being somebody emerges which is called *worthiness*.

A Child Needs to Feel Respected When Corrected

When parents love their child enough to show respect for

the tender, fragile self-esteem just beginning to take shape, they will measure their disciplinary actions with a sense of responsibility for his emotional welfare. They will be guided by the fact that the child's impressionable mind is being molded for good or evil by everything they do with him and to him.

If parents can maintain a perspective on the peculiar privilege and serious responsibility of parenthood, they can do much to motivate their child to want to obey them. The central goal of disciplinary methods is to incite the child to be readily willing to obey parental commands and to heed instruction. When a child is motivated to obey willingly, he develops a character structure in which he wholeheartedly wants to do what is right because he enjoys being right.

When parents become angry at the troubles and inconveniences their child brings into their lives, often resenting the extra work he causes them, they lose this valuable perspective on the privilege and responsibility of parenthood. The child becomes a burden and a bother to them. When this happens, they govern him to reduce their own personal discomforts instead of governing him primarily for his own welfare.

Parental aggravation and anger in the disciplinary process increase the child's sense of separation and loss of belongingness. The parental anger reinforces the child's idea that he is being restricted or punished because his parents do not like him, not because they are concerned for his good.

For this reason, parental anger in discipline incites the child to be defensive with his parents instead of accepting of their authority. This defensiveness increases the child's tendency to be defiant and manipulative. The disrespect which the angry parents show their child promotes the very power struggle between parent and child that frustrates the parent and harms the child's emotional development. Hostilities mount higher and higher, and the struggle can never be resolved.

Angry parents often attempt to frighten their child into being obedient with a wild threat or painful punishment. Some threaten to abandon him if he does not obey, actually playing upon his natural separation anxiety. Fear may subdue the child's will temporarily, but it is cruel and demoralizing and does not incite the child to want to be obedient because the parents are asking him to do what is right. Instead, as soon as the child feels it is safe, he may strive to overcome the domination of his fear and attempt to obtain whatever it was the parents forbade him. Or, the fear may cause him to have a passive-dependent attitude in life and make him unable to be decisive or exercise his own initiative without great anxiety.

Parental anger makes the child tend to feel he is subject to an enemy and must obey against his will. He must compensate for his loss of belongingness and feelings of worth to his parents, so he does things that both express his angry defiance and verify his importance to them. The parents' angry response to his willful defiance verifies in a negative way that he has value to them. The more he aggravates, the more value he feels — though the child learns quickly to measure his conduct so as not to incite parental wrath to such a degree that he will be physically hurt by the punishment.

From the child's point of view, he feels in control of his parents, for he can make them angry and play upon their sense of fairness to the extent that he does not get hurt. He may feel in control of them though he be continually defeated by them and afraid of their wrath. But all sense of positive relationship is lost.

Parents should be alert to the possibility of this reaction pattern developing and defeat it when it arises. The evidence that it might be beginning lies in the parents' noticing that they are continually negative, critical, and aggravated about their child's behavior. They have lost the balance of good feelings and positive relationship with him. The pattern can be defeated if the parents will deliberately set about a program of developing a positive, personal relationship with their child, of minimizing their tendency to nag at him critically, and of conquering their own anger with him because of disobedience. The result of such a threefold program will be a decided increase in understanding and appreciating their child's growing personality, and the child will begin to respond with a more willing obedience. His basic needs for love will be supplied, and he will not have to compensate.

If parents do not respect their child's emotional need for a sense of acceptance as a person during these critical moments of discipline, they automatically instill the idea in the child's mind that he ought only to respect himself if and when his conduct is acceptable. This places the quality of his performance squarely in the middle of his self-identity structure. And this malformation of self-concept will be a constant source of insecurity for the child all his life. Performance must be maintained and improved upon to remain valid as a source of security, and there are many unpredictable factors in life that can limit or destroy one's ability to perform.

If a child does not feel respected when corrected, he is handicapped, for he has no other resource but the attitude of his parents for finding his self-identity. Whenever a child's feelings of being rejected by discipline are not thoroughly restored, he resentfully concludes he is not worthy of acceptance. Such a sense of being nobody is self-destructive and self-effacing, so the child represses the idea of being nobody. He continues to seek some way of finding a sense of being somebody, though he is unconsciously persuaded he is nobody.

Since the parents' rejection of his appearance or performance was probably the cause of the child's feeling like a nobody, he may try to improve upon his appearance or performance to regain his lost self-identity. Relying upon status values for this is a later development, occurring after the child has achieved more competence and has acquired skills he can be proud of. Not only are appearance, performance, and status values insecure and unreliable, but using them in the identity structure creates another problem.

The improvement of appearance or performance or status values can become a way of finding a lost sense of being somebody, and not for self-improvement. The child begins to work hard to prove to himself that he is not a nobody. This introduces a drastic fracture in the child's sense of inner wholeness. His security rests on relative values.

If a child feels respected as a person when he is corrected, he will not lose respect for himself, though he may have done something very wrong. He will naturally feel bad about his mistake, but he will believe in himself that he can overcome the problem and do better next time. The child who does not feel respected when corrected will tend to despair when he does something wrong. He will not only fear the punishment, but be reawakened to the fact that he is nobody and bad. Instead of believing he can correct his problem, he will tend to be anxious or depressed or give up, perhaps feeling sorry for himself, saying, "I can never do anything right!"

Consider two-year-old Jeffrey and three-year-old Claudia at mealtime. They have upset their plates, spilling food on themselves and on the floor.

Jeffrey's mother thought more of her child's feelings than she did about the mess and the work of cleaning it up. "You did not watch what you were doing!" she exclaimed. "You spilled your food all over yourself, and look at the mess of the floor. You had your plate too close to the edge of the table. Now keep your plate here, and this will not happen."

Claudia's mother heard the crash of the plate and yelled, "You did it again! You'll never learn. You dumb idiot! Now look at the mess I have to clean up! I could just shake your teeth loose. You make me so furious!"

Jeffrey was taught how to correct his mistake, and his mother displayed a confidence that he would learn not to spill his food. Claudia's mother, on the other hand, was insulting and degrading in her angry attitude. She was probably feeling pressured by many problems and this was one more problem she was not ready to accept, making her inconsiderate of her child's feelings. Or, she may have been tired and irritable and not well, perhaps enduring a headache, when Claudia spilled her food, and this caused her to be explosive. Or, Claudia's mother may have resented the intrusion of her child into her career, or the feeling of bondage caused by the relentless tedium of overseeing and cleaning up after her. For whatever reason Claudia's mother exploded with wrath, she dumped her feelings on Claudia and gave no instruction about improvement. She called Claudia a bad person because she had made a mistake, and worst of all, she told Claudia she was unable to learn to do better. Yet she expected her daughter to improve!

If Claudia should be subjected to this kind of discipline often when she is very young, she will be convinced she is unwanted and a bother to her mother unless she somehow does just what her mother wants her to and never makes a mistake. She will have no idea how to perform acceptably. If she happens to please her mother, she may feel accepted, but will fear losing her sense of worth suddenly if she happens to cause her mother any problem. So Claudia will have no secure feelings about her own worth as a person, and she will not be able to trust other people's acceptance of her as reliable. We can predict that Claudia will grow to be an emotionally insecure person if this kind of discipline continues.

A New Dimension Is Added to Feeling Loved

A child of two or three years of age might say, "I know I am loved when I am taken care of tenderly. I also know I am loved when I am allowed to have my own way. I do not feel loved when I am forbidden or punished."

Later, after the child has grown a little in his disciplinary experiences, he may change his perception of being loved. He may add to what he previously said, "I feel loved if my parents correct me when I need it and they show me how to do things right. I do not feel loved if they neglect to tell me when I am wrong and I get hurt. I feel rejected if they correct me when they are angry."

Loving parents usually divide an infant's world into part good and part bad when they discipline. They avoid taking something away without giving him something to cling to. "You can have this, or you can do this, but not this" is the essence of their instructions. They divide his perception of his world into part good and part bad and so help him to sacrifice what they do not want him to have. If he chooses to disobey, they reprimand or punish and try to redirect his attention to what he can enjoy safely, but warn him to avoid what they have refused him. This helps him to develop emotional security.

Unloving parents, on the other hand, are basically aggravated by the inconvenience their child causes them. They usually discipline impulsively and in a hurry. They do not divide the child's world and give him something he can hold to. He has no alternative but to stop everything or to quit all he is doing. When the child moves to something else, he has no way of knowing for sure he can have it. It also might be suddenly taken away, and he will again be in trouble with his parents. They fail to take the responsibility for their child's clear understanding of what they want him to do or not to do before they punish him for disobedience. Often the child is confused about just why he is being punished or what his parents want of him. They assume he understands and hold him responsible whether or not he understands them.

Is it any wonder that children become angry with their parents and have no way to resolve those negative feelings? If parents who show so little consideration were employed by someone who treated them the way they demand obedience from their children, they would no doubt seek other employment to resolve their rage. But their children cannot seek other parents! They have to cope with the ones they were born to.

A child's only sense of being somebody at this early age is derived either from being pleasured in some way or by feeling accepted and a delight. He feels separated and alone, sometimes isolated and like a bad nobody, when his parents are angry with him and berate him for unacceptable behavior. When parents forward a sense of being a good somebody to their child in their loving discipline, they motivate him to want to correct his mistakes and do what is expected. When parents attack their child's self-identity for bad conduct, they rob him of a sense of being somebody of worth, and so motivate him to be defiant and independent of them, wishing he could hurt them back for the way he feels hurt by them.

The Impact of Toilet Training

Toilet training begins a process of thinking known as *self-control*. Self-control underlies the ability to be responsible, decisive, and self-governing.

A child needs to learn to obey his parents in eliminating his body wastes at the appointed place. At first this demand probably seems to the child an invasion of his right to do as he pleases. He insists on freedom in these matters by not heeding their instruction.

His parents' disapproval creates many tensions in his relationship with them. The way his parents manage this conflict has lasting effects upon the child's emotional development.

Some parents are consistently casual in their toilet-training discipline. They have a long-range goal in mind, and if their child fails to control his functions, they patiently instruct him and encourage him to do better next time. They seldom, if ever, punish him for a failure. They persistently work with their child until the goal of dependability is achieved. Such parental discipline usually accomplishes the needed self-control with a minimum of unhealthy aftereffects.

Other parents are impatient and severe in the toilet training and insist their child accomplish self-control rapidly. They punish their child verbally, and sometimes physically, shaming him for his mistakes. Such treatment can cause lasting emotional damage. The child may feel insecure about controlling his natural impulses and harbor an underlying fear of responsibility all through life.

A few parents seem to be in some kind of contest, either to prove their own parental superiority or to prove the superiority of their child. They hurry most unrealistically with toilet-training procedures.

Natalie, for instance, boasted to me that her daughter was completely trained at six months of age. She never washed a diaper for her after about eight months. She explained how she awakened her child from her sleep during the night again and again to accomplish her goal. Natalie detested washing diapers. She said she believed other mothers slaved unnecessarily cleaning up after their children.

At the time Natalie told me this, her daughter was fifteen. She was a healthy child but exceedingly insecure and nervous, seldom being able to sleep a night through without waking several times. The slightest noise would disturb her rest. Doctors could find no physical cause for her restlessness. It seemed to me that the extreme methods used in toilet training, coupled with the mother's intense demand that her child not inconvenience her, caused her daughter's nervousness.

Toilet training is exceedingly elementary. It is not rational to relate present personality problems only to bad toilet-training procedures, for that would be an oversimplification. Many other conflicts in a child's experiences negate or reinforce lessons learned in this early period of growth. Nevertheless, we must consider the total parent-child relationship in order to interpret and correct emotional insecurities in adult life.

Toilet Training Awakens a Time-Consciousness

A child has no particular experience by which to be aware of the rapid or slow passage of time until he has to hurry to get to the bathroom. In these crises he learns something about how much or how little he can do under the duress of a time factor.

The polarity of frustration is reversed in toilet training. When the child had to wait for his mother to serve his needs, he was frustrated because she did not obey his wishes, and time passed slowly. In toilet training, the child gets frustrated with himself for not measuring his limitations more accurately, and time seems to pass rapidly. As the child begins to accept various responsibilities in the home, he also becomes aware of the importance of the passage of time. Parents want obedience *now*; the child tends to use time as a controlling agent by procrastinating.

Implications About Personal Worth in Toilet Training

When a child fails to make it to the bathroom, he may be somewhat frustrated with himself because he anticipates his mother's sharp disapproval. He may also feel dirty and ashamed depending, of course, upon how his mother usually feels about such an incident. If he succeeds in making it to the bathroom, he may also have a glowing sense of accomplishment by the same type of mother influence.

If, when he fails, his mother does not become angry but firmly admonishes him to think ahead and try to do better next time, he may easily dismiss any self-rejecting ideas he has. On the other hand, if his mother or father expresses anger and disgust for his untidy behavior, and does so consistently — perhaps communicating in attitude if not in words, "You will never learn; you are just a bad child" — he may harbor deep feelings of self-distrust. He may grow to believe that he is essentially an unpredictable and bad person.

In toilet training, a child may be faced again and again with feelings of being a bad nobody. He cannot bear such ideas. They are devastating and depressing, especially because they are related to controlling impulses that are themselves associated with filth, foul odors, and repulsive materials. For this reason the child quickly denies and represses such an evaluation of himself. This *repression* is a critical factor in personality development.

With this repression, a shift is made in the child's motivation to do what is right. The child begins to do right and seeks to become perfect to prove to himself that he is not bad and no good. He begins to lose sight of doing right for the sake of being more accomplished. His behavior becomes welded to his self-identity structure as a means of rating him as a person. He must become more nearly perfect to prove to himself that he is not a bad nobody.

This repression seems to occur to everyone to some degree, for no one has been loved perfectly by his parents, and no one has ever obeyed with complete self-abandonment in response to parental love. A child has to be defeated in his persistent attempts to exercise his sense of independent prerogative to do as he pleases, and his hostility has to be neutralized toward his parents for being defeated by them. These contrary elements in every child's makeup eventually become self-convicting because they disturb his relationship with his environment and produce overwhelming consequences.

This inherent trait to use one's goodness and perfection as a verification to oneself that he is not a bad person is a key to understanding human behavior. It explains our innate sensitivity to criticism and vulnerability to praise. Criticism verifies our repressed, secret conviction that we are somehow defective and no good. Praise counteracts the repression and helps us to verify to ourselves that we are all right. It also explains why we usually find it difficult to admit our own faults and why we employ so many devices to avoid guilt, such as denial, rationalization, and projection of blame.

Two Kinds of Patience Are Needed

A child needs to develop two kinds of patience in these early years. He cannot do it immediately, for it requires much practice and it can be done only in loving home relationships. He needs to be patient with his parents' delays and denials, trusting in their essential interest in his welfare. He also needs to learn to be patient with himself when he makes a mistake or fails in some way, trusting in his own ability to do better next time.

The parental attitude is a determining influence. If parents are bothered and aggravated by their child's need for attention, the child will naturally lose confidence in his parents' interest in his welfare. If they degrade and insult him when he makes a mistake instead of just dealing with the mistake constructively, he will associate the quality of his character with the mistake and degrade himself as his parents have done. He will not have much incentive to do better, for he will devote most of his attention to condemning himself for not being perfect. It is important to note how destructive impatience actually is. Impatience is a form of anger. When a child does not resolve his anger over having to wait for service, he grows to resent situations that are not to his liking. He tends to insist that circumstances be always according to his expectations, and when they are not, he is not only angry but somewhat confused and discouraged. He is likely to invest so much of his energy in resenting what was disappointing and frustrating to him, that he has no incentive to figure out just how to make the situation better.

Loving parents who understand what is happening can help the child to realize that life situations do not always have to be made to his liking, that he can usually do something to make things better for himself if he will accept the responsibility for trying. They can teach him to regard life problems as a challenge to his creative imagination rather than a threat to his emotional security.

Resenting situations we do not like is probably one of the most evasive and illusionary self-defeating behavior patterns among adults. It is responsible for much of the quick tempers, unreasonable demands, complaining, criticizing, and depressive feelings of self-pity in our society today. In fact, it is one of the root causes of boredom, discontent, loneliness, pessimism, reactive depression, and the general state of unhappiness.

Also, when a child is allowed to be impatient with himself for his own mistakes, he tends to develop an anger toward himself whenever he sees his own imperfections. His secret conviction about being a bad person is being verified by his conduct. He automatically thinks of punishing himself much the same as his parents used to punish him. He has the illusion he is correcting his problem, though this procedure offers him no incentive to develop a plan of attack.

When a person becomes angry with himself because of some foolish action or lack of self-control, he blames the part of himself that did the deed, but the part of himself that motivated the action is not responsible, for he views himself as always intending to do the proper thing. He joins sides with the part of himself that is doing the accusing, not the part that is accused, so he is perpetually innocent and not responsible for the situation. The more viciously he attacks and condemns himself, the more virtuous he feels! For this reason, he has no motivation to correct his mistakes; he merely complains about them and feels helpless, concluding, "That's the way I am." Such a way of coping easily develops into a depressive mood.

Basic Life Styles Result From Parental Discipline and Example

A small child experiments with three different modalities of behavior in order to rescue his failing sense of being somebody. For long periods of time he may try one and then the other, depending on the governmental pressure of his parents and how they cope with his defiance of their authority. Whichever mode of reacting provides the greater sense of being somebody is the one he will use the most. Thus the child's life style of interacting with his environment will form around one of these three compensating ways of finding self-identity.

These three modalities are *defiance, compliance,* and *withdrawal*.[6] The more the parents meet the child's basic need for a sense of being somebody by their loving, understanding, restorative attitude during the disciplinary experiences, the less the child will tend to be either defiant, compliant, or withdrawn in his life style. Conversely, the less a child feels loved by his parents, the more intensely his life style will orient around one of these modalities. He will become more rigidly defiant of authority, compliant with his environment, or withdrawn from meaningful social relationships.

It is natural for a child to defy his parents' authority. He may attempt to bluff them out of their stated position, or he may seek devious ways of outsmarting and outmaneuvering them. When he employs a defiant mode of behavior, he is obviously hostile, self-assertive, and self-willed.

The defiant child develops this modality as pattern because he is able during his early developmental years to bypass his parents' governmental controls and to get his own way regardless of their demands, instructions, or threats. He tends to view their requests and orders as an infringement upon his liberties, and he develops strong resentment against *having* to do anything they try to force him to do. When a defiant child becomes an adult, he tends to resent anyone making demands upon him. He seems to have no fear of openly confronting people in order to get what he wants. He will tend to be excessively aggressive and will tend to blame others for his failures.

The compliant child develops this modality as his pattern because he is unable to get his own way openly. He fears his parents' disapproval and their discipline at a very early age. In the chastisement he loses so much of a sense of worth that he is willing to compromise to preserve his own sense of self. Out of the fear of being a nobody he makes sure he obeys explicitly. He feeds on the praise he receives for obedience and represses his own defiant wishes in order to win a sense of being somebody. His theme seems to be peace at all costs.

The compliant child inadvertently finds himself secretive, somewhat cunning and deceptive in getting his own way. This is his manner of expressing his resentment and defiance of his parents' authority. He tends to behave well in order to relax his parents' surveillance of his behavior, but attempts to do as he pleases behind their backs. He is quite unaware of being defiant or rebellious, for he believes himself to be good, and in this image he finds a sense of being somebody.

When he grows to adulthood, he tends to be passive, fearful of open confrontations, and somewhat insensitive to his own true feelings. He is actually a hostile person, but he expresses his hostility in passive, dependent ways. He lacks the ability to be appropriately aggressive. He is easily overcome by guilt feelings and is frequently depressed. He may tend to be pessimistic and negative, though he may try to conceal these unhappy feelings.

The withdrawn child develops this modality as his pattern because he is unable to be defiant or compliant — he fears the wrath of his parents too intensely at a very early age. He complies with his parents and with others as he must, but he essentially fears being hurt by life situations. He attempts to avoid feeling dependent upon others, and when he must rely on other people, he is very careful to maintain enough control in the circumstance so that he will not feel rejected. He may resort to much fantasy and daydreaming, often enjoying relationships with imaginary people, but this does not always happen. He may substitute things and activities for relationships with people. In his busyness he ingeniously maintains a legitimate, and often praiseworthy, occupation of his time. He keeps himself too busy for socializing on every level. Conversation is concerned with trivialities and the affairs of others, seldom with any personal feelings or concerns.

The withdrawn person may be secretive, sometimes devious, but his behavior is always calculated to avoid needing others to the point where they can hurt him if they do not conform to his wishes. He is just as hostile as if he were defiant, but he is fearful of revealing his feelings if they might cause others to reject him. When provoked beyond his ability to contain his wrath, he usually strikes at his offender and then retreats to his imaginary world for safety, hoping to avoid any further relationship with the offender.

All three of these modes of adaptation contain some element of defiance of parental control, either openly or secretly. Each mode blocks emotional development and emotional security, for each interferes with enjoying fulfillment in personal relationships. Each modality views others as the source of insecurity. Each is a defense against the sensation of being nobody. Each modality places the source of relationship in the other person's initiative. Secretly he feels, "I will know they love me if they seek me out." At the same time, accepting love that is shown feels most threatening, for it reactivates the danger of being rejected and controlled or used.

The defiant person easily offends others, but is unaware of how he is robbing them of their sense of autonomy by his inappropriate need to be in control of the situation. The compliant person makes friends easily, but he is unaware of how his passive dependency upon others to lead in situations robs his relationships of meaning. The withdrawn person is fearful of people and of situations, so he usually robs himself of exposure to opportunity to have good relationships. When he does relate, he is overly careful and does not invest enough of himself to have a significant relationship.

Some Basic Considerations for Parents

It is important for parents to realize that a child naturally has a strong drive to do as he pleases and that this drive will express itself more emphatically as the child increases in his ability to do a variety of things.

For a child to develop a strong character and become a well-adjusted personality, he must be free to attempt to thwart his parents' authoritative control in every way he can creatively conceive. Ideally, it is equally imperative that all his efforts to overpower his parents be negated and defeated. During this parent-child conflict, it is vital to the child's emotional welfare that he always feel respected and loved as a person by his parents, even though his defiance may at times be highly aggravating. *Obedience should never be taught at the expense of a loving relationship with the child.*

Parental discipline might be viewed as an impervious fence. The child needs to feel free to do many things inside the fence and have abundant instruction supported by genuine example about the best way of handling privileges. The child also needs to be free to examine the fence and test it in every way he can, but the fence must remain insurmountable and impermeable.

As time passes and the child grows up, the fence of restriction as well as the freedom of privilege becomes a part of the unconscious controlling and liberating forces within his mind. Wherever the child has been able to penetrate the fence of his parental restrictions, he will be unclear about what is right and wrong, and he will tend to be hostile because of the uncertainty. He also will be hostile because he can succeed in overpowering his authorities even though he may consciously enjoy his unrealistic sense of liberty.

Children attempt many manipulative devices in order to keep a sense of control in the situation. They may nag and try to wear the parents' patience down to a point at which they will be granted what they desire. They may bargain with their parents and try to earn their privileges. They may throw temper tantrums, procrastinate, feign illness, or sneak behind the parents' back to get what they want. When caught, they may lie, blame someone else, or excuse themselves in some way to avoid responsibility for their willfulness. There are few arts of psychological intrigue that the child of average intelligence fails to employ in seeking to defeat his parents' governmental control.

Parents should take note of ineffective disciplinary procedures and make necessary revision. Wise parents exercise creative imagination in child discipline to maintain a high level of efficiency. Long before children become teenagers, they usually know pretty well where their parents' blind spots in discipline are. They usually know how far they can go in defying their orders before losing the battle for what they want. Because of parental inefficiencies, children often grow up believing certain unacceptable behavior is wrong *only if* they get caught.

The values and ideals of parents are riveted into the minds of their children by parental discipline. If parents are unclear in their own values and priorities, they pass these uncertainties on to their children. If they are unkind, unloving, and insensitive to their child's feelings, they influence accordingly. If they are careless about fairness and justice in their administrative control, and if they consistently hush their child when he tries to debate or defend himself, they incite a high level of hostility and disrespect in the mind of the child.

It is very important that fathers and mothers arrive at and maintain an agreement between themselves about child discipline. One parent should not be negating the efforts of the other. The child needs to feel that both his parents are equally interested in his welfare, though one parent may seem to be more in command.

The child should have no reason to doubt what his privileges and limits actually are. Whenever he is not clear about an instruction, he will naturally consider his punishment totally unfair. Ignorance of the law may not be a valid excuse in civil matters, but to a child's mind it most certainly is valid. A child's resentment over being treated unfairly ruptures his respect for the parent's right to govern him, and it defeats the purpose of the discipline.

Grandparents and other relatives should not be allowed to interfere with the execution of parental authority in the home. Baby-sitters who have any extended care of the child should also cooperate with the parental attitudes. Too many bosses, and especially those who tend to cancel the parents' essential control, rob the child of developing the ability to accept wholeheartedly what is good for him and to reject what may be harmful. The confusion this inconsistency causes opens the way for irresponsible conduct later in life.

Whatever habits a child develops in relationship to his parents' authority stay with him through life until circumstances force him to change. Unfortunately, when a child carries infantile attitudes into his adult relationships, he is usually insensitive to the inappropriateness of his behavior. For instance, a husband who treats his wife as if she were his mother (or conversely, a wife who treats her husband as if he were a disobedient son) perpetuates his own unhappiness and seldom realizes how he does it. Adults with infantile attitudes toward authority figures tend to leave one failing relationship to begin another failing relationship. They maintain their own loss of fulfillment and are unaware how they are defeating themselves.

Restored Belongingness Becomes the Basis for Worthiness

In summary, we note that a child begins to experience a restored sense of belongingness because of his parents' loving forgiveness and redirection of his actions. In his restored belongingness he senses a feeling of value and quality in his self-identity. This feeling is a sense of worthiness. After many encounters with doing as he pleases, getting into trouble with his parents, being punished and forgiven, the child ordinarily learns a measure of respect for himself when he does what is right without having to be told or threatened. When this happens, it is a mark of good character in the making.

Because a child is idealistic in his thinking, he tends to view himself as ideal if he fulfills his parents' ideals for him. This is the essence of the second element of self-concept, worthiness.

Cultivating Autonomy Strengthens Self-Concept

Competence, the third element of self-concept, begins to evolve in about the third year of life. It continues to develop through the preadolescent and adolescent years to complete the attainment of self-concept by the time the child becomes an adult. Competence, like belongingness and worthiness, is the end result of loving relationships in the home.

In this third period of a child's emotional growth, he normally grows to perfect some sense of autonomy and a measure of being independent, decisive, and responsible. In doing so, he encounters numerous conflicts with a variety of people — his parents, other authority figures, relatives, certain friends and associates.

This period is characterized by competitive activities, and they cause him many anxious moments and times of despair. The way in which his parents become involved in these conflicts and guide him in facing his competitive activities determines to a large extent the quality of competence he will develop.

Competence is based on a sense of belongingness and a sense of worthiness; one is the state of feeling ''in'' with people, the other is the state of feeling ''good'' among people and of having worth. Competence is a feeling that sums it up with a sense of functioning among people.

As the very small child becomes more able to talk, to run,

to interact with other people in his environment, he becomes more of a social being. He is interested naturally in people and animals and things in nature. He wants to know more about his interesting world. He expresses his interest by asking many questions and experimenting.

Growing toward school age, the child widens his circle of interest in people and the world about him and discovers ideas and relationships he never knew existed. Lifelong habits of relating to people become fairly well established in this third period of maturation.

Many Factors Influence Early Development

As a child nears his third or fourth birthday, he becomes aware of being a part of a community of people. He may be in a preschool class, Sunday school, or a daytime nursery. The child has watched television, has had books read to him, and has made a host of interesting contacts with society.

The child is exposed to teasing and to ridicule among his playmates. Small children are frank with each other, sometimes heartless in their quarrels and with no regard for feelings. These conflicts present a variety of new problems to the child's sense of being somebody. Often his socializing with other children brings him into conflict with their parents, who pass judgment upon him. Also, as he is involved in certain group activities, other adults become authority figures in his life. He must make choices and decisions and abide by them. He feels accountable in many directions. He usually seeks to measure up to the expectations of a variety of people.

Almost every day the growing child experiences some sort of an identity crisis. He must cope with disappointment, frustration, rejection, isolation, and frequent humiliation. His established feelings of belongingness and worthiness are challenged and threatened again and again.

The child normally returns home to his parents' loving understanding and support to find relief from the recurring feelings of separation and aloneness and nothingness that keep recurring. When these two elements of belongingness and worthiness are reaffirmed by the parents' loving counsel and support, a new sense of being somebody begins to emerge. It is a feeling of competence. Eventually, as he is able to endure and overcome through a wide variety of experiences, the child feels increasingly confident that he can manage himself amid social difficulties.

It takes fifteen or more years to complete the development of a sense of competence. During this span of time, the child matures in every way.

For instance, he or she becomes a full-grown man or woman physically. Intellectually the child receives a major part of his education; he learns many valuable skills during this period and gains a vast amount of knowledge. Socially the youth emerges from the home into the community of the church, the school, and group activities of various sorts. He learns teamwork and sportsmanship. Many children are gainfully employed, at least on a part-time level, by the time they are eighteen, and some are beginning to serve in the military; a few are self-supporting.

During the middle and late teens, the young person usually shows a definite interest in dating the opposite sex and forms long-distance goals regarding his own marriage. The preadolescent is highly competitive in his activities, but in adolescence social life is often shrewdly discriminating.

By the time the child has grown to be adult, his development should be complete enough that he feels like an adult, poised with a sense of competence. Hopefully he has acquired an adequate self-concept by this time and is able to face life's unpredictable contingencies with a minimum of emotional insecurity and disabling anxiety.

A Child Needs His Parents' Undivided Attention

From the time a child is three or four years old until he is sixteen or eighteen, he normally seeks occasions when he can have his parents all to himself. He will seek this special relationship with first one parent and then the other. He needs to feel worthy of being that important to his parents. This special relationship with his parents undergirds his sense of worthiness during the time he is undergoing emotional turbulence. The child not only wants but needs equal access to either parent as he chooses if he is to develop a sense of inner unity.

Solo parents are an exception here, for a child with only one parent will compensate for the loss of the other parent by relating to other people in the community. The situation that most greatly damages personality development is where a parent abides in the home but is indifferent to his child.

Many parents do not realize this need in their children and, because of their own preoccupations, consistently push them aside. This cripples the parent-child relationship and forces the child to function independently of his parents before he is emotionally ready.

When parents have a contentious relationship and depreciate each other in front of their children, the children often take sides and tend to reject one parent in favor of the other. Sometimes they reject both parents. This causes the conflict between the parents to be internalized in the children, which is responsible for a variety of emotional disturbances later on.

As a child is exposed to various threats to his budding sense of self-identity, he needs to identify with his parents as ideals to emulate. The child naturally views his parents as completely adult. In his close association with them, he looks to them as a prophetic example of what he is destined to become. This helps him to maintain a goal for his ambitions to change and mature. Parents who maintain a close loving relationship between themselves automatically fulfill this emotional need for their children.

The Ideal of Feeling Special

When parents value their children enough to give them personal attention and display an interest in their intimate feelings without being critical or degrading, they speed their child on to becoming emotionally mature. Such an experience with parents helps the child to reaffirm his belongingness and worthiness when he is threatened to feel like a nobody. It helps him to idealize his parents and empathically to model after them in establishing his own sense of competence.

Being special involves an emotional openness that can occur only when the parties involved are not afraid of making incriminating disclosures. Feeling special provides an opportunity for a child to verify himself as a budding male or female, and it also provides an opportunity to discover areas that are deficient and need attention.

The experience of feeling special to parents is also a preparation for the romantic relationship of marriage. Ideally, in marriage each partner holds the other in highest esteem and seeks to find in the other an exclusive sense of belonging and union. Usually when a couple are romantically related, they enjoy being unguarded and open with each other; they voluntarily seek to reveal their personal feelings. In this way they discover a fulfillment in a reliable emotional unity.

Three qualities of parenthood help resolve for the child his need to feel special to his parents. The parent must be respected as an ideal person, be respected as a competent authority, and must communicate to the child that he truly loves him. To a large extent this love is communicated through compassionate interest and a desire to understand thoroughly situations from the child's point of view. When these three components are present in the parent-child relationship, the child's need for feeling special is met in life situations. Each contain an element of threat to his sense of being, but the parent's love and treatment of him as a special person resolve his jealousies and help him advance in his social relationships.

Some Parents Are Not Ideal

Some children do not have ideal parents with whom to relate. A parent may lose his child's respect. This can happen because of the parent's own emotional immaturities: he feigns sickness or has temper tantrums or turns silent or indifferent in manipulating to get his way in the home. Another parent may lose the admiration of his children because he consistently treats them as though they were a bother and in the way. He disciplines in anger and insults his children by the names he calls them and by his rejecting attitude.

Sometimes one parent spoils the relationship between his child and the other parent. For example, one parent may downgrade the other parent consistently in front of the child, giving orders angrily, making corrections in disgust, speaking insultingly. Occasionally one parent may be possessive of his child and imply that the child is disloyal if he enjoys the affection of the other parent. Some fathers have been known to be jealous of the wife's affection for their newborn infant and despise their child for coming between him and his wife. Some mothers have made their daughters afraid to relate to their father freely, especially during puberty, by telling them to avoid physical affection with their father, saying, "Men think of only one thing, sex!"

If a child disrespects his parent's integrity, he will attempt not to imitate him. To compensate, the child often tries to develop opposite characteristics. But the problem with trying to be different from the disliked parent lies in the hostility the child feels toward the parent who failed to be ideal. An interesting truism is that we tend to copy those we hate as much as we copy those we love.

Such a child lives with a person who has authority over him, but who does not measure up to being ideal. A child naturally tries to find a special relationship through ideals, but if he cannot, he will seek feelings of being special through arousing anger in the unloving parent. He then uses the intensity of the parent's anger to find his special value, but he does not have to feel related to that disliked parent in order to get the special feelings.

Finding a special relationship with the parent through the intensity of negative feelings only fosters the child's habits of being rebellious to authority. In his defensiveness with the parent, the child unconsciously copies the parent's undesirable habits of violence. For this reason the child who is trying to mold his personality to be different from his parent usually deceives himself. He may think he is different, but unwittingly he has shaped his personality after the undesirable traits he despises.

Lorin as a child was mercilessly beaten by his father for the slightest violation of his wishes. He vowed he would never be like his father. But Lorin was startled to discover that he treated his own son about the same way his father had treated him. The son was aggravating by his defiance, but Lorin said he flew into a rage before he knew what was happening and beat his son. The incident unnerved him so much, he came to me seeking help.

Growth of Feeling Responsible

The child's first sense of responsibility begins as he is able to control his body eliminations and not soil himself. As he grows a little older, the same feeling of responsibility is applied to doing various chores around the house. He learns to tidy his room and be responsible for keeping it in order. He learns to groom himself and be responsible for preparing himself for meals and going places. He learns to help clean the house and yard, and these tasks become part of his set of responsibilities. He also learns that a promise must be kept, so he becomes responsible for keeping his word.

Being responsible means learning to manage time and to determine priorities. It means making choices and sticking with those choices with a sense of the consequence of decisions. It also means learning to be considerate of the feelings of others. Being responsible means accepting blame for being wrong or incorrect and doing one's best to resolve the problem. It means apologizing for times when one has offended another person. It means righting wrongs committed.

A child naturally tends to delegate responsibility to others when he is required to exert himself in doing something unpleasant. Wise parents teach their children that they should do things for themselves as much as possible and delegate only what they cannot do for themselves. Being responsible requires self-control and also being expendable.

Children naturally follow their parents' example in being responsible. If one parent is lacking in this ability, a child is likely to model after his excesses. On the other hand, if the irresponsible parent loses the respect of his child, the child will probably model after the more responsible parent in order to avoid being like the undesirable parent.

Facing Competition Courageously Is a Part of Life

In the play yard a child faces a variety of competitive

situations. Each contains an element of threat to his sense of being somebody. He feels he must win, be better than, be the best, in order to be an acceptable person. In reality only one can win, so every child needs to learn to lose gracefully with little discouragement or loss of self-identity.

The problem lies in the child's need to feel special. He confuses his winning the game with being special and important. A child is evidencing maturity when he can put his best into winning. If he loses, he simply considers it a game and does not feel as though he has failed as a person and has become a bad nobody. If a child can be taught to regard the game as entertainment in which he exercises his best skills and not to think of it as being on trial to prove his worth, he can concentrate on the game and enjoy it. He will be more likely to play fair and to insist that others do so as well.

Unfortunately, however, parents often project their own emotional needs upon their children and give them more love for winning. They rate their child as excellent if he wins and "dumb" or "stupid" if he loses. When parents fail to regard the child's self-esteem as important in these matters, they cause him to associate his performance with his sense of being somebody, and the unrealism of this association undercuts emotional security.

Loving parents enjoy their child's victories and share in his excitement. If he loses, they sympathize with his feelings of disappointment, but encourage him to overcome his deficiencies so he can play a better game next time. They do not humiliate their child by blaming him for his errors, and they do not point out discrepancies in the way the game was managed so as to make their child feel he was facing unfair odds. Loving parents do not have to prove their own worth through the accomplishments of their children.

Healthy Struggle With Inferiority Feelings

A child seven or eight years old begins to wrestle with inferiority feelings. These feelings accelerate to a maximum during the teenage years until the child learns to accept his limitations and make the best of his capabilities.

Early in this period, the child naturally feels threatened with being a reject in his society if he is not a winner every time. He tends to feel ashamed of himself if he acts foolishly or loses a victory because of carelessness.

This period is characterized by many fights and quarrels with his peers. These combats add to or diminish the child's sense of competence. Naturally he has a lesser sense of competence if he continually loses than if he is able to win some of the time.

Children want their parents to defend them and help them to win. How parents relate to childhood quarrels has a great effect upon the child's sense of competence. Some parents want peace at all costs and forbid their child to fight and defend himself. This causes a child always to feel like a coward and believe there is virtue somehow in not defending his rights. Other parents seem to enjoy a sort of spectator's sport in watching their child win over the others; they take sides in favor of their own child. Occasionally parents will be inclined to blame their own child for the disagreement regardless of the evidence to the contrary. The parental attitude is a key factor in the child's sense of being somebody during these struggles.

A child in this period of development needs to prove to himself the extent of his own strengths and weaknesses and to dissociate his self-identity from either factor. It is the duty of loving parents to help him not to confuse his limitations with feelings of being disqualified for love and acceptance as a person.

When parents can assume a neutral, advisory role in their child's quarrels, teaching him fairness, justice, and responsibility, they help him to mature emotionally. When parents become embroiled in their children's playmate quarrels, they are inclined to be biased unfairly in their judgment. If they refuse to be involved at all, the child may feel abandoned and rejected.

As the child is encouraged to do his best in competitive events and to be fair and honest in his conflicts with others, he can learn to accept the fact that living with others is a cooperative endeavor. He can learn that disagreement need not always break relationships and that most conflicts can be resolved if dealt with properly. There is usually a good way to resolve interpersonal conflicts, a way that not only preserves the relationship but possibly strengthens it.

Fantasy and Idealization Are Valuable Assets

Through grade school and until late in the teens, a child normally tends to idealize his parents when there are loving relationships in the home. Idealization seems to become most intense from about ages eight to fourteen. The child also idealizes persons outside the home, leaders in the community, actors, singers, and heroes of past and present. The child is a kind of hero-worshiper; he tends to copy the virtues — sometimes the vices — and to emulate the values of those he idealizes.

This is one reason why children reach for their parents' undivided attention during this important period of development. If they can feel totally accepted by their ideal, they know they have a chance of becoming somewhat like them or better. A child identifies with his parents to maintain a sense of being somebody during the perilous situations of facing combat, competition, decisions, responsibility, and individuality that threaten to make him feel cut off from his peers as a reject. Though the child is influenced by others outside the home, he still regards his parents' values and ways of doing things as basically right and proper. Though a child may try to reject his parents by being opposite in many ways, their influence remains primary.

A New Dimension Added to Feeling Loved

Love grows another giant step during this period of a child's life.

Parental love is received by a child in several ways during his childhood. At first a child felt loved when he was made comfortable, then when allowed to have his own way, when governed fairly, when forgiven for his faults, when understood, when encouraged to do his best. In this period the child feels love also when he can enjoy feeling special because he captures his parents' undivided attention.

Whatever has felt like love will always feel like love. All through life we feel loved when someone takes the initiative to make us comfortable, allows us to have our own way, and so on. But love needs to take one more giant step in completing its development as an emotion of fulfilling relationship. Love needs the embossing of a feeling of being special to the one who loves us or whom we love.

Eventually, if a person develops a good self-concept, he will naturally develop an altruism in his love relationships and feel loved when others accept his love and desire to relate openly to him. Mature love is sharing feelings with self-abandon in the context of mutually respecting each other's integrity as peers. Such maturity occurs when the antecedent levels of emotional development have occurred.

10

Sex-Role Development
Completes
Self-Concept

As we have discussed in the previous chapter, a sense of competence grows through a variety of situations. But at the heart of this very important element of self-concept is a maturing sense of sex-role adequacy.

From the time a child discovers he is either male or female, he feels destined to a certain role in life. Usually one of his parents exemplifies that role for him. He identifies with that parent as a model and seeks the other parent's approval for validation of his sex appeal.

During the child's preadolescent and early adolescent years, the sense of sex-role destiny intensifies. For some children it is almost a compulsion that dominates practically everything they do. Competing and comparing form the dynamics of thinking for this period of emotional development. The child is driven by insecurity to establish his sense of being somebody, but most of all, he seeks self-verification as an adequate man or an adequate woman.

A child climbs fences, balances himself to walk on a narrow rail, plays house and pretends to be the parent or the child, determines to win a game every time, fights for a sense of superiority and independence, makes things of utility value that simulate adult achievements, involves himself in sports, attempts to acquire skill in some of the arts in which he may be particularly gifted, and experiments with various social activities in which he is personally involved with the opposite sex in his own age-group. In a thousand-and-one ways the child practices a variety of skills to prepare and establish himself as a promising adult.

The child seeks to fulfill his sex-role destiny and to prove to himself he is not defective, as he is inclined to suspect from his various failures. It seems that all activities of the growing child augment and support the goal of developing sex appeal, and this continues until he becomes established as an adult with a completed sense of competence.

The Child's First Awareness of Sex

During the first two or three years of a child's life, he or she is not aware of the significance of being a boy or a girl. The child begins to realize a certain distinction to the fact that he is consistently dressed in boy's clothes and called a boy, or that she is dressed in girl's clothes and called a girl. But the import of that classification does not seize the child's mind until one day he or she makes a momentous discovery.

"I'm like Daddy; Mommy is different! That's why I'm a boy." Or, "I'm like Mommy; Daddy is different! That's why I'm a girl."

This discovery is shrouded in mystery for the young child, and it is infused with curiosity. He begins to think about his body and himself as a person in a new way. The incident may escape parental notice — it often does — but when it occurs, it adds a new dimension to the child's sense of being somebody.

Previously he had been identifying with his parents to discover in a general way how to do various things. Now the child begins to identify with his parents with a more specific goal in mind. The child seeks to discover the meaning of being a boy or a girl, a husband or a wife, a father or a mother.

This new awareness tends to make the boys feel somewhat set apart from the girls; nevertheless, they do not cease to be mutually interested in each other. Some children, more curious than others, investigate and try to discover overtly just what makes the difference between the sexes. When they do actually disrobe their playmates, or try to see their parents' nakedness, they usually bring a crashing blow of disapproval upon themselves from their parents for their curiosity. Other children who seem less curious, or are less inclined to act upon their curiosity for some reason, may not actually sense that there is an anatomical difference between the sexes for several years. They seem more inclined to deny or sublimate their sexual curiosities.

The parental attitude strongly affects the child's thinking

about sexual matters. Everything the mother does — from changing the baby's diapers to bathing and dressing her youngster — influences the child's attitude about sexuality. The child empathically identifies with the mother's general attitude about his or her body and its various parts. The child senses the parents' appreciation and pleasure and revulsion and feelings of taboo. Some parents are much more intent on governing their child's inquisitive investigations of his own body or his parents' bodies than others; some are graciously casual about sexual matters; a few are overly permissive.

Parents need to deal with sexual matters in the context of the child's thinking and level of maturity. Early investigations have no moral value. Feelings of right and wrong associated with moral guilt do not begin to have significance for a child until he is at least six or seven years old. Prior to this, parental instruction or reprimand should be simple and clear without moral implication, such as, "No. Don't do that. You do not take your clothes off here; you do that in the bedroom or the bathroom. You do not let other children play with you sexually, and you do not play with them. If any of your playmates undress for you, leave. Do something else."

At this early age a child is simply curious. His interest in sexual matters really has no moral value. He needs clear instruction about what he should or should not do, but he does not need feelings of shame for being curious. The parent can recognize the child's interest as perfectly normal, and a child should not be made to feel guilty for having the interest. Parents can answer the child's questions in a general way, indicating there is a difference between girls' and boys' bodies. God made us this way, and it is good. It is good for the parent only to answer what the child is asking, and when it is appropriate, tell him he will understand more when he is older. But when he is older, make sure you tell him.

Value of Sexual Fantasies

Sexual fulfillment in adult life is highly invested in fantasies. Adults who have few or no sexual fantasies are much more inhibited sexually than people who experience a more active fantasy life. The development of sexual fantasies are, therefore, beneficial as long as it is clearly understood at an early age that the sexual expression itself is reserved for the special, responsible relationship of marriage. Since fantasies of actual sexual activity are laden with guilt feelings and fears of acting out, it is good to sublimate with fantasies of romantic adventures and delightful social activities with the opposite sex.

If a child is exposed to the frank details of actual adult

genitalia, and especially the act of coitus, when his own organs and psyche are undeveloped he becomes frightened and burdened with guilt due to frustration and other factors. Usually the child's fear and guilt feelings cause him to be sexually inhibited and to defend against sexual fantasies. Instead of sexual feelings being associated with ideals, they are rejected as repulsive and bad. Too much exposure to adult sexuality can also have the opposite effect upon the child. He can become preoccupied with sexual ideas excessively and he does not have a healthy interest in other activities important to his development.

In such cases, the child's natural curiosity about sex somehow becomes associated with his need to be defiant of his parents, and sexual investigations become a way of acting out his independence of their authority. Gratification for the child seems to lie mostly in his ability to get by with doing forbidden things secretly, and it is not an expression of a meaningful relationship with his sexual partners. In fact, promiscuity in a child's sexual contacts can interfere with his developing meaningful relationships with the opposite sex later in life.

It is good for parents to discuss freely, honestly, and without embarrassment matters of sexual interest to the child, but in general terms. The child needs to feel a security in his communication with his parents in these matters, knowing they will tell him all he needs to know when it is necessary to understand. This allows his fantasy life to mature normally. It keeps the romantic ideas among the ideals for relationship with the opposite sex. It helps him to sublimate his sexual interests in a variety of character-building activities. Through sublimation, a child is able to develop a sense of morality and confidence in his own self-control. He can feel confident that by the time he is old enough to participate in sexual intercourse, he will also have wisdom in his selection of a mate. He very likely will want his sexual fulfillment to be an expression of an exclusive relationship with the one person with whom he chooses to spend his life.

By insisting that sexual intercourse be reserved for the special relationship of marriage, parents are not only teaching their child to do the responsible thing, but also helping him to keep the sexual relationship ideal where it can provide the greatest fulfillment. When sexual intercourse is primarily an expression of a physical need for sensual gratification, it lacks the ideal elements of being a manifestation of responsible love and it becomes degrading to self-esteem; the person denies his total involvement in the sexual relationship. This causes a split between his needs for physical and emotional gratification. He sacrifices the meaning of loving relationship for the immediate gratification of a physical appetite and thus does violence to his own better judgment and sense of wholeness.

While the individuals involved in solely sensual gratification may rationalize their situation so as to believe it is normal, they still at times yearn for the sexual experience to be an expression of an abiding relationship that affords a sense of emotional oneness with one's mate. These are some of the psychological implications of sexual promiscuity that have little or nothing to do with moral code yet undergird the purpose for the code.

When a growing child has been taught to exercise self-control toward the opposite sex, he is taught the highest form of responsibility, which pays a great reward of emotional gratification. He is investing in his future married happiness and qualifying in his own mind for the pleasures of sexual ecstasy in marriage and for the relationship that experience affords. Nothing compares with the sense of rightness which sexual innocence affords.

Innocence should not be confused with ignorance. Knowledge in sexual matters based upon actual experience can be self-incriminating and deface the possible beauty of a good marriage. It arouses fears of unfavorable comparisons and the possibility of other loyalties.

Sex-Role Development

Boys normally tend to identify with their fathers more than with their mothers; this helps them to feel like little men. Girls tend normally to identify with their mothers; this helps them to feel like little ladies. At about three years of age, a boy or a girl becomes aware for the first time that the father is male and the mother is female, with feelings of both appreciation and curiosity. Prior to this time, father served his child in the role of being an extension of mother; he is now regarded as father with increasing significance.

In a year or so after the momentous discovery about sexuality, boys become exceedingly proud of the fact they are boys and not girls. Likewise, girls develop a pride in their own physical charm and attractiveness and are usually glad they are not boys, though they may at times envy boys because they seem to do more interesting things. Boys and girls imitate other children of their own sex as well as copy the traits of their parents. Each is searching for the meaning of his or her particular role in life as male or female.

Three issues in the parent-child relationship contribute to a healthy emotional development. They are *idealization of both parents, respect for their governing authority,* and *a sense of the parents' loving understanding.*

Parents will automatically be held up as ideals by their children if they do not in some way disqualify themselves. Idealization of parents depends on the child's sense of being a pleasure to his parents. If a parent answers his child's need to feel special, the child will almost always consider his parent as ideal.

An optimistic, happy attitude toward life situations contributes to being ideal in the child's mind. A child likes to think he has a chance to succeed in life and be happy. When parents are pessimistic, derogatory, critical, and generally negative in their attitudes, they depress the child with ideas that he is faced with insurmountable obstacles in becoming a total adult. This may cause him to turn to others who are more cheerful and optimistic, more positive and less self-concerned, as ideals. But the parents' attitudes will have a controlling influence for good or bad.

Another factor contributing greatly to idealization is the parents' ability to cope realistically with problematic situations. To the degree the parent is competent, the child will tend to idealize. If the parent is passively dependent or fearful of undertaking new things, the child will have no reason to idealize. If parents are manipulative and inappropriately domineering, they lose the child's admiration and respect. If they are themselves emotionally immature and ineffective as adults, children lose respect sooner or later.

The romantic unity enjoyed between the parents also contributes to the idealization. Children want to believe they will be happy in marriage; parental quarrels left unresolved discourage them, lead them to take sides, and cause them to internalize the parents' problems. Children find it difficult to idealize parents who are not romantic. In fact, they may idealize the parents' unromantic attitudes and find themselves handicapped later on.

Children have a dynamic need for their parents to govern them. They will respect parental authority if the parents are respectful of them as sensitive persons who really want to do what is right. Parents show this respect by being consistently clear in their instructions, making sure their children understand what is expected and how to perform it. They also show respect by being fair in their judgments and punishments, preserving their children's self-esteem when disciplining them.

The parents' abiding love for their child is manifested mostly in their understanding of him and their sincere interest in his total welfare. Understanding parents listen to what their child is trying to communicate to them, are patient and forgiving, and are encouraging in helping the child to improve. Parents who know they love their children might double-check themselves once in a while to determine whether the love they feel is actually being communicated.

It is a relief to know that a child wants his parents to function as good parents and succeed with him, and whenever parents have fallen short in any way, they can reclaim their lost position of respect by admitting honestly their mistakes and doing their best to overcome whatever is deficient. Children usually are glad to forgive when their parents are sincere and honest with them.

Importance of Father and Mother Roles

About the time that boys and girls begin to realize their father is a man and their mother is a woman, they both turn to their father with a peculiar interest. At first the reason may be to find relief from mother's persistent surveillance, to divide and to conquer the governing authority. But soon the interest in father becomes a sort of idealistic, infantile love affair. This special love for father usually continues until it matures in the middle or late teens. Love for mother does not become less significant, but it tends to change in its quality and meaning for boys and girls as years pass.

As we have said, a child is extremely idealistic. There is no room for mediocrity in the child's thinking. A boy wants to become the strongest, the biggest, the greatest man living; to achieve this goal obviously requires modeling after the man he believes embodies all these traits — father. A girl wants to be the prettiest, the most charming, the nicest, and most adequate woman ever to live; to achieve this goal naturally means to model after the woman who seems to embody all these traits — mother. As boys and girls grow into their school-age years, they discover other great people from stories they hear or read; or someone in their circle of social contacts stands out as ideal, perhaps a grandparent. They model after them also.

Children observe how mother and father interact with each other. This is easily verified by watching small children play house; they assume to be one parent and then the other and act accordingly. This mimicry is a way of practicing the personality traits they have observed. Also, in the games children play, one notices how children observe the way father manages the household affairs, disciplines the children, copes with his business problems. And they reveal they are just as observant of mother as she manages her daily affairs. Boys learn much about being men; girls learn much about being women. The influence of the parents teaches children their roles as husband and wife and father and mother, and they learn the fundamentals of their system of moral values and priorities by copying their parents.

Jealousy Comes Into Full Bloom

Children naturally become extremely jealous of each other and of first one parent and then the other. This jealousy plays an important part in emotional maturation and should not be ignored. A child can be guided by loving parents to work through this negative emotion so as to outgrow the feelings which cause it. Parents need not quash jealousy as an evil feeling that must be forbidden any expression, for this brings no growth and resolution. If a child finds no adequate resolution for his normal jealous feelings when he is small, he will tend to be jealous later in life until he hopefully encounters circumstances that help him to overcome his emotional insecurity. In the meantime, he spoils many promising relationships with his jealousy.

To understand the emotion of jealousy, we need to realize the general setting for its occurrence. During a child's second and third years, especially, the emphasis in parental discipline is self-control. "Watch what you are doing," "Look where you are going," "Be careful," or "Think before you act" are constant instructions. Thus control and mastery at this time become the major values in the child's sense of being somebody. His sense of worthiness begins to be established and validated by his ability to control himself, and his sense of belongingness is reaffirmed when he pleases his parents.

Now that the child is becoming more of a social being, he naturally employs control and mastery in his love relationships. In his play he tries to dominate his friends. Often a paralyzing contest goes on as to who is going to be the leader.

At the time the child reaches toward father, differentiating more clearly between father and mother, his love for each of his parents manifests a controlling, manipulative quality invested with many unrealistic expectations. The child will frankly tell his parent, "You don't love me" or "You hate me." The reason he gives is that they did not do what he wanted them to or they forbade him something he wanted.

To explain it briefly, the child is beginning to seek a special relationship with his parents, first with one and then the other. His innate need for exclusive rights to the parent of his choice makes the child exceedingly possessive in his relationships and jealous of any intruders.

Many parents are amused at the triangular contest a child feels with his parents. At this early age, he may snuggle to one parent and tell the other, "This is my daddy; you can't have him" or "This is my mommy; you can't have her." This little maneuver indicates the child is beginning an important phase of his emotional development. Parents should not make fun of him, but simply in their own way communicate the message, "We all love each other. No one is excluded."

When children manifest jealousy of other siblings, they are expressing the same need to be special to their parents. They need to be taught that love is not quantitative so that it is divided when shared, but qualitative so that it grows when expressed.

As an example of sibling rivalry, Tim complained to his mother that she gave Jennie, his sister, a bigger piece of cake. Jennie, on the other hand, accused her mother of letting Tim watch television longer at night. This argument was scarcely quieted when a new one arose. Tim accused his mother of favoring Jennie because she was a girl; he said he had to do all the hard work because he was a boy. Jennie, on the other hand, accused mother of letting Tim do more fun things because he was a boy. Each child was obviously seeking to find an exclusive relationship with mother, and each was jealous because she seemed to be divided in her loyalty.

It requires unusual understanding and love for a parent under such harassing pressure to maintain patience. If the parent can maintain a perspective on the child's fundamental emotional need, he can address himself to the issue of the child's need to feel special instead of the issue that the child presents of being slighted.

Every child naturally goes through a period in his development when he feels possessive of others and wants to feel exclusive in his relationships. Ordinarily, in a home that is graced with loving relationships, these possessive feelings are easily resolved. Where a lack of such relationships exists, the jealous emotions are not resolved, but become compounded with other unresolved hostile feelings. As a result, it is not at all uncommon to find this same possessiveness and jealousy among adults. Their expression of jealous anger, however, is usually more disguised than the child's.

Threat to Being Special for Boys and Girls

We discussed the need to be special in the previous chapter, but we must add a few observations regarding the influence this emotional need has upon the development of the child's sense of sex-role competence. Unresolved jealousies play a big part in the feelings of inadequacy often suffered in adulthood.

The need to feel special becomes intense for children of six or eight years of age. They often seek satisfaction among animal friends. In the affection of pets they find a measure of exclusive love, for they can maintain a level of control and possessiveness. By the time the child is seven or older, he usually begins to turn to other children of his own age and sex to find a special friend, or pal. The need to have special friends continues through life. It is interesting that the friends made during the teenage years often have lifelong significance.

Jealousy is the anger felt when one fails to hold onto the special feeling of being exclusively important to some one person. That person seems to enjoy a relationship with someone else. Briefly the love one wishes for himself is given to another, and jealousy is the anger that results. There need be no actual rejection or slight intended; the person feels jealous simply because the person he loves seems to enjoy someone else.

The loss of being special seems to imply that the slighted one comparatively has no worth. The rejected one feels like a nobody, a "nothing" person. This is the source of the anger, for he desires to punish someone for his loss of self-identity. He may attack either the desired lover or the usurper who seems to have taken his place. Jealousy incites a person to spite, to antagonize, and to humiliate the offender.

Like anger on other levels of development, jealousy is self-defeating and adds to the sense of being unloved and unlovable. A brief review of the development of hostility might be helpful.

One of the first causes for anger is having to wait for service, which threatens to make the child feel separated and alone. To compensate, the infant tries to eat enough or to gather enough possessions around him so as not to need others. A person's attempt at being self-sufficient has in it an element of divesting others of the power to deprive him of whatever he may want. Later in life we label this tendency greed, avarice, or cupidity.

When a child becomes angry over being restricted or forbidden by parents, he envies others who seem to have what he wants for himself. His envy is a hatred for others, and this causes him to be unwilling to try to acquire or to achieve the object for himself. This envy interferes with developing feelings of worthiness, for it blocks relationships vitally needed for emotional growth. Envy destroys faith in the goodness of others and sponsors negative, suspicious, pessimistic attitudes. Envy blocks idealization of the very persons who are actually concerned for the child's welfare and are able to help him. Envy is considered the most destructive of all the hostile feelings.

In this third level of development, the child is angry again over being deprived of the love he wants, for it seems to be given to someone else. If this anger is not resolved, he will not want to be special to his parents, who appear to be unfaithful to him. For this reason, jealousy blocks the development of competence.

Parents should take note of these various forms of hostility and do what they can to understand their child's feelings at every age. Hostile reactions are inevitable, and certain distortions in interpersonal relationships develop if each type of hostility is not resolved when it occurs. Parental understanding and appropriate reactions to the child's feelings help to prevent repression from occurring. Repression usually takes place when the child is afraid to reveal his true feelings.

In the first level of development, the child's feelings of rejection cause most of his angry reactions; this is because he interprets having to wait for service as a rejection. In the second level of development, the child's feelings of frustration as well as rejection cause his angry reactions; he tends to interpret restrictions and parental control as rejection. In the third level of development, the child's feelings of humiliation as well as frustration and rejection incite his anger; he tends to interpret any failure to measure up to expectations as his being a bad person and unworthy of acceptance.

Loving parents thoughtfully consider their child's resentments as significant. They attempt to help their child resolve his negative feelings by talking about them. This does not mean they condone his acting them out, but they discuss his feelings openly even though he may be expressing hate feelings for his own parents. They can admit they understand how he feels, but assure him that he also has other feelings. When he decides to accept his parents' control, he can have a better attitude. If the child is not afraid to reveal his true feelings to his parents, he is not so likely to repress them. In being free to discuss his feelings with his parents, he can discover a more responsible and appropriate mode of behavior. Parents who work with their children during outbursts of angry reaction when they are young, find their children experiencing a minimum of rebellion against their authority when they become teenagers.

When a child tries to control his parents' love and fails, yet continues to be impressed that his parents sincerely love him, he learns a new dimension of himself. He learns he is a unique, special person and does not have to maintain a special, exclusive relationship to verify his own sense of being somebody. He learns to live and to let live. He does not have to control his love objects. In fact, he learns that he loses the love he desires when he attempts to control, for he has robbed the lover of being voluntary in his expression of love. If the child takes this step in emotional growth, he can love others and not feel the least bit threatened by their having other relationships that are more intimate than his is with them.

Other Factors That Mold Sex-Role Development

The pathway of sexual development is slightly different for boys than for girls. We will treat each separately.

Boys in a loving home idealize their father and identify with him, respect his authority, copy his ways, and develop a confidence in their own maturing sense of manhood. They respect their mother's authority if it corresponds with their father's attitude. Boys seek the delightful admiration and confidence of their mother as a verification of their own achievement of manhood.

Girls in a loving home idealize their mother and model after her to find a sense of their own womanhood. Mother is a living picture for her daughter of how a lady conducts herself. Girls respect their father's authority as prime and submit to him and his government. They respect their mother's authority when it is subordinate to their father's attitude. They seek their father's delightful admiration as a verification of their achievement of being desirably feminine.

In an ideal home, love binds father and mother together in a state of pleasant agreement. Differences are not harbored, but settled. The two parents act as one in their execution of governing authority. While mother may be the one to execute the details of the home rules, father abides as the underlying strength of those rules. His leadership is manifested in many ways, but particularly in assuming the initiative to make decisions final and to see that they are carried out.

A wife usually enjoys being subordinate to her husband when she is treated with sensitive understanding and genuine respect for the person she is. A loving husband does not dominate his wife, but honors her as someone he idealizes. He values her opinions and treats her as a peer with deep affection. A wife who is thus regarded usually finds it natural to be submissive and responsive. She and her husband hold each other in an idealism that is second only to the devotion they may feel for God.

Pathway for Boys Briefly Stated

Since father normally feels romantic toward mother, the son who models after him not only loves his mother, but also tends to feel romantic toward her. He may tell himself that he is rehearsing for his marriage someday in showing her affection, but he loves her with a sexually oriented affection nevertheless.

The boy naturally respects his father's prior claim to a sexual relationship with his mother, and this respect is a security for him in controlling his impulses when alone with his mother. Should the boy be tempted to act out his sexual fantasies with his mother, he would tend to feel terribly inadequate in being able to please her and tend to feel in frightening jeopardy of his father's wrath.

A boy may feel guilty for having sexual fantasies about his father and mother's relationship and so refuse to allow the fantasies. Boys sublimate their sexual drives in many ways. Nevertheless, they do experience some romantic feelings about mother now and then, and this may occur until the middle teens.

The mother who loves her son properly does not have romantic feelings about him. She always regards him as her son, and she is careful never to relate to him in a way that makes up for any disappointment she may be experiencing with her husband.

For example, Dwight was busy with his vocation, trying to develop his new business. He did not realize how little time he allowed for his wife and family just to enjoy being with them. Sally, his wife, was increasingly lonely for the companionship with him she once knew.

As the years passed, it seemed that Gregory, their son, had the capacity to understand the feelings she longed to find in Dwight. She found herself confiding in Gregory about many personal anxieties. At first Gregory felt a strange sense of importance in this confidential relationship, but before long he discovered he deeply resented the situation. He felt robbed of an aspect of his childhood by having to assume the burden of substituting for his father. Also, he grew to resent his father for his devotion to business instead of being romantic with his mother, to say nothing of his resentment over having no time with Gregory himself. Gregory had a growing sense of insecurity at home and longed for the time when he could get away from it all.

Moreover, a good mother does not seduce her son to obey her wishes because she is frail and sickly, or because she is attractive and it is beneath her femininity to work. Whatever the service she wants him to render, she should ask for it simply; the son should not feel manipulated. A good mother relates to her son lovingly, instructing and correcting him as she deems necessary and praising him appropriately.

Sons do not always respect their mother's authority. Instead, they may coldly, often disrespectfully, defy her orders. In a boy's romantic frame of mind, it is impossible for him to accept his mother's commands or corrections without feeling put down and rejected. From his point of view, he has ceased to be special to her and is valued only for the service he might render. His negative attitude naturally makes his mother reinforce her instructions. This intensifies the problem, making him still more defiant; he feels he has to protect his sense of manhood by angry defiance.

It is good at this point in the discipline for the father to reinforce the mother's instructions. "You obey your mother. I refuse to allow you to speak to her so disrespectfully!" he may say firmly. Ideally, the father refuses to allow his son to sulk, to act out his anger, or to defy his mother. He must obey. This frame of reference kills the romantic admiration for his mother for that particular situation. The proper, platonic mother-son relationship is reestablished by the father's firmness.

He needs to feel loved by both parents and sense their love for each other at the same time. The boy's terrible sense of separation felt by the emotional bind of the situation is healed when he obeys and senses their forgiveness and restoration. These experiences normally happen many times during this period of growth, but by the time he is seventeen or so, the boy will normally find virtue in assuming responsibility and accepting instruction without feeling rejected in the process.

Belongingness and worthiness are doubly reinforced by the parental attitude when he is obedient. The boy's maleness is verified because his mother is pleased with his conduct and improved attitude, and his father is reassuring by his companioning interest in his son's affairs. Eventually the boy feels a love for his mother that is no longer romantic in nature. He feels a competitive sense of being a peer with his father in work and at play.

The restored sense of belongingness and worthiness from both parents that occurs in these troublesome years finishes the development of the boy's sense of competence, He has finally proven to himself that he is a worthy, independent individual and a responsible, decisive, adequate male.

By the end of his teens, a son should be sufficiently comfortable with his manhood to function as an adult. He can meet the daily competition at work and at play. He can launch his career and can woo and win a desirable mate to establish a home of his own. In that relationship with his mate, many of the frustrations and deprivations of childhood deriving from his romantic desires and fantasies with his parents will find a fulfillment.

Pathway for Girls Briefly Stated

Girls experience a similar threat to their belongingness and worthiness when mother corrects them, but for a very different reason. Since a girl idealizes her mother and has love feelings for her father that become romantic in character, she submits to her father's authority in order to be pleasing to him, for she feels he loves her. She desires to be a delight to her father, so she obeys him. Because of her romantic feelings for her father, his disapproval of her conduct makes her feel she has lost her attractiveness to him. Thus the girl learns to be submissive to her father as her natural love response. His pleasure in her attitude validates the feminine attractiveness she is trying to establish.

For this reason girls often seem to obey their fathers more readily than they do their mothers. They often tend to be insulted or humiliated when mother corrects or punishes. This is especially true when mother, in exasperation, reinforces her commands by saying, "I am your mother. You must obey me because I am your mother!" Since the daughter has romantic feelings of a sort for her father, she feels somewhat in competition with her mother for his affection. When mother corrects, she feels her mother has "pulled rank" and squelched her.

In a loving home, when girls express anger toward their mother, they receive their father's sharp reprimand. "You do not talk that way to your mother! You must speak respectfully. Obey what she says." This firmness squelches any and all romantic idealization of father for that particular situation. Such experiences happen many times during the teenage years, but finally the daughter senses the loving embrace of both parents and discovers a restored sense of belongingness and worthiness in their mutual love for her. This completes her sense of competence as an adequate woman.

Good fathers have a deep respect for a daughter's emotional struggles in developing her femininity. They appreciate her sex appeal and take note of her attempts to experiment with her sense of being attractive. They do not belittle her for her sometimes bizarre dress or use of makeup; instead they indicate pleasantly, but firmly, what is or is not appropriate. They do not have a sense of protective jealousy toward their daughter that can make them overly critical of her attempts at being stylish and seductively attractive. They help her develop good sense in these matters. While a father may appreciate his daughter's sex appeal, he does not act toward her romantically in any way that might imply to the child that she is somehow taking her mother's place.

Moreover, a good father does not seek solace in his daughter's voluntary and sometimes aggressive love for him. He does his best to maintain a strictly platonic father-daughter relationship that is sensitive to her emotional needs, not his own. If there happens to be husband-wife conflicts, he tries to be wise enough to deal with them in ways that do not involve his daughter.

The fear of mother's jealousy over her feelings of romantic

admiration for her father, or over the closeness of their relationship, also helps to squelch her romantic feelings for her father. If the mother is emotionally mature enough to see the issues as developmental and not be actually jealous of her daughter's affection for the father, the daughter's emotional development will be greatly enhanced. The girl will be freer to experience her total love feelings for a man later on in marriage and at the same time know she is good in doing so. She has her parent's approval for her natural feelings. This provides her with a secure sense of competence in her womanhood and at the same time gives her a basis for an impeccable moral character.

Ideally both boys and girls resolve these kinds of conflicts with their parents by the time they are seventeen or eighteen. At this time mother is usually treated with complimentary respect and with affection. Both boys and girls begin at this age, if not sooner, to seek a sort of peerlike relationship with both their parents. Wise parents begin to rest in the sense that their child-rearing task is approaching an end, and they can enjoy a peerlike relationship with their children.

11

False Security Factors in Self-Concept

Self-concept is an illusive image of self, an intuitive sense of being somebody. Cognitively we know we are somebody — there is no doubt about this; but emotionally we may have difficulty at times believing we are not actually just a nobody. This is because of certain false security factors in our self-concept.

Our sense of being somebody at a particular moment relates to at least three factors: the present environmental situation, which seems either to be for us or against us; the way we have been conditioned from childhood to view ourselves in such situations; and a variety of unconscious memories that condition our perception of what is happening.

We must understand something about the unconscious memories that cause distortion in our perception. We cannot change the bad experiences we have had, but we can alter the perception of our position in the environmental situation. The power of these memories over our way of thinking lies in the fact that the reason for such misperceptions remains unconscious. We do not know just why we think as we do; we have to trust our perception of reality until we can somehow see things differently.

These unconscious memories introduce unrealistic elements into our present situation. Some of these elements cause false security. Many of us, for example, may notice that certain friends seem to believe they are indispensable and everyone likes them and folks are always admiring whatever they do. They seem not to realize that they are being tolerated, not enjoyed, and that people are being too courteous to tell them how boring they actually are. On the other hand, some of these elements from unconscious memories cause people to feel insecure and like an intruder in a situation even while their friends are thoroughly desiring their presence and admiring them in certain ways. For instance, some persons feel ugly and unattractive regardless of how they are dressed; people may be complimenting them, but they seem always to disregard the reality of the praise.

All of this means that to some degree most of us possess elements of insecurity in our self-concept. These elements are self-perpetuating instead of self-correcting or self-nullifying.

Unloving Factors in Relationships Leave Lasting Effects

Loving and unloving factors in relationships incite contrasting ideas about one's sense of being somebody. As we know, loving relationships instill stable feelings of belongingness, worthiness, and competence in the mind of a growing child. On the other hand, loveless factors in relationships create insecure feelings of separation, isolation, and aloneness. Love unites people in a bond of oneness; loveless factors disunite people, making them defensive with one another regardless of age.

Love is the dynamic of true, positive, liberating fellowship. "There is no fear in love" (1 John 4:18 RSV). In a loving relationship there is a minimum of needing to be on guard and a maximum of freedom in self-revelation to the other person. Each social interaction reinforces for the persons involved a sense of being somebody, for the love that is felt validates the elements of self-concept — that they are accepted and wanted, right and good, adequate and competent. Loving relationships tend to lay anxieties to rest and promote peace of mind.

Unloving relationships not only promote negative, defensive attitudes, but also make each person involved aware of being a separate individual who must lean entirely upon his own resources for a sense of being somebody.

Since an unloved child does not sense belongingness in the parental attitude, he sets about to win his acceptance by capturing the attention of others with a distinctive appearance, or an unusual performance, or by taking pride in some excellence rating which gives him a feeling of status. Not being awarded belongingness in love, he finds a false sense of belongingness through capturing attention. The insecurity factor lies in his having to hold the attention and keep the center of the stage in order to avert a feeling of loss of belonging with others.

When a child does not feel loved, he attempts to capture a sense of worthiness from his parents through defiance or compliance. He discovers in his defiance, if he can get away with it, a sense of being autonomous by overpowering the people who attempt to govern him. The insecurity factor lies in his needing to remain a rebel in order to hold onto his sense of autonomy; this automatically positions him in an independent, defensive, aggressive attitude of mind. He cannot help being involved occasionally in situations where this attitude does not work, and he is devastated by the consequences of his own willfulness.

When a child must be compliant, he discovers in his compliance a sense of worthiness in winning parental approval through ascertaining their wishes and complying with them. He must deny and negate his own wishes and feelings to be accepted and feel good about himself. This develops a false security factor, for he is certain to encounter many situations in his lifetime in which he must be clear about his own wishes and feelings and be aggressive in making confrontations; otherwise he will be overpowered by those who are more defiant in their patterns of interaction.

The defiant personality is obviously independent, critical of others who disagree with him, aggressively controlling in most any situation, seldom critical of himself, and more or less insensitive to the feelings of others. These traits continually interfere with his establishing any meaningful peer relationships, and they make him insensitive to the actual love others may be feeling for him. Thus the defiant person tends to isolate himself from loving relationships. He needs to verify his sense of being somebody by taking notice of how effective he is in the administrative position. So he maintains a false security factor in his self-concept.

The compliant personality is plainly more or less dependent, passively manipulative, and often critical of itself, and it has the facade of caring for the feelings of others. The compliant person is trying to keep peace at all costs. He tends to avoid any open, unpleasant confrontations that might irritate others. In doing this, he anticipates their wishes and attempts to be pleasing to them. Thus he denies his natural desires and tends to subjugate himself to others who are more aggressive, or avoid them if he can. He has such an intense need to be liked by others that he functions under the illusion he is always giving himself lovingly to others. This he secretly resents, for he feels used. He is just as blind to the actual love of others for him as is the defiant person, for he assumes he merits that love by some excellence they find in him.

Situations naturally occur which demand realistically that he be aggressive and forthright. The compliant person is too passive to manage the problem, and he loses. He is unable to correct his deficiency, so he criticizes himself mercilessly, or feels sorry for himself, and possibly becomes depressed. He loses his sense of being somebody. Thus the compliant person is continually perpetuating a false security factor in his self-concept by being pleasing and congratulating himself for being such a nice person.

When a child cannot get away with being defiant with his parents, and he is too afraid of their wrath to want to try to be pleasing in the compliant modality, he withdraws to himself and becomes somewhat autistic. His fear of his parents is too intense for him to want their love. He actually wants nothing to do with them, for they are like enemies to him, but the problem is, he is dependent on them for his essential needs.

In this frame of reference, he complies with his parents to get his basic needs, then retreats to himself and to his fantasies for a sense of being somebody. While the defiant person congratulates himself for being able to control others, and the compliant person congratulates himself for being able to anticipate the wishes of others and be regarded as very nice and agreeable, the withdrawn person congratulates himself for being able to hide his true feelings and keep others from bothering him with their wishes or demands. Thus the withdrawn person, by his indifference to others, prevents loving relationships from occurring. He seeks to be so self-sufficient that he will never need anyone — then he can never be hurt.

When a child is deprived of loving relationships in the home, the unloving attitudes he must live with teach him that he is undesirable, no good, or inferior. He is persuaded he is not much of a person, just a nobody. Regardless of which of the three basic modalities he may use in coping with the unloving environment, he must repress the idea that he is a nobody and try to prove to himself he is somebody.

His resources for proving to himself that he has value as a person are threefold: He can reflect upon how others regard his appearance and find in their opinion a sense of being somebody. He can reflect upon his own accomplishments as he has met competition and perhaps won trophies for excellence, achieved certain educational degrees, climbed to certain heights on the social status ladder of success in business, clubs, or lodges, etc. The third is the status value he is able to derive from his social position and his accomplishments.

In each of these three resources is a false security factor. If the person is using appearance, he must always remain attractive. If he uses performance, he must always achieve greater degrees of skill and perfection. If he uses status values, he must maintain his ratings and improve them if possible. He may use one or all three resources. He may feel like somebody today, but his security is based on variables and is ephemeral and unstable.

A person deprived of love relationships in childhood is locked into a narcissistic, self-centered, self-congratulatory mode of thinking. In this mode of thinking he has to use his environment to verify himself either subtly or openly. If he cannot find sufficient self-verification from the admiration of others or from their envious attitudes toward him, he will invert his thinking and criticize himself, pity himself, and complain about his helplessness, or find a sense of being somebody through sickness and being helpless. Even depression, as miserable as that feeling is, can be a way of being somebody by the helplessness of the debilitation it causes. The depressed person derives some sense of being somebody out of being afflicted with a problem that seems utterly impossible to overcome.

Loving relationships build strength and stability into self-concept. Unloving relationships produce these insecurities. To the degree that a person has felt unloved he is therefore afflicted with times when he is distressed with anxiety and emotional insecurity.

Polarity in Relationships Maintains False Security

Wishing to be liked by others creates a polarity in relationships that is self-defeating, but scarcely anyone is able to change that polarity. In wanting to be liked, we focus our attention primarily on ourselves and how we are impressing the other person. We are not really thinking much about the other person's needs or his value as a person. Momentarily we acknowledge his virtues and express an admiration, but often those gratuities are in the service of needing to receive approval ourselves. We often express a like for people that is beyond our actual interest in them. We are seeking self-verification by being friendly. Few people are sufficiently assured within themselves of their own self-identity to give approval to others without expecting as much in return. We usually act loving in order to incite the other person to be loving, but the relationship is void of real love. We identify with others in need and feel compassion. This is good, but not enough.

Self-verification needs introduce false security factors into relationships. The polarization toward self contaminates relationships with hypocrisy and expectation. We tend to feign love that is not so real as we pretend. We do not carry through with the concern we manifest. We tend to expect others to notice us and to reward us for our investment in their happiness. We feel offended if this does not occur. The polarization caused by our need for self-verification causes us to be defensive and easily offended. We tend to be occupied with curiosity about other people's affairs, to be caustic, sarcastic, and cynical, to ask people's opinions and be offended if they differ from our own.

Every effort to find self-verification has within it a subtle element of control of some factor that needs to be voluntarily displayed by the other person involved. Because of this, we can never be sure the love we receive is genuine, for we have in some way or other asked to be loved or done something to merit it.

Projected Images Disturb Honest Relationships

When we meet a person, I have heard, we meet three people: the person he wants us to think he is, the person he thinks he is, and the person he really is. We all tend to project an image to others when we communicate with them. We each employ empathy and try to read what the other is feeling by his projected image.

There are at least two reasons for projecting images to others. One is that we naturally are self-conscious, that is, conscious of ourselves as though we were viewing ourselves from a distance. When we speak of self-concept, we speak of our image of ourselves. Introspection is a function of this ability to analyze oneself. We may describe something we do and say, "That's the way I am." In doing this we are stating how we view ourselves.

The other factor that incites us to project an image is our unsatisfied need to be loved, which has left us with an uncertainty about being lovable. We try to project an image that is lovable unless we are angry, and then we usually don't care what others think.

It is interesting to think of a few of the images we attempt to project in social situations. We will try to determine the possible reason for each such image.

A person afflicted with inferiority feelings might try to project the I-know-what-I'm-doing image. He might try to impress with an I-can-do-anything image or a Nothing-ever-bothers-me image. He could on occasion use the I-don't-care image.

If a person were hostile, he might easily project the I-hate-everyone image. On other occasions he might employ the Don't-get-too-close image. He might project the Who-cares-about-you image.

The person who is discouraged or depressed may project the I'm-always-wrong image, the I-never-do-anything-right image, or perhaps the I-can't-win image. He could easily project a No-one-knows-the-trouble-I'm-in image.

Someone who is lonely might project the Please-notice-me image or I'm-neglected image.

A person habitually insecure and fearful will project a No-one-can-be-trusted image or Something-terrible-is-about-to-happen image.

The list of images is endless, but a second look indicates all are self-centered and self-concerned. None of these does anything to verify someone else in a social relationship. When someone is needing self-verification and is exposed to any of these images, he tries to avoid getting overly involved. Thus these images are all self-defeating and self-perpetuating.

When a person is secure within himself, he is able to love others with a desire to be expendable for the others' welfare. The acceptance of his love is in itself gratifying and fulfilling. Because of the relationship he feels he has been allowed to know and to understand another person more profoundly; the voluntary trust and self-disclosure are fulfilling. A secure person is likely to project an I'm-interested-in-you image. He communicates by this image the message, "I accept you as you are; I respect you even though we may see things differently."

The insecurity factor in self-centered images is also in the parental component implied by the image. The person awards the other person some authority value and then subjects himself to the reaction of this other person. Almost any image projected for self-verification is intended to win a response that will aid the person in his attempt to feel like somebody. If others react as he anticipates, all is well for that situation. If others do not react as anticipated, but perhaps negatively, he feels deflated and upset.

Underlying Factor in False Security

The principal cause of false security is the mind's ability to repress unwanted feelings and keep such ideas out of awareness. The emotion that holds these ideas in the unconscious is the fear of reactivating whatever caused them to be repressed in the first place. Some forms of repression are valuable and constructive, but when hostility, guilt, or fear is being repressed, we can expect certain insecurities to follow.

When such ideas are repressed, the person consciously

tries to prove to himself in a compensating attitude that the repressed idea never existed. As long as he can keep his mind occupied on other issues, he lives as though he never had the unwanted experience. Since the person felt insecure with hostility, guilt, or fear, he retains a sense of security as long as he can keep out of awareness the issues that made him insecure. When circumstances threaten to reawaken those repressed feelings or ideas, a person becomes anxious, fearful, and sometimes depressed. The person may unwittingly employ a variety of reactions in his anxiety to distract himself from the unwanted idea or feeling that is about to come from the repressed.

Lynwood came to my office to discuss certain feelings of anxiety he was experiencing. Christmas was approaching, and he was planning a trip east with his wife and two children to visit parents and relatives. As the day of departure drew near, he became more and more anxious. Instead of anticipating a delightful visit, he was filled with dread.

Lynwood explained that his parents had made fun of his mistakes at family gatherings when he was a child, using his blunders as items of amusing conversation. He reported they would say, ''You can't guess what Lynwood did this time,'' then proceeded to mortify him with the details of some childish behavior. ''Then,'' he said, ''they'd all laugh at me. I was the butt of their jokes. I don't believe I can take it if they do that this Christmas.''

What will you feel like doing if they do?'' I asked.

''I'd like to hurt them someway,'' he responded impulsively, ''the way they have hurt me over and over again all my life!''

''You'd like to hurt them,'' I echoed.

''Yes,'' he continued, ''I have a rage inside me. It's violent. I want to do something terrible! I don't dare feel that rage. It scares me!''

''You've never told them how angry they make you?'' I enquired.

''No,'' he replied, agitated. ''If I told them how I feel, they'd just have something more to laugh about next time. I'd just be a sorehead!''

''But you are an adult, and you do have the right to express your disapproval of what they do,'' I said to start him thinking more realistically.

''Yes, I guess I could speak up,'' he replied thoughtfully. ''But the thought of it scares me silly.''

Lynwood did go home for Christmas, and he did speak up. He reported he simply told them to stop and talk about something else, and to his surprise, they seemed embarrassed and changed the subject.

As long as Lynwood was away from his parents, he could feel somewhat secure in his love for them, but when faced with the prospect of actually being with them, he became anxious over the hostile feelings he had never been able to face. Fortunately he recognized his tendency to blame himself for his bad feelings instead of doing something about them. He had a constructive confrontation with his parents, which led to a more complete disclosure of his feelings later. Though his parents were a bit defensive, they did listen, and his total relationship with them improved.

A False Security Common to All People

Regardless of how loving parents may be, they cannot meet the child's idealistic demands for perfection. They cannot come the instant he feels a need; they cannot allow him to do just as he pleases all the time; they cannot give him their undivided attention whenever he needs it. Life normally has frustrations on all levels of development. Furthermore, the child's own ability to perceive the parental attitude is not completely accurate, due to his lack of maturity and experience. Also, a child has an innate willfulness, a self-determination, which must be harnessed for productive living and fulfillment.

For these reasons no child ever completely resolves his feelings of separation, isolation, and aloneness. He never feels totally secure in his sense of being somebody. Today he may be very happy, but something will happen sooner or later to rekindle feelings of being just a nobody. He never can seem to get away from the possibility of losing his sense of self-identity, his self-esteem, his somebody feelings. These momentary feelings of being a nobody linger, so the child represses them. They devastate his ability to think about what is happening.

When the idea that "I am a nobody" is repressed out of awareness, the conscious thought is "I look good" or "I did this well" or "I am important — so I am somebody." The child proves to himself by his appearance, performance, or status that he is not a nobody; but on a conscious level he takes notice that he is somebody. This is called *self-verification*. The child has an innate need to verify himself as a person, as somebody, for somewhere lurking in his unconscious self is a conviction that he is a nonentity, a nobody.

This is why parental love is especially important to growing children. By the process of identification, loving relationships in the home build an organization of feeling experiences in the child's mind called a *self-concept* — that is, belongingness, worthiness, and competence. Self-concept negates the need for self-verification in the immediate situation. The more a child has felt loved, the less will be his need for self-verification as an adult; the less a child has felt loved, the greater will be his need for self-verification.

Self-verification is essentially proving to oneself that he is not a nobody. Self-verification relates to three basic desires and feelings: being wanted, being good, and being adequate.

As a child develops in his first phase of growth, he tries to prove to himself that he is not unwanted. Parental love fulfills his desire and validates his belongingness. He does not have to appear well or to perform well or to hear some compliment that makes him feel important in order to verify to himself that he is not unwanted. He knows he belongs.

When a child progresses into his second phase of growth, he tries to prove to himself not only that he is not unwanted, but that he is not "no good," or bad. Parental love validates his worthiness, and he does not have to use appearance or performance or status to verify to himself that he is somebody.

Growing into his third phase, a child tries to prove to himself not only that he is not unwanted, that he is not bad, but that he is not inferior. Again, parental love validates his desire for competence. He does not have to use self-verification strategies to feel validated as an adequate, competent person.

Bear in mind that self-verification is a source of false security in the self-concept. Self-verification is essential when there is an absence of love, but the process never validates, it only tentatively verifies. In self-verification we are trying to disprove something to ourselves on a conscious level that unconsciously we are persuaded exists. More exactly, *we are convinced of being a nobody, a nonentity, but we have repressed that idea out of awareness, and this conviction remains because it is out of reach of conscious change until we can bear to lift the repressed idea and have some way to change it.* On a conscious level we must keep proving to ourselves by certain reflections of our influence upon our environment that we are somebody. We maintain a continual distraction of our attention from our inner reality feelings. Thus we perpetuate our own insecurity.

To demonstrate how we maintain a distraction from our secret conviction about ourselves, ask anyone this question: "If ever I could really get to know all about you, do you think I'd like you?" I have asked that question of audiences many times, and the response is always the same. Some of the people will thoughtfully say no, or they will express an uncertainty. Fear of death and judgment by a holy

God may also relate to this sense of being no good, a nobody, a bad person, yet accountable.

Self-Verification Polarizes Our Thinking

The need for self-verification tends to polarize our thinking in three basic ways. We need to be either *strong* or *weak* or *evasive* in the situations of life.

The Need to Be Strong

The need to be strong is a modification of the defiant personality structure. When we need to be strong, we have to maintain an image of strength in all situations. Insecurity manifests itself in that we are not appropriately flexible. For instance, we may never be able to show emotion — to weep — because that would be weakness. Or, we may not be able appropriately to leave a problematic situation alone; we may feel a sense of having to display our strength by getting involved. We may feel we have good answers to all problems, and so we are critical of the attempts others make.

The need to be strong means that we seek self-verification out of the way we attract to our radiance people who admire us and praise what we do. We gain a sense of being somebody by the impact of our influence upon others.

The need to be strong makes us avoid situations where we might need to follow the leadership or advice of someone else. We resist being dependent on others. We stubbornly insist upon having our way in most situations. Though we glean a great deal of verification from our positive, optimistic attitude, we are actually quite insensitive to the feelings of others and unable to give them proper value. We are often considered conceited and unable to accept blame when we are in the wrong.

The Need to Be Weak

The need to be weak is a modification of the compliant personality structure. When we need to be weak, we have to maintain an image of weakness and dependency in all situations. There are times naturally when we feel weak and dependent, but to use dependency and weakness as a way of finding self-verification is most self-defeating. When we do this, we are inviting sympathetic assistance and can never learn to overcome our weaknesses, for then we would have to seek different means of self-verification.

When we need to be weak, we may seek self-verification out of illnesses and frailty. We are bidding for the gracious concern of others and for their willingness to make life easier for us. Thus such weakness becomes highly manipulative. The need to be weak may relate to the fear of making a bad decision, so we continually seek advice from others. We may not be able to delight appropriately in our own accomplishments, so we need others to praise us for our efforts. We may feel as if life is very hard for us, so we are filled with self-pity and feelings of being a martyr. All these attitudes are attempts to find a measure of being somebody without assuming a normal sense of responsibility for our problems.

The Need to Be Evasive

The need to be evasive is a modification of the withdrawn personality structure. If we are evasive, we are attempting not to be involved. The self-verification in being evasive lies in being able to preserve one's present level of self-identity and not letting anything disturb. The insecurity arises in that while avoiding issues may give us a sense of security for the moment, we still have to face those issues sometime in some way. The more we avoid, the more we need to be evasive to hold onto our sense of security.

When we are evasive, we are indifferent, often silent when normally we might speak. We may be evasive by changing the subject, or getting involved in some other project more to our liking. If we are evasive as a way of maintaining a sense of security, we are exceedingly careful not to reveal our true feelings. We are slow at offering opinions. We may hold the stance, "What difference does it make?" We try to hold to the idea that nothing is really very important. The evasive person really has few friends!

False Security Is Self-Perpetuating

Self-verification gives only momentary feelings of being somebody, and the need for it keeps recurring. The underlying problem is never dealt with — that we are trying to disprove to ourselves on a conscious level something we unconsciously believe is so.

When we attempt to find self-verification by overemphasizing our strengths, we cannot admit our normal weaknesses and need for dependence. Thus we have to stay strong whether we actually feel strong or not.

In attempting to find self-verification by capitalizing on our weaknesses and need to be dependent, we must not exercise our normal strengths or be conscious of having those strengths. We must stay weak and miserable and dependent.

When we attempt to find self-verification by being evasive and uninvolved, our indifference keeps us out of touch with others and having to rely upon our imaginary feelings of being somebody.

One of the most effective insights a person can obtain in this regard is to discover how he is perpetuating his own misery and maintaining his own insecurity. Then he needs some insight about how to go about stopping the habit of maintaining his insecurity. He needs insight into where his true securities are and how to claim them for himself.

Part 3
What We Can Become

Self-concept has a new, stable premise in spiritual conversion. How we can relate to God for basic emotional needs. New self-concept changes personal relationships and gives new meaning to living. Perfecting the new self-concept and continuing to grow into emotional maturity.

12

Stable Premise for a Secure Self-Concept

The need to determine a sense of being somebody is universal. No one can function efficiently when he feels like a nobody. We are aware of needing self-verification because we have not been adequately validated in our self-identity by loving relationships in childhood.

We are all creatures of relationship. We desire first of all in our relationships to feel accepted. Second, we are concerned about feeling a sense of goodness, of having quality. Third, we are intent on feeling adequate as we face life situations and fulfill our particular sex roles. It is exceedingly difficult to bear the feelings of being unwanted, no good, or inferior. Thus we consciously or unconsciously distill evidences from our life situations that will verify for us that we are actually somebody who is accepted, good, and adequate.

Like any other type of validation, there must be a sound premise, or the verification we feel is of little consequence. In other chapters we have discussed at length the virtues of identifying with the accepting and approving attitudes manifested in loving relationships. We also have discussed the self-defeating inadequacies of self-verification that continually introduce false security factors into self-concept.

The effects of loving relationships upon self-concept might be compared with building a house upon a rock. Love is a valid premise for self-concept, for the relationship of love is consonant with our nature.

The effects of self-verification upon self-concept might be compared with building a house upon sand. The premise is not consonant with our nature, but is a result of our own effort. The premise is somewhat illusory, for it is actually what we believe the other person thinks of us. Self-verification, by its nature, is completely entangled with variable, unpredictable, subjective, and relative factors.

Some Insecurity Factors in Self-Verification

Let us remind ourselves of a few of the insecurity factors incorporated in self-verification.

One factor is that we seek a reaction from others that is possible only if they love us unconditionally. Our expectations of their reactions are usually tinged with idealization; yet at the same time we are depending upon their verifying us, they usually are expecting us to verify them. They are no more able to love us unconditionally than we are able to love them. Because each wants verification and is trying to impress the other for that purpose, neither is actually attending to the other person's welfare.

How often we have wished for reality in relationships, something with a little depth, something dependable below the level of the common courtesies. Isabelle exclaimed, "I wish I could depend on what others say. People talk so friendly and they seem to be loving, but when I begin to believe in them, I get let down. I find they don't really mean all the love they seem to show. I give up trying to understand people."

Isabelle was apparently looking for unconditional love. She made the discovery that others were just as manipulative and unable to love her unconditionally as she was. The big question is: How can we find a verification from people who are just as much in need of being verified as we? The best we can provide each other is the illusion that we are accepted and loved. When we become frustrated and angry with others because of our disappointments, either we try to hurt them back — which may mean some type of open confrontation — or we try to "get even" more subtly, or perhaps we just withdraw and break the relationship.

We want the feeling of being loved unconditionally, but we have been prepared in our childhood experiences to believe that somehow we must qualify for it. Yet in tiny infancy we concluded we were nobodies unless somehow we behaved in a way that pleased others, especially our parents. This nobody feeling was reinforced many times through most of our youth. Therefore, to keep the idea of being a nobody out of awareness, we did the things that rendered the greatest sense of being somebody. Some of our conduct was pleasing; some was displeasing. By displeasing, we in hostility were proving we were greater than those who tried to govern us.

Another factor contributing to our insecurity as a result of attempting self-verification is our own perception of what others mean by what they say or do. Our perception is conditioned by our own mental attitude at the moment, but we do not usually think about this. For instance, if we are in a hostile, antagonistic mood, we tend to ascribe negative, selfish, corrupt motives to what others say or do. We are not likely to make any allowance for their poor choice of words in expressing themselves, or we might maintain that they had some implied meaning, something evil in mind. We may be offended by the other person's preoccupation with some other matter that made him seem disinterested in us. Our hostility makes us take any offense personally.

Or, on the other hand, if we happen to be down on ourselves for some reason and in a somewhat depressed mood, we might be embarrassed to accept a compliment or be irritated by the other person's joyfulness. If someone should criticize us, we might assume we deserve it and make a bigger issue of the criticism than is warranted.

If we happen to be overly anxious at the time someone extends a friendly gesture, we will probably be so preoccupied with ourselves and our problems that we overlook what was said. We might give a negative reaction that nullifies whatever value we could have received.

These distortions in perception of our relationships based upon our own frame of mind cause self-verification to fail.

The greatest insecurity factor in self-verification, however, is self-deception. We are unrealistic with ourselves, and we cannot have a stable sense of security when we base our self-confidence upon self-deception.

We need to keep the infantile idea that we are a nobody out of awareness. We do this by taking note of how others rate us for our appearance, performance, and status, and then we congratulate ourselves as though this proves we are somebody. Pride or conceit is a self-congratulatory mechanism of thinking. The problem with pride, as far as our own emotional growth is concerned, is that the energies of life are all focused upon proving to ourselves that we are somebody.

Whatever physical beauty, whatever excellence in our performance, or whatever status rating we proudly display is all dedicated to keeping the idea of being a nobody out of awareness. Having to prove anything to ourselves about our self-identity keeps us from actually feeling like somebody. We soon have to do better than we did previously in order to maintain the sense of being somebody; any fault we find in ourselves becomes self-convicting and threatens to awaken the idea that we are nobody.

We glory in our self-improvements, but since we have never rid ourselves of the idea of being a nobody, our self-improvements do not give us a stable sense of being somebody; they only make us less likely to think about being a nobody.

Spiritual Dimension to Thinking Provides a Stable Premise

Unconditional love is apparently the only parental attitude that can condition a child to develop an adequate self-concept, for true love is not conditional and it does not change. It is easily verified. The Bible says, "Love never faileth" and "Now abideth . . . love" (1 Cor. 13:8,13).

People at their best do not love unconditionally in any consistent way. A few of our relationships may gratify us with expressions of true love, but living involves a wide variety of interactions with people which may range from love to bitter hate, from compassion to malicious violence. While we desire unconditional love, we often do much to destroy the value of that love when we have it. We may want it so much, we will be afraid to trust it.

The only reliable source of true love is God. "God is love" (1 John 4:8). God loves us unconditionally, for He is love. We are created in the image of God, so we have an innate need to be loved unconditionally.

Several values are apparent in considering God's love. We know of God's love by the Bible. The Bible claims to be the Word of God, and it does not change. Jesus said, "Verily I say unto you, Till heaven and earth pass, one jot or one tittle shall in no wise pass from the law, till all be fulfilled" (Matt. 5:18). "Heaven and earth shall pass away, but my words shall not pass away" (Matt. 24:35).

One value is that the Bible is an objective source for learning of God's love as well as His other attributes. This source does not change. Furthermore, the message is not obscurely written; anyone can read and understand the love of God.

Another value is that God's love has been demonstrated in an historical event, the crucifixion and resurrection of Jesus Christ. "God commendeth his love toward us, in that, while we were yet sinners, Christ died for us" (Rom. 5:8). "In this was manifested the love of God toward us, because that God sent his only begotten Son into the world, that we might live through him. Herein is love, not that we loved God, but that he loved us, and sent his Son to be the propitiation for our sins. Beloved, if God so loved us, we ought also to love one another. No man hath seen God at any time. If we love one another, God dwelleth in us, and his love is perfected in us'' (1 John 4:9-12). Thus the Bible clearly indicates how God has affectionately and compassionately concerned Himself about our welfare, not only for our immediate needs but for our eternal destiny as well.

God is invisible. This is also of great value. He is available by faith to each person living in the whole world at any moment of time. ''Draw nigh to God, and he will draw nigh to you'' (James 4:8).

When we are seeking self-verification, we try to condition those from whom we want love and contact them at a time when they will be most likely to accept us. The very fact that we do this makes the love we receive from them less reliable and more questionable. Are they responding to us because we have intrinsic value, or are they giving us attention because they need our approval? This is a hard question to answer conclusively. But God is always available. He cannot be manipulated. He does not need our love for His sense of identity. He is God. He loves us because we are somebody to Him; we have intrinsic value! ''For God so loved the world, that he gave his only begotten Son, that whosoever believeth in him should not perish, but have everlasting life'' (John 3:16). God loved us with unconditional love.

We need not only unconditional love for verification of our sense of being somebody, but also someone in authority who will be honest and fair. In self-verification we project parental components to others to give them the authority to rate us. We want them to be honest and fair, but we doubt that they are, for we have influenced their reaction.

God is not that way. He is sovereign in His authority over everyone. He is God. He is also honest. He does not hide the truth from us about ourselves. He starts with the fact that we are sinners. We have a reason for feeling as if we are nobody! We are guilty before Him, but He doesn't stop there. He has provided us a way of forgiveness and restoration. We cannot make ourselves acceptable; we must accept His grace to truly feel like somebody. When we do, we find that we always have been somebody to God, and His grace opens up a whole new premise for self-concept.

Stable Premise Available by Spiritual Conversion

God is the Person; we are created in His image. He lovingly

invites us to come to Him, to believe in Him, to know His love. "Come unto me," Jesus said, "all ye that labour and are heavy laden, and I will give you rest" (Matt. 11:28).

By faith we accept God's love as we accept Jesus Christ as our personal Savior from sin. The decision to receive Christ makes us spiritually and personally related to the invisible God. "As many as received him [Christ], to them gave he power to become the sons of God, even to them that believe on his name: Which were born . . . of God" (John 1:12,13). "Of his own will begat he us with the word of truth, that we should be a kind of firstfruits of his creatures" (James 1:18). He is unseen but real to each one who trusts in Him. This makes us aware of being somebody to God. We know we are *really* somebody, for we are somebody to God!

Once we have this assurance of being someone because we know we are loved unconditionally by the living God, we can dare to disregard the idea that we are nobody. We no longer need to deceive ourselves about our true self-identity; we know we are somebody to God.

This reality about our identity puts our personal relationships with others on an entirely different plane of reference. We can love because we have been loved; we have been redeemed from the idea of being a nobody, which relieves us of relating to others in order to verify ourselves as we have done previously. We can begin to love others unconditionally because God has loved us unconditionally; furthermore, God loves them as He loves us.

We have discovered our true sense of identity; we are God's somebody. Because we have experienced God's love, we can forgive others for not meeting all our ideal expectations of them, for not being as perfect as we want them to be, for being hostile, for not loving us unconditionally. We have discovered that we have been seeking love horizontally when we have needed a vertical dimension to give meaning to horizontal relationships.

As 1 John 4:12 indicates, our love for each other becomes a manifestation of God's love in us, and as we continue to love others, His love is made more complete in us. In other words, we do not turn to people to establish our self-identity by some device of self-verification; we find our self-identity in our loving relationship with God. Then we are able to love people more nearly unconditionally, and in so doing we establish our self-identity and perfect our sense of being somebody.

When we exercise faith in God through Jesus Christ, we no longer need self-verification; we are validated. The Word of God is our assurance of this relationship. We trust in the promises of God as our security. Whatever pride we take in our excellencies does not unite us to God. We are united to Him by faith in Christ's atonement for us because of his love. He took our sense of being a nobody into Himself when He died for us. He became a nonentity, a nobody for us when He died on that cross. We felt His love when we realized that He loves us just as we are, a nobody, a nonentity.

All our efforts at self-verification are instantly canceled. "Not by works of righteousness which we have done, but according to his mercy he saved us" (Titus 3:5). "For by grace are ye saved through faith; and that not of yourselves: it is the gift of God: not of works, lest any man should boast. For we are his workmanship, created in Christ Jesus unto good works, which God hath before ordained that we should walk in them" (Eph. 2:8-10).

Self-verification is a works program for saving our sense of being somebody. Actually we are saved by faith, not by works. By faith we understand that we are somebody to God, who loves us with unconditional love. In fact, we are a creation of God; He creates a new self-concept within us. Our new self-concept is His workmanship in us. Because we know we are somebody, we can be somebody to others and do them good. This is our "ministry of reconciliation" (2 Cor. 5:18) — to represent the unconditional love of Christ to others.

Three fundamental yearnings in relationships are satisfied by faith in God and relating to Him by His Word: We know we are accepted by God; we belong, for "he hath made us accepted in the beloved" (Eph. 1:6). We know we are good, for He has forgiven and cleansed us from sin. "Being justified by faith, we have peace with God through our Lord Jesus Christ" (Rom. 5:1). We know we are not inferior or inadequate in life situations, for He is with us at all times. "But thanks be to God, who in Christ always leads us in triumph, and through us spreads the fragrance of the knowledge of him everywhere. For we are the aroma of Christ to God among those who are being saved and among those who are perishing, to one a fragrance from death to death, to the other a fragrance from life to life" (2 Cor. 2:14-16 RSV). In Christ we have overcome the fear of being inadequate and inferior; we are committed to doing our best for Him.

Spiritual Explanation for Emotional Insecurity

According to the Bible, man is created in the image of God (Gen. 1:26,27). All God's attributes are absolute; man has similar attributes, but on a finite scale. All our attributes are responsive except one, and that attribute is willful self-determination.

God is life, the source of all life (Gen. 2:7). We do not

create life; we have merely the ability to reproduce living persons like ourselves. We live, are alive as living persons, but God is life (John 5:26).

God is the source of all truth and knowledge and exact justice. "The Spirit is truth" (1 John 5:6). "The heavens declare the glory of God; and the firmament sheweth his handiwork" (Ps. 19:1). "All things are naked and opened unto the eyes of him with whom we have to do" (Heb. 4:13). We do not create reality or truth; we only respond to it. We comprehend truth, acquire knowledge, appreciate justice.

God is love (1 John 4:8). We are unable to create love, but we readily respond to being loved. Having been loved, we can love others.

God is one. God, though a holy Trinity, is a perfect unity (Deut. 6:4). We seek a sense of inner wholeness. We want a unity with others as we relate to them. God is a unit, but God is not alone; He is Three-in-One: Father, Son, and Holy Spirit. Christ prayed for our oneness with each other and our oneness with Him (John 17:22-24). It is our innate need for a homogeneous wholeness within that causes us to seek to overcome our inner conflicts and externalize our negative emotions.

God's sovereignty necessitates His being self-determining. He is almighty and rules the universe. He is responsible to Himself in His exercise of willful choice, for He is God. "Who hath known the mind of the Lord? or who hath been his counsellor?" (Rom. 11:34). God is One, and whatever He does is consistent with what He is. God is always functioning in perfect harmony with Himself. He is the Author of law and order on an infinite scale of values. He is holy, and all He ordains is good.

When we consider the fact of man being created in the image of God, we must realize that this attribute of self-determinism is not a responsive attribute. We are self-willed and self-determining as though we were gods, but we are not almighty to execute our schemes. We are finite and dependent, therefore responsible to conform to our source of supply. Herein lies the bind that causes emotional insecurity. We want what we want, and we resist any limitations; yet we must accept our limitations and our dependency upon others and cooperate with them in order to obtain our basic needs. We may feel like gods in our sense of self-sovereignty, but we have not the power to execute our reign as we wish.

From infancy we are pleasure seeking and determined to do as we please. We resist being governed and restricted. We become angry when we do not get our way. Anger is an attempt to assert our sense of self-sovereignty.

Our irresponsible demand for sensual pleasure, for the possession of things, and for the admiration of others puts us in conflict with our environment. Our lack of consideration for the rights of others not only causes them to be defensive with us, but compels us to defend ourselves against losing to those who are also irresponsible in their demands upon us. In other words, our instinctive need for security — while at the same time meeting our physical and emotional needs — puts us in conflict with our environment, and this reflectively puts us in conflict within ourselves.

We must exercise self-control in obtaining sensual pleasure or possessions. Our self-control and respect for others' needs and rights gain for us a certain degree of admiration from others. If we do not exercise this self-control, we are liable to be in jeopardy of the wrath of our society, causing us greater loss, deprivation, pain, or for some offenses, possibly death.

We note another source of inner conflict. We become divided in our enjoyment of pleasure. We learn that some pleasurable activities are wrong. We gain pleasure sometimes in doing what is right and sometimes in doing what is wrong. Whatever we enjoy, we accept as part of ourselves. This makes our judgment in conflict with our desire for pleasure in doing what is wrong.

Whenever we violate our own good judgment for the sake of immediate gratification, we encourage a split to grow within ourselves. Our conscience and faculties of judgment are less able to control our impulses. This occurs as a result of making compromises within ourselves in our thinking. For instance, we may reason "Just this once" or "A little bit won't hurt."

The conscience is an organ of the mind that controls our impulses so that we conform willingly to what is right and shun what is wrong. This controlling organ of the mind was developed by parental influences in the home during childhood. It causes us to feel good about ourselves when we do what is right and to feel bad and guilty when we do what we know is wrong. Even though our conscience may be overly punitive or inclined to be overly lenient, we must respect its voice. "Rulers are not a terror to good conduct, but to bad. . . .Do what is good, and you will receive his approval, for he is God's servant for your good. But if you do wrong, be afraid, for he does not bear the sword in vain; he is the servant of God to execute his wrath on the wrongdoer. Therefore one must be subject, not only to avoid God's wrath but also for the sake of conscience" (Rom. 13:3-5 RSV). Other Scripture passages recommend living in such a way as to maintain a good conscience, e.g., 1 Peter 3:15,16,21.

In other words, we need to forbid ourselves the pleasures of sin in order to maintain inner wholeness. "To him that knoweth to do good, and doeth it not, to him it is sin" (James 4:17). Once we have violated ourselves by yielding to temptation, we have no way to restore inner peace apart from the grace of God. We can deny our mischief and try to forget it happened, but we only repress it and discover later that we are doing little things to punish ourselves. The anxiety some people feel when they begin to be happy and the things they do to keep themselves from becoming too excited are often manifestations of the need for self-punishment. We can rationalize away the immediate feelings of guilt, but we cannot stop remembering.

Guilt feelings over violating one's conscience are nobody feelings. Some people I have counseled have explained that they are not just a nonentity, but a minus quantity; they would have to improve to be considered a nothing!

One great source of emotional insecurity is the loose hold that our conscience and good judgment have upon our ability to control our impulses. When we speak of impulses, we must not overlook the pleasure of vengeance found in exercising hostility. This pleasure is akin to the pleasure derived from sensual gratification; it is as difficult to control hostile drives as it is to control sexual drives. Both types of impulses cause much emotional insecurity because pleasure is a common denominator.

Adam and Eve sinned by disobeying God (Gen. 3:1-6). They exercised self-determination in a willful, defiant manner. They both knew they were disobeying God, but they were offered an immediate gratification if they ate of the forbidden fruit. The original rupture in the governmental system of the mind seems to have occurred at this time (see Rom. 5:12-19). Ever since Adam sinned, man has been insecure, willful, disobedient, in conflict with others, and in conflict within himself.

How Faith in God Solves the Insecurity Problem

Faith in God can be explained dynamically as a surrender of our right to exercise an independent prerogative to anything we desire. Faith harnesses our attribute of self-determination to the will of God, for we accept our responsibility to God for our willfulness. Faith is dependence upon God, but we must not overlook the fact that faith is also a responsible exercise of autonomy, creative imagination, and decisiveness. Faith is the heart of man reaching out to God in response to the written Word of God, the Bible, with a commitment of oneself to all one understands about God.

Faith in God can bring one into a vital relationship with God only when one believes in Jesus Christ. "Ye believe in God, believe also in me" (John 14:1). Faith in God surrenders our willfulness to Him; faith in Jesus Christ, His Son, clears the record of all our rebellious acts of self-determined willfulness — our sins (John 3:18).

This faith through Jesus Christ brings us into union with God so that we become born again in His spiritual family of believers called the Church (Eph. 1:13; 1 Peter 1:23). We are united to God and to each other. We are born again, regenerated by His Spirit, and adopted into His family (Rom. 8:15; Gal. 4:5). As children of God, we are in contact with God's Spirit, who leads us in daily situations (Rom. 8:14).

We read, "The wages of sin is death; but the gift of God is eternal life through Jesus Christ our Lord" (Rom 6:23). Death is a process of fragmentation, reducing the organization of components that life built back to their original elements. When we violate our consciences, we promote the split within our minds. This increases the loss in our sense of wholeness because it increases the fragmentation already present. The ultimate result of fragmentation is death to the feeling of being somebody.

In other words, as we give in to our impulses against our better judgment, we encourage a process of thinking that ultimately leads to guilt feelings and a sense of being a nobody, a nothing. We have furthered the process of death within us, for we are more disorganized within. When we come to God and confess our sins, we admit we are violating His Word and ourselves, and we find His forgiveness. We accept His gift of life. Being justified from all sin — that is, coming to a state of mind of no condemnation (Rom. 5:1; 8:1) — we are healed of the effects of the splitting. We are restored in the sense of being somebody. We are somebody to God.

Coming to God through Jesus Christ means that we identify with Christ in His sufferings for our sins. Our sins cause Him to suffer in atonement vicariously for us. When we sense the impact that our willful disobedience has upon the heart of God, we lose the value in the pleasure we take in our sins. How can we enjoy doing what will cause our Lord to suffer when we love Him? Thus we can devote ourselves more consistently to doing what is right; we take a greater pleasure in doing the will of God.

Romans 12:1,2 speaks to the issue: "I beseech you therefore, brethren, by the mercies of God, that ye present your bodies a living sacrifice, holy, acceptable unto God, which is your reasonable service. And be not conformed to this world: but be ye transformed by the renewing of your mind, that ye may prove what is that good, and acceptable, and perfect, will of God.''

As we consider His sufferings for our sins as an expression of His love, we are motivated by gratitude to make a present of our bodies, the seat of our desires, to God. By doing this we make a gift of our bodies to Him, that is, the house in which we live, the temple of His Holy Spirit.

This commitment aligns the source of our desires with the governing forces within our conscience, the faculties of good judgment. On an idealistic level, we have resolved the rupture within our psyche between the governing forces of the mind and the source of desires. We resolve the conflict between what we want to do and what we should do, because during the moments when we are aware of our commitment, we want to do what we should do. We have exercised our self-determination, our self-sovereignty, in a way that conforms to the will of God. We are being responsible to God for the satisfaction of our desires.

This is the idealistic step which corrects our motivations. The last part of this passage indicates the practical step which corrects our conduct: ''Be not conformed to this world,'' I believe, needs to be applied to the strategies of self-verification. Everyone in the world, generally speaking, practices self-verification in order to determine a sense of being somebody. We who appreciate the love of God for us in Christ and have made a present of our bodies to Him have a sense of being somebody to God. Our Christian fellowship validates on a realistic level this self-identity: *God + Me = a Whole Person.*

Maintaining this equation for our sense of being somebody transforms our total behavior because it renews our mind, provides a sense of wholeness, establishes us on a no-condemnation plane of living, and weans us from the need for self-verification. In this new sense of secure self-identity based upon a loving relationship with God, we prove to ourselves in the daily circumstances ''what is that good, and acceptable, and perfect, will of God.'' Our minds have the proper attitude to discern His will and be willing with a whole heart to do it. Our life style verifies that we are motivated from within to be in the will of God in our thinking and actions. We are better able to cast ''down imaginations, and every high thing that exalteth itself against the knowledge of God, and bringing into captivity every thought to the obedience of Christ'' (2 Cor. 10:5).

As we determine to follow this twofold pattern for the correction of our godless ways of living, we ''grow in grace, and in the knowledge of our Lord and Saviour Jesus Christ'' (2 Peter 3:18). We begin to taste of the ''peace of God, which passeth all understanding" (Phil. 4:7; cf. John 14:27). This is the fulfillment of John 10:10: "I am come that they might have life, and that they might have it more abundantly."

Faith in God Provides Elements Needed for Development

We find in our God, as the Bible describes Him, a perfect blending of the three attributes of parental control that we need for peace of mind and an emotionally mature sense of self-identity. On an absolute level they fulfill our ideals. These attributes are *almighty sovereignty, realism manifested in perfect justice, unconditional love manifested in grace and mercy.*

We need to be governed by and responsible to an absolutely sovereign one who is perfectly consistent, unchangeable, and impossible to manipulate. At the same time, we need a parent who never varies in his ability to consider all the facts, our understanding of those facts, our motives and intentions and abilities. He also must never vary in his ability to be totally fair in his evaluations. Also, we need the same parent to love us unconditionally with a changeless love charged with grace and mercy. Such a love is primarily interested in the child's overcoming his deficiencies and will use discipline as a means of both instruction and correction. All these basic needs are satisfied in our relationship with God as Parent.

Our earthly parents were appointed by God to stand in for Him and to relate to us in His place until such a time as we were mature enough to relate to God personally. They were the living representatives of God to our child mind. The problem we encountered with our earthly parents was that they did not balance these three attributes, but related to us more with one attribute than with another. They sometimes exercised sovereign authority without a balance of realism in considering our understanding of their orders, so we tend now to view God as a tyrant who must have His way regardless of human suffering.

Or, our parents may have tried to consider our abilities and the facts but were weak in their governmental controls, for they allowed us to manipulate them. Now we are not sure God controls all things. Perhaps He is just an ambiguous controlling force.

Or, perhaps our parents were loving us because we were able to perform for them satisfactorily, and we learned to believe that we needed to earn the love we wanted. They loved us conditionally. We tend now to think of God as being conditional in His love for us, and we may fear His sudden disapproval or punishment.

We might think of many combinations of emphasizing one or two of these three attributes at the expense of the others. We all have certain distortions in our apprehension of God, but these can be corrected if we will take the trouble to determine from the Scriptures who God is and what He is like. As we consider the true nature of God, we must keep in mind that these three fundamental parental attributes are in perfect, immutable balance in Him. Holding to that essential concept and making sure to relate one attribute to the other will speed us on to a more complete and accurate perception of God. It will help us to relate to Him more satisfactorily.

Faith is Fundamental to Hope and Love

Faith in God through Jesus Christ aligns our inner selves with the absolute values found in God, and this incites a process of thinking that completely transforms our determination of a sense of being somebody. The inner conflict between our sense of righteousness, or what is right, and the desire to do as we please in an immediate opportunity afforded by a situation is potentially resolved as we exercise faith in God and make a present of ourselves to Him.

The problem of obedience is not positioned upon trying to be accepted by God. Rather, because He has accepted us with forgiveness we can trust Him to be with us in our temptations to give us the power to resist. He is able always to give the ability to do what is right (see 1 Cor. 10:13).

This new sense of awareness of self as a whole person inspires a sense of hope in God. Life in Christ becomes so involved with the eternal purposes of God and so embellished with immediate securities in the present that our minds are redeemed from the domination of negative, pessimistic thinking and ignited with positive, incurable optimism. We tend to have a sense of being indestructible; the experience of physical death becomes in our thinking only an experience that opens the gateway to a perfect life.

Having faith and hope, we are inspired to reach for new dimensions in experiencing the love of God and in developing our own ability to love. Love becomes more than an ability to be loving; love becomes a dynamic of life.

Faith incites obedience to God. "Faith without works is dead" (James 2:20; cf. v.26). Hope inspires self-discipline. "Every man that hath this hope in him [hope of eternal life] purifieth himself, even as he is pure" (1 John 3:3). Love encourages obedience with new motivation: "If ye love me, keep my commandments" (John 14:15).

How Faith in God Closes the Separation Gap

After spiritual conversion occurs, the sense of separation

on a fundamental level is ended. Though we cannot see God, by faith we know we are never alone; He is always with us. Any distance we may feel between God and us is within our own minds. Our minds are in an unrelating attitude, and we project the idea that God is distant.

Jesus said to His followers just before He ascended to heaven, "Lo, I am with you alway, even unto the end of the world" (Matt. 28:20). Jesus promised that the Holy Spirit would "abide with you forever" (John 14:16). A timeless promise was given to Isaiah (41:10): "Fear thou not; for I am with thee: be not dismayed; for I am thy God: I will strengthen thee; yea, I will help thee; yea, I will uphold thee with the right hand of my righteousness."

Now we can understand a deeper significance to the separation problem. Being separated from mother was in God's design a way of getting us to recognize that we were separated from Him because of sin. We have been filled with terror at the thought of being separated, isolated, and alone. Such feelings imply rejection as a nonentity, a nobody. We are actually a nonentity, a person without a true self-identity, when we are godless in our living, employing self-verification as a means of being somebody.

We can quiet these anxieties about our self-identity by spiritual conversion. When we get back to God, we can truly know ourselves, and this prepares us for improved relationships with people. As we needed to feel a sense of being somebody to our parents, we can now actually feel a sense of being somebody to God, and we can validate this self-identity in the Word of God and in Christian fellowship.

13

Permeate the Relative With the Absolute

A. *In Our Perception of the Situation*

Our self-concept may seem fairly stable when life's ebb and flow of problems stays within acceptable limits. Occasionally, however, a tidal wave of unexpected difficulties overwhelms us. It may be a surprise illness, the sudden death of a loved one, a business failure, or a marriage or family problem we cannot handle. Our boat is not only rocked; it seems as if it is about to split in the middle and take water.

At these times of unusual stress we become conscious of how strong or how weak our inner security really is. We seem to get in touch with our inner selves best in times of crisis. It is then that we begin to reach desperately for some resource to hold onto, some relationship that is available and reliable.

When these critical times occur, we are occasionally surprised by just who our true friends really are. Often someone whom we least expected to be concerned shows compassionate understanding. But again, we may find everyone very much preoccupied with his own concerns, and we feel alone in our distress.

We are all interdependent upon one another for many things. This interdependence might work much more satisfactorily if it were not for many relative factors in circumstances that continually make almost everything conditional. For instance, the very people who seem to be too preoccupied with themselves to stand by us with encouragement and support when we are in distress probably would be more attentive *if* they were not also feeling many pressures. While we want their attention because of our own anxiety, they probably wish we were not so preoccupied with ourselves and could give *them* some support.

Nearly everything in life appears related to how fortunate or unfortunate we happen to be. Often circumstances seem to be governed by chance or luck. Some people conclude it is ludicrous to believe in security because the variable, the unpredictable, and the chance elements seem to dominate so many situations. They decide that it is not so much what you know as whom you know that counts for success, and that life is mostly a matter of manipulative skill in getting what you want, in using people, in being able to get by within the framework of civil law. But this plane of reference leaves much to be desired. One might achieve a measure of happiness in what he is able to do and in the accumulation of things, but fulfillment will escape him.

The Heart Cries for the Absolute

Human nature yearns for something absolute in life, something real and reliable, something independent of circumstances. We want to reduce the controlling power of so many variables. We wish for a few guarantees that might remove some of the elements of chance or luck from life's situations. As in algebra, when it is necessary to solve an equation containing several variables, we need to reduce our considerations to just one variable at a time. The human mind staggers at any concept that contains relationships expressing the function of more than one variable.

Though we long for the absolute in terms of fulfilling our ideals, we tend to resist the idea of an absolute in regard to standards of right and wrong. We would like to make legalistic constructs relative to culture, to the times, to custom, or to religious dogma. This is, no doubt, a reaction against being governed, limited, and restricted by an authority that has power to stop us from doing as we please or to impose an arbitrary penalty upon us for violations.

When we feel guilty, we naturally rationalize, "Just how wrong is it?" or "Is the law a good law?" or "Why must I obey when others are getting away with violating the law?" Sometimes we would like to believe that all moral values are relative, that there is no absolute truth, no absolute honesty, no absolute sexual morality. If this were true, it would relieve us of a certain degree of responsibility for our actions and thus help us resolve some of our guilt feelings.

This relativism is also partly due to the unfairness in our civil government. For example, suppose we are involved in an automobile accident. In a few cases we might be as innocent as if a runaway auto crashed into our parked vehicle. But suppose both cars were moving and neither party was able to prevent the accident at the intersection. Actually both parties might have some responsibility. Each in retrospect might be able to say to himself, "It would not have happened if I had done thus or so." But the law determines one party guilty and the other the innocent victim, only one as responsible for the accident, and settlements are made accordingly.

This kind of justice occurs in our civil courts in a wide variety of situations besides automobile accidents. One is determined as the guilty party and totally responsible for the problem, though both parties may honestly have some responsibility and should share in the settlement.

From the way justice is administered in our civil government, it might seem that right and wrong are relative values. Essentially, however, we need a system of absolute justice in order for good government to exist, and on a human level this is unattainable even though ideal.

According to the Bible, God's sovereign government is absolutely just. In His economy there is an absolute right and wrong. He does not govern as people do, according to conduct only; He considers the dimensions of motivation and of knowledge. "Whoever knows what is right to do and fails to do it, for him it is sin" (James 4:17 RSV). "He that doubteth is damned, . . . for whatsoever is not of faith is sin" (Rom. 14:23). There is no way to manipulate or avoid God's just evaluation, for He is holy. "So then every one of us shall give account of himself to God" (Rom. 14:12; cf. Rev. 20:11-15).

While "it is a fearful thing to fall into the hands of the living God" (Heb. 10:31), because His justice is exact, this truth actually emphasizes the great value of His forgiveness. If His justice is absolute, His remission of sins is equally absolute! "Therefore being justified by faith, we have peace with God through our Lord Jesus Christ" (Rom. 5:1). "There is therefore now no condemnation to them which are in Christ Jesus" (Rom 8:1). "As far as the east is from the west, so far hath he removed our transgressions from us" (Ps. 103:12; cf. Isa. 53).

True Security Available by Accepting the Absolute

God is absolute in all His attributes. He is holy and just and good. This means He is greater than any constant or variable we know about. He is greater than all relative values, for He is the Creator of them. All constants and variables express finite details and concepts. God is greater than anything He has created, and we read that He not only transcends the universe, but inhabits it. "Thou, Lord, didst found the earth in the beginning, and the heavens are the work of thy hands; they will perish, but thou remainest; they will all grow old like a garment, like a mantle thou wilt roll them up, and they will be changed. But thou art the same, and thy years will never end" (Heb. 1:10-12 RSV).

The security of the believer in Christ lies in the fact that God does not change; He is greater than all things; He encompasses and ordains all the variables and is fully capable of leading us in our efforts to cope with them. "Jesus Christ the same yesterday, and today, and for ever" (Heb 13:8).

God does not promise to change the variableness and conditional factors in our circumstances to meet our whims or to resolve any of the relative values in our relationships; He does not promise to make life easier for us to cope with, but He does promise to be with us in our situations. We are not alone in our distress. Whether or not people have time for us or are sensitive to our needs, He is with us. The sense of being separated, alone, or isolated is gone. We know He is with us in everything that happens. "Whither shall I go from thy spirit? or whither shall I flee from thy presence? If I ascend up into heaven, thou art there: if I make my bed in hell, behold, thou art there. If I take the wings of the morning, and dwell in the uttermost parts of the sea; Even there shall thy hand lead me, and thy right hand shall hold me" (Ps. 139:7-10).

Furthermore, we know that whatever happens to us is for a good purpose, though we may not at the time discern it. God is able to make good derive from what is actually evil because He is greater than Satan and all evil forces. He has conquered through the death and resurrection of Christ all man's sin and defiance. Thus He continually causes "all things [to] work together for good to them that love God, to them who are the called according to his purpose" (Rom. 8:28; cf. 1 Cor. 15:53-58). After He forgives our sin, He uses the regrettable experiences as a positive influence for good in our lives.

The believer is personally related to, and a child of, the Absolute God. This sense of being a part of the total of life makes the relative, the variable, and the unpredictable seem more acceptable. It is impossible for anything finite to overpower or destroy a person whose mind is anchored by faith in the One who is absolute and in sovereign control of all that is happening. The anchor of faith incites optimistic hope in God, and these intimately relate to the love we feel for Him who has loved us. The very circumstance that without faith in God seems related to our destruction becomes by faith in God related to our benefit and contributes to our future destiny. Seven times in seven different types of overpowering problems God promised a special blessing to the overcomer — see Revelation 2:7,11,17,16; 3:5,12,21.

Our security in the thick of life's chaotic turbulence is God's infinite transcendency over all circumstances. He is sovereign over all things and He is almighty. At the same time, He is personally invested by all the sufferings of Calvary in the welfare of each one of us as a good Parent who knows our actual needs. Our security is not in our ability by faith in God to get Him to change our situations so that we will be less disturbed by the conditional and variable factors, nor is it in the fact that He might heal our bodies or reduce our pain. Our security is in our submission to His divine scheme of things and in our accepting what He can and does mean to our sense of true self-identity. In Christ each of us is a whole person (Col. 2:10).

One reason why life's situations are so difficult for us to cope with is, we are out of touch with the total scheme of life. From our childhood we have grown to assume that life centers around our own personal interests and needs, that the goal of life is our own happiness. We do not seem to realize that we are an integral part of a greater whole. We do not seem to comprehend the pattern that we are designed by God to be a manifestation of His character in a world of people who do not know Him and His love and grace. The goal of life is not really our own personal satisfaction, but to live for His glory. As the apostle Paul expressed it, the goal of life is that "Christ shall be magnified in my body, whether it be by life, or by death. For to me to live is Christ, and to die is gain" (Phil. 1:20,21).

The beauty of this self-sacrificing attitude to the greater purposes of life is that we experience His joy. We may not always have happiness in the sense of continually enjoying pleasant circumstances, but we do have His abiding joy within. "These things have I spoken unto you, that my joy might remain in you, and that your joy might be full" (John 15:11). We experience a greater satisfaction when life is fulfilling than when we simply experience immediate pleasure.

When we come to realize this great, timeless truth about life through a personal spiritual conversion, we sense an expanse to life, a thread of great meaning and purpose in everything that happens. This makes living an exciting challenge to tackle whatever happens and to observe how God is working in the intricate, minute details of everyday events. We find ourselves both participants and observers as we sense being in His will.

We find ourselves like pinballs of human light moving on a timeline stretching from eternity past to eternity future. Each of us has his own situational frame of reference designed by God to act out His divine attributes in a tangible time-space context. Though we must function autonomously with decisiveness, we nevertheless are fully dependent upon God and responsible to Him for every thought and action. He is glorified in that our freedom of choice in the exercise of our own will never fails to perform the intricacies of His inscrutable design for the destiny of His creation according to His divine foreknowledge.

God's One Great Frustration

God has allowed Himself to be frustrated in one matter regarding the freewill choices of mankind. To preserve the integrity of every individual human personality, He has decreed that the man He has created should have the right of choice to defy Him. He is "not willing that any should perish, but that all should come to repentance" (2 Peter 3:9). "God sent . . . His Son into the world . . . that the world through him might be saved" (John 3:17). Many Scripture passages reveal God's yearning for the salvation of everyone, that all mankind would turn to Him and relate to Him with love in response to His great love for them. In fact, the event of the crucifixion of Christ can be understood as an unveiling of the heart of God for the sins of the world (see 1 Peter 1:19,10; Rev. 13:8).

The greatest frustration to God is that Jesus Christ died in vain for those who choose not to believe in Him. Nothing is as frustrating as to make a sacrifice of love for someone and have that one refuse to accept it. We experience frustration on a finite, human level; how much greater would be the frustration of an unaccepted love-gift on an absolute, divine level! The whole heart of God is committed to our eternal welfare; no wonder there is "joy . . . in heaven over one sinner that repenteth" (Luke 15:7,10)! "Thanks be unto God for his unspeakable gift" (2 Cor. 9:15).

Faith in God Permeates the Relative with the Absolute

When we trust God and love Him with all our hearts, we associate ourselves with the One who transcends everything happening to us. When we do not trust God or consider Him as a vital part of our thinking, we tend to feel closed in by life's circumstances, and we have to fight to stay alive. But faith in God lifts a person out of domination by the relative values and permeates his thinking with the absolute so that he is free to live at his best.

God manifests His greatness in His condescension to minute details. Man created in the image of God lives in a context of minute details, fluid circumstances impregnated with relative values, and exacting limitations. But man manifests his greatness in accepting his place in God's great scheme of things, believing that God will lead him either to accept or to surmount his limitations. By faith in God's sovereign government of all things, His personal love, and His ability to communicate His wisdom and strength, man can consider the relative values in circumstances and the frustrating limitations as not actually antagonistic to his ultimate fulfillment in life, but rather as contributing to his ultimate growth in grace and opportunity to glorify God.

We tend to resist, and sometimes to resent, anything not ideal. In the archaic memories of our minds is an ideal experience. The prenatal state was an ideal condition because of the immaturity of the unborn infant. Even though he was exceedingly confined and limited by his mother's womb, nevertheless, to him he had all he could ever want, and he had to do nothing toward his own satisfaction. It is because he outgrew the womb and was born and continued growing that he became conscious of limitations. Growth always causes a person to occupy completely his present perimeters of life and to need to expand. This naturally forces him to face and to surmount, if possible, certain limitations.

Three kinds of limitations occur because of growth. There are many more, but we will limit our considerations to these basic three.

1. *One limitation is time*. The tiny child feels hungry or in need of some attention, and he has to wait for service. He is limited in having his own way with regard to time. He must wait until the person caring for him can bring him what he wants. He can become angry, but he still has to wait for service.

This limitation abides with us throughout life. We have to wait for others to attend to our needs whenever we are dependent, and we can become angry because we have to wait. We also must manage our time so that we can do what we need to do within the limitations of the day. We develop time priorities. Though we try to control and master the time factor in life, we are continually faced with the omnipotent reality that we cannot change; time continues to move along at its own pace regardless of how hastily or how slowly we move.

As we trust God, the Author of time and the One who

governs our personal time factor in life, timing our situations, we realize He always does things at the right time. We can be patient with God as we trust Him to be managing our time factor. Patience is a virtue of Christian maturation (James 1:3-5). It is the ability to abide by what is happening without being angry or resentful.

2. *Another limitation concerns space and things.* The child grows until he is able to move about the house by himself. Immediately he is confined to certain safe areas — he can go here, but not there; he can climb on this, but not on that; he can hold this object, but he must not touch that one. He feels fenced in. All through life we must cope with being limited in space and in the possession of things.

We find an innate sense of security in being able to move about as we like without being limited. We also find an innate sense of security in the possession of things. The accomplishments of life are commonly rated according to how much freedom one has to move about and how much wealth he has accumulated.

But we can become exceedingly frustrated in our management of space and things. Since a sense of security is implied in these commodities, we always want more than we have. When we turn to God for our inner securities, we find ourselves accepting His government of these matters in our lives. Such commodities are a stewardship to God, and we are responsible to Him for our use of them. We cannot take them with us when we die, and they have utility value only. So faith in God leads us to be generous with others who are in need (James 2:14-17). Generosity is another virtue of Christian maturation.

3. *A third limitation lies in ability.* The child grows old enough to begin to compare himself with older, more capable people. He begins to encounter feelings of inferiority. He is faced with his own limited abilities. He grows as he overcomes these limitations.

But all through life we face the problem of having limited skills and limited energies to perform those skills. It seems the more we grow in our ability to do things, the more things we become interested in doing. We can never escape the boundaries of our own limited knowledge, wisdom, and energy to perform what we wish we could achieve. We impute certain security factors to our abilities to perform adequately, for we tend to use our achievements as a means of self-verification.

By faith in God, we accept our limitations as being of His design. Moses, for example, was afraid to return to Egypt and lead the Israelites out according to God's command (Exod. 3,4). He objected several times, but when he told God he was not eloquent of speech, God replied indignantly, ''Who hath made man's mouth? or who maketh the dumb, or deaf, or the seeing, or the blind? have not I the Lord?'' (4:11). Moses learned to accept both his limitations and his abilities as from the Lord. Thus as we also exercise faith in God, we can accept our abilities and limitations with gratitude, for our faith divests them of their usual threat to our inner security.

Faith in God leads one to accept his limitations in ability, and this leads to a quality of character called humility. We humble ourselves under the mighty hand of God because He cares for us with tender, loving care (1 Peter 5:6,7). Humility is another virtue which reveals Christian maturity.

As we exercise faith in God while encountering our limitations of time, space and things, and abilities, we grow to overcome the domination of that particular limitation in a situation. In overcoming, we mature emotionally to develop the virtues of patience, generosity, and humility. Faith permeates the relative aspects of our lives with the absolute and is a means of maturing strength of character.

We grow up to adulthood holding on to our ideals and infantile wishes, yet at the same time we have to cope with our various limitations; these limitations make our life anything but ideal, for they threaten our sense of inner security. Faith in God affirms our sense of inner security so that our various limitations become related to His divine will for us and are no longer a threat. By faith we enter into a third dimension of thinking that provides a peace of mind established on the absolute instead of the relative, the variable, and the unpredictable.

Faith in God inspires hope in a life beyond this one in which time limitations will not exist. Also, our future life has no space limitations. Only those who have not received Jesus as personal Savior will be confined to one place, the lake of fire (Rev. 20:15). Any future limitations in our abilities seem from the Scripture not to be of any significance, because ''we shall be like him; for we shall see him as he is'' (1 John 3:2).

Indeed, faith in God permeates our perception of the relative values in our world with aspects of the absolute!

B. In the Functioning of the Inner Self

We have considered the effect of faith in God upon our perception of life situations. Now we will consider the effect of faith in God on the functioning of the inner self.

Apart from faith in God, man is fragmented in his thinking; he has an unresolvable split within his mind. He is continually aspiring to exercise the freedom of self-determination to possess or to do whatever his heart desires as though he were the sovereign owner of all things. At the same time, he is having to admit his limitations of energy, knowledge, skill, time, and dominion in accomplishing what he wishes. Moreover, he is continually reminded of his dependence on others and his subjection to the government of the society of which he is a part.

Man has a basic loyalty to two opposing issues: one is the irresponsible satisfaction of his desires, and the other is the gratification he receives from others as he conforms to the folkways of his society. Man has the ability to feel as sovereign as though he were God, but he does not have the sense of inner wholeness to exercise his sense of autonomy in a totally responsible manner. When man commits himself to God by faith, that split is healed.

It is easy to understand how this occurs when we study the historical account of man's relationship with God from its beginning.

God said of the forbidden tree in the Garden, "In the day that thou eatest thereof thou shalt surely die" (Gen. 2:17). Adam and Eve ate, and they started the process of death within themselves. Splitting and fragmentation are related to death. Life is a force that builds unities of essential elements; death is a force that disconnects those unities, fragments the structures, and returns them to their original elements. Life is a unifying force; death is a fragmenting force. Without doing injustice to the original wording of the command, we could understand it to say, "In the day you eat of the fruit you will break your spiritual union with God and begin to fragment emotionally. You will no longer sense being at one with the living God, and you will have caused a split within yourself that will fragment you into a state of death."

Man's first sin caused him to lose direct access to God. Ever since then, man has had access to God only by faith. "No man hath seen God at any time; the only begotten Son, which is in the bosom of the Father, he hath declared him" (John 1:18).

God made a provision for access to himself immediately after He punished man by evicting him from the Garden (Gen. 3:24). Man could come with his sin offering to an appointed spot where cherubim provided a point of contact with God (Gen. 4:3-5).

Later in man's history, in the life of Abraham, we read of man meeting God by faith at an altar with a burning animal sacrifice. When Abraham's descendants became the nation of Israel, man met God at an altar of burnt offerings with a tabernacle and many rituals. Inside was a mercy seat with cherubim and a Shekinah light and priests.

Still later in human history, Christ came as God's sacrifice for man's sin and offered Himself on the altar of Calvary (Heb. 13:8-16). Christ Himself is our High Priest. Since that time, man comes to God by faith in Christ's atoning sacrifice. "By [Jesus Christ] also we have access by faith into this grace wherein we stand" (Rom. 5:2). This is the gospel message: "I declare unto you the gospel which I preached unto you, which also ye have received, and wherein ye stand; by which also ye are saved, . . . how that Christ died for our sins according to the scriptures; and that he was buried, and that he rose again the third day according to the scriptures" (1 Cor. 15:1-4).

The gospel is the message of salvation offered to us by God for the split and fragmentation within our minds. The Bible speaks of that split as a result of the first sin: "Behold, the man is become as one of us, to know good and evil" (Gen. 3:22). To know is to experience, and this means making that knowledge or experience a part of oneself. Man has taken two polarities within himself. In the mind of man is the memory of the pleasure derived from both good and evil, both of being in harmony with God and in being dissonant to Him. Pleasure is the feeling which galvanizes an experience into us, making it a part of ourselves.

Adam and Eve ate of the forbidden fruit, and in doing so they willfully defied God's commandment. They were no longer willing subjects to the Word of God, but the record indicates they were both guilty and fearful (Gen. 3:7-10). They had accepted God's providential benefits freely and enjoyed them; these pleasures related them to God as accepted by Him. The pleasures they derived from eating disobediently made them feel unrelated to God and subject to His wrath. Their willful disobedience trapped them, in that they remained dependent on and responsible to the God they had just defied by the exercise of their own willfulness.

It is logical that God should punish man for his disobedience and defiance of His authority by spoiling his pleasure in his independent exercise of self-determination. Why should God support a disobedient child by allowing him to continue enjoying pleasure he derived from direct disobedience? Thus in the punishment God promised sorrow, pain, frustration, misery, and death to occur in the world He had created and provided for man (see Gen. 3:17-19).

The pleasures Adam and Eve enjoyed by eating of the forbidden fruit were ephemeral. "The tree was good for food [pleasant tasting], and . . . pleasant to the eyes [nice to look at], and to be desired to make one wise [enjoyable to know something forbidden]" (Gen. 3:6). They enjoyed their disobedience. Sin is pleasurable, but only temporarily (Heb. 11:25). It was not long before they were hiding from God in the Garden in terror at the sound of his voice.

Adam and Eve enjoyed doing what God allowed, and they enjoyed doing what He had forbidden. Pleasure invites us to give ourselves to whatever is pleasurable and to be interested in that object. Pain, on the other hand, repels us so that we avoid whatever is making us miserable and we lose interest in that object. Adam and Eve had enjoyed being at one with God and, no doubt, enjoyed the freedom of partaking of the many pleasant foods in the Garden. They also enjoyed eating of the one tree that separated them from God and brought upon them fear and guilt. Their investment in pleasure split them emotionally into two polarities.

This same dichotomy is true in man today. We enjoy good things, and we enjoy "the pleasures of sin." We accept God's provision, but not His regulations. We want fun, but not the penalties of wrongdoing. We tend to believe the world belongs to us, and if we do our best, we like to believe we will be rewarded with happiness. But this is not the message of God's Word.

Because of Adam's sin, all his descendants are in a state of existence contaminated with problems. "Man that is born of woman is of few days, and full of trouble" (Job 14:1). We all have problems and unhappiness whether or not we believe in God, but God uses our troubles to draw us to Himself, for He promises to be with us in our problems. It is not until we receive our glorified bodies that we will be in a world free from distressing troubles. The distresses of life are related directly or indirectly to spoiling the pleasure we may derive from willfully seeking our own self-determined goals.

Man Has a Privilege of Choice With Responsibility

We have a choice in life. We can choose to be defiant of God, or we can choose to live in a loving relationship with Him. We do not have the right to establish a system of living that is not responsible to God, and God will one day destroy our attempts to do just that. Ultimately any system of being somebody that we might develop on our own without regard for God will be destroyed by Him.

We live under the illusion that we have a choice between living in obedience to or living in defiance of God. It is true we can ignore God or decide to defy His Word, but only for a time. Sooner or later we will face the ultimate fact that we are responsible to Him. "So then every one of us shall give account of himself to God" (Rom. 14:12). "Marvel not at this: for the hour is coming, in the which all that are in the graves shall hear his [Christ's] voice, and shall come forth; they that have done good, unto the resurrection of life; and they that have done evil, unto the resurrection of damnation'' (John 5:28,29).

It is improper to apply the gospel of saving grace only to the future life of being admitted to heaven. The gospel of saving grace also applies now to delivering us from the ravages of the death forces within us that daily torment and frustrate us with relative values, inhibiting limitations, and yearnings for something more reliable than self-verification for finding a sense of being somebody.

Self-verification is a works program for salvation that has nothing to do with God. If it does involve religion, it is not biblical but hypocritical. Self-verification offers the equation for self-identity that *Man + What he believes others think of him = a Confident Person.* This formula is only tentatively and partially true. Man continually perpetuates his own insecurities, for he lives in a context of circumstances he cannot completely control.

God knows, and He has told us, that we have a split within ourselves. We know both good and evil. When Adam, our first parent, chose to be in this dilemma, he caused all his descendants to be afflicted by the same dilemma. We all want to exercise an independent self-determination, but we are frustrated by our limitations when we attempt to do it.

If Adam had not defied God willfully, any one of us in any generation since that time would surely have done it. ''As by one man sin entered into the world, and death by sin; and so death passed upon all men, for that all have sinned'' (Rom. 5:12). ''The carnal mind is enmity against God'' (Rom. 8:7). Yet at the same time we all seem to feel we have a right to good things that God provides. We are split in our interests.

Since Adam chose to be in this dilemma, and we were born victims of an environment that has resulted from his choice, God by his loving grace has offered us a choice through the gospel to escape the consequences of that original dilemma. If we use our self-determination to obey the gospel, He promises to forgive us and receive us and make us ''accepted in His beloved'' as his dear children.

Man knows both good and evil, and the evil condemns him and fragments him from within. God has taken the responsibility for the evil in man. God offers to accept man and make him one of His own children, *if* man will determine to accept God's offering for sin on Calvary in the person of His Son. Christ's offering for our sin relieves us of the responsibility for our evil nature. He forgives us and thus frees us from the dilemma, for we need no longer feel condemned. Our love for God and identification with His sufferings for our sins spoil the pleasure we have in sinning. We are healed of our split and free to serve God with a whole heart and a clean conscience (Heb. 9:14).

When man refuses to turn to God and accept His grace, he determines by the exercise of his independent self-determination to live with his dilemma, to perpetuate his split and continue fragmenting himself from within. He chooses to remain as he is and be responsible for himself and for his guilt before the holy God.

Thus man without God always has the knowledge that he is both good and evil. He can never completely deliver himself from this knowledge regardless of how thoroughly he tries to deny the reality of God or of his own sinfulness. His internal split, manifested by many anxieties about life, continually reminds him that he is not a whole person, not at one with himself.

Man philosophizes and teaches himself to be responsible as a person, but avoids accepting his responsibility to God. He tries to improve his state of mind, but he can never erase the memory of his violation of his own better judgment and knowledge of what is right. He may deny the fact of sin, but he can never erase its effect upon himself, for he has an abiding guilt that can be conscious or unconscious. The telltale is his abiding need for self-verification.

Because man enjoys his pleasures of disobedience to God, the evil remains a part of himself. Since he enjoys the pleasures derived from doing what is good and right, these values also remain a part of himself. Because of this, man without redemption from God is locked into a condition of thinking that is always based upon relative values and never upon absolutes. He manages to live in the illusion he creates for himself in his personal relationships with others that he is all right and acceptable. He uses self-verification as a means of holding onto the idea that he is somebody, but when self-verification fails, he returns to the sense of being unwhole, a nobody who is unwanted, no good, or inferior. He can only aspire to experience the absolute sense of being right; he can never actually possess such virtue within himself.

By contrast, the person who accepts God's grace in Christ accepts for himself God's responsibility for his sinful nature and so experiences God's forgiveness. His mind is free from struggling with the dilemma of a split within. He is free from sin and rid of abiding guilt, for he has accepted the fact that by God's grace he is somebody to God. When he errs, he simply turns to God, against whom he has sinned, and admits his mistake. Instantly he knows he is forgiven and cleansed (1 John 1:9). Since he is free from the responsibility for his sin, he can concentrate on overcoming his disobedience and improving his conduct.

When a person is in a loving relationship with God, he is conscious of being a whole person (Col 2:10). God is a unity, a whole Person. We are in His image and struggle to approach an inner unity, and we can find that sense of wholeness only in our union with God. We relate to the Absolute by faith, and we find a healing for the schism within ourselves.

The Christian can accept himself as being bad, a nobody, because God does (Rom 7:14-8:17). He is free to move toward God and to become godly. He can "reckon [himself] to be dead indeed unto sin, but alive unto God through Jesus Christ" (Rom. 6:11).

He is free to "yield [his] members as instruments of righteousness" (Rom. 6:13). He has, by God's forgiveness and cleansing, a unity within. He can then concentrate on the tasks at hand without having to extract from the circumstance at the same time some value for his own self-identity. He can function because he knows who he is; he does not need to prove anything to himself about himself. He is free to apply himself to doing the will of God. He can "walk in newness of life" (Rom. 6:4), for the pleasure he found in sin is on the cross, crucified with Christ. The dilemma is effectively gone.

By faith in God we have a vital relationship with the Absolute and this gives us the ability to cope with the relative values in life.

14

Reorient Self-Concept to the Absolute

For our self-concept to be purified from the relative values that continually disturb our sense of inner wholeness and peace of mind, we need to reorient our thinking to the absolute values found in the Scriptures. These absolute values provide a new premise for self-concept that is stable and unchangeable.

As soon as we accept Christ as our personal Savior and experience spiritual conversion, we discover a new sense of self-identity. "If any one is in Christ, he is a new creation; the old has passed away, behold, the new has come. All this is from God, who through Christ reconciled us to himself . . . " (2 Cor. 5:17,18 RSV).

Not only do we find a new sense of wholeness within ourselves because we are forgiven, but we begin to realize a new meaning to living and a sense of destiny. We are His; He is ours; and we are at last gripped by a feeling of being complete. "Ye are complete in him, which is the head of all principality and power" (Col. 2:10).

When a man and a woman fall in love and are at last committed to each other in marriage, they experience a sexual union and often exclaim, "Now I feel complete. I have found my mate."

On a spiritual plane, a similar thing happens when we receive Jesus Christ. He has loved us, and we have responded to His love with our love. We commit ourselves to Him and become joined

161

to Him as His bride, the church (Eph. 5:22-33). In this bond of love He infuses us with His Holy Spirit; we respond with our total being in utter self-abandonment to Him. The result is a sense of being complete in Him. We have found our spiritual mate, the Lord Jesus Christ. We are complete in Him as a bride is with her husband.

By identification with Christ we have found our true self-identity. We are somebody because we belong to someone who is truly Somebody! He has accepted us and made us His own. We are somebody to God.

Spiritual Premise Gives New Equation to Self-Identity

Man is created in God's image. Because God is perfect and ideal, we tend to be perfectionistic and idealistic. We grew up trying to relate to imperfect people, but we wanted our parents and others to be ideal. We were disappointed because they did not measure up; many of the grudges we hold against family members are due to our inability to forgive them for being human and imperfect. We cannot accept them as they are.

We have developed several equations for our sense of being a somebody, but none of them really balances. They are not true. One such equation is *Appearance + Admiration = a Whole Person*. This equation does not balance because we are not the sum and total of how we appear or what others admiringly think of us.

Another such equation which does not balance is *Performance + Accomplishments = a Whole Person*. We are more than the sum total of our skills and the recognized abilities we have developed.

A third equation might be *Status + Recognition = a Whole Person*. This equation is also untrue, for we are more than anyone thinks of us.

Try as we might by our appearance, performance, or social status to find self-verification for a sense of being somebody, we always come short of satisfaction. Whatever pinnacle of self-identity we achieve soon crumbles under the pressure of hostile rejection or criticism, introspection or guilt, fear or anxiety. *We cannot do anything to qualify for the by-product of being loved unconditionally and voluntarily.*

We have been loved unconditionally and voluntarily by God, and He has manifested that love at Calvary. When we stop trying to qualify for His love and simply accept Him as our Savior, we enter into a new set of values, a new dimension of self-identity. We find a new equation for our sense of being somebody, and this one truly balances. It is *God + Me = a Whole Person*.

This equation is consistent with being in the image of God. An image has meaning only because of the object it represents. A picture is worthless if it does not portray a certain object, and it finds its value primarily through the value of the object it represents. So it is with us. We have meaning, and life has meaning, only because of God in whose image we have been created. He is the Person; we display personality. We can know who we are, what we are, and why we are only because of Him. He has revealed Himself in His Word.

The term *in Christ* often appears in the New Testament when speaking of the relationship between Christians and God. By faith we are "in Christ," and Christ is in us by His Holy Spirit. "Ye are not in the flesh, but in the Spirit, if so be that the Spirit of God dwell in you. Now if any man have not the Spirit of Christ, he is none of his" (Rom. 8:9).

We are partakers of the divine nature. "Whereby are given unto us exceeding great and precious promises: that by these we might be partakers of the divine nature" (2 Peter 1:4).

We are partakers of His holiness. The Father chastens us "for our profit, that we might be partakers of his holiness" (Heb. 12:10).

Being "in Christ" means we "are partakers of the sufferings, so shall ye be also of the consolation" (2 Cor. 1:7) of Christ. We share in His life, and He shares ours. In a very real sense He is incarnate in each one of us who love Him; yet we never cease to be totally ourselves and responsible to Him as autonomous individuals. "For none of us liveth to himself, and no man dieth to himself. For whether we live, we live unto the Lord; and whether we die, we die unto the Lord: whether we live therefore, or die, we are the Lord's" (Rom. 14:7,8).

When we accept Christ as our personal Savior, we implement the equation for a true sense of self-identity: *God + Me = a Whole Person.* We are sealed by the Holy Spirit (Eph. 1:13; 4:30). The Holy Spirit of God enters the believer and makes his body His temple: "What? know ye not that your body is the temple of the Holy Ghost which is in you, which ye have of God, and ye are not your own? For ye are bought with a price: therefore glorify God in your body, and in your spirit, which are God's" (1 Cor. 6:19,20). Receiving Christ is a spiritual transaction that binds a person to God in a secure love relationship and provides a stable premise for a self-concept with a new dimension of reality.

Discovering a new sense of being somebody by relating to Jesus Christ personally by faith has the potential for a sense of inner wholeness. We "are complete in him" (Col. 2:10) potentially.

During the moments that we sense our intimate union with Christ, we are usually aware of an inner wholeness. As we practice this sense of being somebody "in Christ," we develop feelings of inner peace which are somewhat independent of whatever turbulence we may be experiencing in our daily circumstances. The equation *God + Me = a Whole Person* has a fundamental meaning in our sense of self-identity.

Relate to God the Father, Validate Belongingness

In our relationship with God the Father we are assured of belongingness.

We never outgrow the need for a parent even though we may be parents ourselves. We are responsible to God, and we relate to Him as our heavenly Parent. There is deep emotional satisfaction in relating to God as Father. Jesus recommended this relationship with God: "After this manner therefore pray ye: Our Father which art in heaven, Hallowed be thy name" (Matt. 6:9).

Perhaps the greatest security to be found is in the sense of parental acceptance. We read, "He [the Father] hath made us accepted in the beloved [Christ]" (Eph. 1:6). We did absolutely nothing to earn that acceptance; we submitted to Him, and He made us accepted to Himself! "God so loved the world, that he gave his only begotten Son" (John 3:16). He made us accepted because He loved us!

This great truth reinforces our sense of belongingness; indeed, it validates it. We are loved by God the Father with an unconditional, voluntary love. We know we belong to Him because of His immutable promises. "As many as received him, to them gave he power to become the sons of God: . . . which were born . . . of God" (John 1:12,13). "Ye have received the Spirit of adoption, whereby we cry, Abba, Father. The Spirit itself beareth witness with our spirit, that we are the children of God: and if children, then heirs; heirs of God, and joint-heirs with Christ" (Rom. 8:15-17).

He is pleased to call us His sons. This gives us a position with Him in His family. We know we are somebody to God; we have been redeemed from being a nobody! The idea of being a nobody never again will have any validity. When it threatens us, we can firmly reject it in the reassurance of God's promises! We are always wanted by God.

Relate to God the Son, Validate Worthiness

In our relationship with the Son of God we are assured of worthiness. Being forgiven all sin, we lose our sense of guilt and the associated feelings of being a nobody, a bad person.

God has "reconciled us to himself" in the death of His Son (2 Cor. 5:18). This means God holds nothing against the sinner for being a sinner. Because of Christ's atonement, He is immediately ready to accept anyone who will believe in Him. The only factor that will condemn anyone is unbelief in Jesus Christ: "He that believeth on the Son hath everlasting life: and he that believeth not the Son shall not see life; but the wrath of God abideth on him" (John 3:36). When we trust in Jesus Christ as our Savior, we need never fear being rejected by God, because He is reconciled to us. He promises to forgive when we confess our sins to Him (1 John 1:9). So we never need to fear ever being rejected by God: "My sheep hear my voice, and I know them, and they follow me: and I give unto them eternal life; and they shall never perish, neither shall any man pluck them out of my hand. My Father, which gave them me, is greater than all; and no man is able to pluck them out of my Father's hand. I and my Father are one" (John 10:27-30).

Feeling a secure belongingness, we identify with the Sinless One, Jesus Christ. This means we accept His forgiveness and regard ourselves as righteous because of His grace. In trusting Him, we have rejected our godless self-determination, which tends to motivate us to sin. Thus our thinking is premised upon a new plane of reference when we trust in God. We can regard ourselves as guiltless. This is the basis for a true sense of worthiness. It is established in a reaffirmed sense of belongingness validated by God's Word.

This freedom from guilt gives us no excuse to continue sinning, but to the contrary, actually motivates us to do what pleases God. "How shall we, that are dead to sin, live any longer therein?" (Rom. 6:2; cf. 1 John 1:7-2:3). Also, "every man that hath this hope in him purifieth himself, even as he is pure" (1 John 3:3). We sincerely want to become more Christlike so that we can realize all that His grace can mean.

Our security in His grace is expressed in 1 John 2:1: "My little children, these things write I unto you, that ye sin not. And if any man sin, we have an advocate with the Father, Jesus Christ the righteous: and he is the propitiation for our sins." When we sin against God, we will be pestered by the devastating feelings of being wrong and a nobody, because the Holy Spirit will be convicting us of our sin until we confess and forsake the evil. "If our heart condemn us, God is greater than our heart, and knoweth all things. Beloved, if our heart condemn us not, then have we confidence toward God. And whatsoever we ask, we receive of him, because we keep his commandments, and do those things that are pleasing in his sight" (1 John 3:20-22).

The condemnation-free plane of reference means we are secure in Christ and need not fear His punishment. ''There is no fear in love; but perfect love casteth out fear: because fear hath torment. He that feareth is not made perfect in love'' (1 John 4:18). His perfect love provides a condemnation-free plane of living that makes us free from the fear of being punished for sins (Rom. 8:1). As we grow in grace and in knowledge of Christ, we are able to live on that plane and accept all that His forgiveness means. Our love for Him is perfected, and our fear of Him diminishes. At the same time, our zeal for Him and for doing His will increases.

The freer we feel of guilt, the more complete will be our sense of worthiness. We will be identifying with the One who is righteous, and we will attempt to live by His Holy Spirit and His Word.

Relate to God the Holy Spirit, Validate Competence

We have stated that we have a secure sense of belonging-ness as we relate to God as our heavenly Father. We have a secure sense of worthiness as we relate to Christ the Son as our righteous-ness.

We also have a secure sense of competence as we relate to the Holy Spirit as our Comforter, Guide, and Source of strength. He is with us daily to face our situations with us, and He is in sovereign control of the situations that He allows us to experience.

The Holy Spirit has been sent to us after the death, resurrection, and ascension of Jesus Christ. He is Christ's other self, our Comforter (John 14:26). Christ is now in heaven interceding for us (Heb. 7:25), and the Holy Spirit inhabits our bodies as His temple (John 14:17), maintaining our sense of the presence of God in our circumstances.

The Holy Spirit directs our attention to Christ: ''He shall testify of me'' (John 15:26). He teaches us: ''He shall teach you all things, and bring all things to your remembrance, whatever I have said unto you'' (John 14:26).

He imparts the love of God: ''The love of God is shed abroad in our hearts by the Holy Ghost which is given unto us'' (Rom. 5:5).

He imparts hope: ''The God of hope fill you with all joy and peace in believing, that ye may abound in hope, through the power of the Holy Ghost'' (Rom. 15:13).

He imparts joy (Rom. 14:17; Gal. 5:22; 1 Thess. 1:6). Among other blessings, He imparts the ability to live a godly life and maintain a relationship with God in spite of the undertow of habit and the emotional insecurities we derived from our childhood. He is our competence, making it possible to live the Christian life and hold onto the sense of being somebody to God.

The meaning of the equation of self-identity, *God + Me = a Whole Person,* is this: My belongingness is secured and reaffirmed by my love for God my Father and validated by His love for me. My worthiness is secured and reaffirmed by my love for Jesus Christ His Son and validated by His love for me. My competence is secured and reaffirmed in daily situations of life through the ministry and love of the Holy Spirit as He uses the Word of God to instruct, correct, and reassure me; my competence is validated as I live by the Word of God.

"All scripture is given by inspiration of God, and is profitable for doctrine, for reproof, for correction, for instruction in righteousness: that the man of God may be perfect, throughly furnished unto all good works" (2 Tim. 3:16,17).

Reorient by Obeying the First Great Commandment

One commandment transcends all others in the Bible. Jesus called this "the first and great commandment": "Thou shalt love the Lord thy God with all thy heart, and with all thy soul, and with all thy mind" (Matt. 22:37). Jesus continued, "The second is like unto it, Thou shalt love thy neighbour as thyself. On these two commandments hang all the law and the prophets" (Matt. 22:39,40).

Jesus indicates here that two relationships are of great importance. One is a love relationship with God. This is primary. The other is a love relationship with others.

To be a complete person, to know yourself and be glad about what you know, it is essential to commit yourself completely to God in total love. This means going far beyond the usual, perfunctory ritual of worship. It means relating to God as a living Person. We do this best by relating to Jesus Christ, the Son of God and Second Person of the blessed Trinity.

Christ was incarnate in human flesh: "The Word became flesh and dwelt among us, full of grace and truth; we have beheld his glory, glory as of the only Son from the Father" (John 1:14 RSV). Jesus told His disciples He was a manifestation of God, and what we know of God is seen in Christ: "He that hath seen me hath seen the Father" (John 14:9). The apostle John was explaining who Christ was; He said, "No man hath seen God at any time; the only begotten Son, which is in the bosom of the Father, he has declared him" (John 1:18).

Furthermore, the Holy Spirit does not speak to us of Himself, though He is here with us and in us. "When he, the Spirit of truth, is come, he will guide you into all truth: for he shall not speak of himself" (John 16:13). "When the Comforter is come, whom I will send unto you from the Father, even the Spirit of truth, which proceedeth from the Father, he shall testify of me" (John 15:26).

Because the Father is revealed in Jesus Christ, and the Holy Spirit only directs our attention to Jesus Christ, it is appropriate that we speak of loving Christ. It is much easier to visualize the Person we are loving if we remember that all we can ever know of God is revealed to us in Jesus Christ through His Word.

"We love him, because he first loved us" (1 John 4:19). We are not told to create love for God, but we respond to the love of God with love. He is the Lover; we are loved by Him, and we respond with love.

The commandment to love God is clearly threefold. We are to love God with all our heart, with all our soul, and with all our mind. Loving God with all the heart means to love Him with all our affection; loving God with all the soul means to love Him with all our will according to our knowledge of Him; loving God with all the mind means to love with a total commitment of ourselves to Him.

It is reasonable to expect God to command this quality of devotion from us, since He created us in His own image to live in a vital relationship with Himself. He did not create us to live independently of Him. Relationship with God must take precedence over our instinctive drives for sensual pleasure, as great as these drives are. We discipline ourselves to satisfy these natural desires *because* we have a relationship with Him, and we do it in a way that pleases Him, or we wait until such gratification is possible.

This great commandment implies that loving God takes precedence over our ambition to own and control properties. Relationship, not the acquisition of things, is the meaning of life. When life is over, we leave our things, but we take our relationships with us. "Now abideth . . . love" (1 Cor. 13:13). When we hold relationship primary as the meaning of life, then we are able to be objective about things so that they only have utility value as God intended.

The commandment to love God with one's total self cancels pride. True love always idealizes the object loved. We will, indeed, want Him to be glorified in everything when we are in love with Him. Love inspires gratitude and happiness. When we love God with all our heart, soul, and mind, our total self, the admonition of Colossians 3:14-17 will become more of a way of life than a duty to be performed: "Above all these put on love, which binds everything together in perfect harmony. And let the peace of Christ rule in your hearts, to which indeed you were called in one body. And be thankful. Let the Word of Christ dwell in you richly, teach and admonish one another in all wisdom, and sing psalms and hymns and spiritual songs with thankfulness in your hearts to God. And whatever you do, in word or deed, do everything in the name of the Lord Jesus, giving thanks to God the Father through him'' (RSV).

Loving God with our total self according to the first great commandment settles once and for all our search for self-identity. We know who we are: we are His, and we belong to Him. We know what we are: we are good and acceptable, for He has atoned for our sins. We know why we are: we have a good destiny, being created in His image and for His glory to live forever with Him. By His grace we can face life situations regardless of the pain involved, for He is working in us "both to will and to do of his good pleasure" (Phil. 2:13, cf. 1 Cor. 10:13; Rom. 8:28,29).

These great certainties directly contradict every dynamic and device of our lifetime habit of self-verification. In self-verification we feel unloved and are attempting to find some reason to idealize ourselves so we can feel acceptable. In the walk of faith we realize we were not acceptable until we repented of our sins and received Jesus Christ as our Savior. We discovered that we were loved by God even though we were nobody, unwanted, bad, and inferior. He took us as nobodies and revealed to us that we were somebody to Him!

In self-verification we look to people to accept us, to admire us, to love us, so we can feel as if we are somebody. This keeps us from resolving our infantile conviction that we are nobody. In self-verification we tend to avoid responsibility for our mistakes and faults by making various excuses and rationalizations. We do this because we cannot bear to lose self-esteem and feel like nobody.

As Christians we can accept responsibility for our faults, for we are basing our feelings of being somebody on God's love and forgiveness of us. When we do this, we have an incentive to attack our faults and overcome them. We want to grow in Christ.

Belief in God's existence without love for Him usually leads us to depersonalize God into being only a force or a supreme being. We may hope that God will providentially attend to our welfare, but we usually trust to fate or luck.

When we actually love God with our total selves, He comes into focus as a Person, an absolute Person. We cannot see our love Object, but He is real; He is known to us by faith in His Word.

This fact is exceedingly important. God is infinite and

absolute in all His attributes. If He could be seen, He would be finite; but because of the incarnation of Christ His Son, God has appeared finite and knowable and perceivable. God becomes real to each of us as we trust in Him. He has revealed Himself in the Bible so that He can be understood as we need to know Him. We clarify our thinking about God as we grow in our knowledge of Scriptures. The ministry of the Holy Spirit is to enlighten our minds about Jesus Christ, who is God's manifestation of Himself in human flesh (John 1:14).

Because God is invisible, He can be unlimited by time and space. He is universally available to every person at any place in the universe, and He always has been available in any time of history. The apostle Paul prayed, "That Christ may dwell in your hearts by faith; that ye, being rooted and grounded in love, may be able to comprehend with all saints what is the breadth, and length, and depth, and height; and to know the love of Christ, which passeth knowledge, that ye might be filled with all the fullness of God. Now unto him that is able to do exceeding abundantly above all that we ask or think, according to the power that worketh in us, unto him be glory in the church by Christ Jesus unto all generations of the ages of the ages. Amen" (Eph. 3:17-21 marg.).

To obey the first commandment means trusting Him implicitly regardless of what may be happening, believing that He is doing what is right and just and tenderly caring for us. "Humble yourselves therefore under the mighty hand of God, that in due time he may exalt you. Cast all your anxieties on him, for he cares about you" (1 Peter 5:6,7 rsv). This is exceedingly difficult, for it means surrendering our presumed control of life situations to His sovereign will.

Love is often tested by self-sacrifice. God's love was tested at Calvary for us. "That the trial of your faith, being much more precious than of gold that perisheth, though it be tried with fire, might be found unto praise and honour and glory at the appearing of Jesus Christ" (1 Peter 1:7).

Obeying the first commandment means we can feel secure enough in our self-identity to be able to dispel our anger whenever it occurs. We can quickly reorient ourselves to the fact that we do not need to be defensive if someone treats us unfairly, critically, with hostility, or in some way that fails to measure up to our expectations. We can conclude that whatever happens in a situation, God expects us to handle it with His guidance in a good and appropriate manner.

Leonard, a Christian friend, said when a certain difficulty arose, "I wonder how God wants me to handle this situation." He had stopped fighting the situations he did not like as though they were impositions or burdens. At the time he said this, he was accepting the frustration of his problem as a challenge allowed by God for his good. Leonard was living confidently in his relationship with God.

It is important to keep in mind that love is an emotion that cannot be forced. Love must be a response; love cannot be coerced any more than it can be earned. Love is also consonant with our nature; this means that we will have a love response when the obstructing emotions are externalized, identified, and dissipated. If we have trouble loving as we should, we should investigate what is preventing our love from coming into awareness.

As we think of God's love and read about it in the Bible, we ordinarily feel a response to Him as though He were tangibly present with us. When we take notice of how much He has forgiven, accepting us when we could not accept ourselves, we begin to sense the greatness of His love. "To whom little is forgiven, the same loveth little," our Lord said (Luke 7:47).

I believe God is pleased with any love we feel for Him. As we sense His love more completely, our response will be more profound and self-involving.

As we reorient ourselves to the new premise for self-concept, we prepare our minds to accept the challenges of everyday living and to discover the dimension of usefulness and fulfillment God intended for us when He redeemed us.

15

Find New Meaning in Personal Relationships

We continue in this chapter our consideration of the two great commandments, which appear in the Old Testament and are reemphasized by Jesus in the New Testament. They deserve our careful and persistent attention.

The first commandment is "Thou shalt love the Lord thy God with all thy heart, and with all thy soul, and with all thy mind" (Matt. 22:37; cf. Deut. 6:5; Mark 12:30). The second commandment is "Thou shalt love thy neighbour as thyself" (Matt. 22:39; cf. Lev. 19:18; Mark 12:31). Speaking of their importance, Jesus said, "There is none other commandment greater than these" (Mark 12:31). "On these two commandments hang all the law and the prophets" (Matt. 22:40).

Obedience to the first great commandment relates us to God. It orients our thinking so that we are willingly committed to Him completely with our total self. Obedience to the second great commandment relates us to people. As a result of obeying the first, we can obey the second. When we do, we love others with a mature, genuine, unconditional love. Loving God with our total self settles our need for a sense of being somebody, and this settled sense of self-identity provides a base from which we can relate to others with every concern we naturally would like them to have for us.

Jesus showed us by His life how the second commandment

172

relates to the first. There is no question from the record that Jesus loved God with His total self during His incarnation, and because He loved God, He manifested His love for us by dying for us.

Jesus was motivated by the love of the Father. "The Father loveth the Son" (John 5:20). In Jesus' great prayer to His Father, He indicated plainly that He came as a sacrifice for our sins because of His Father's love for Him and His love for us. He prayed for us who believe in Him that we may be one in a covenant of love. "That they also may be one in us: that the world may believe that thou hast sent me. . . . that they may be one, even as we are one. . . . that the love wherewith thou hast loved me may be in them, and I in them" (John 17:21,22,26).

For this reason Jesus gave us a new commandment: "A new commandment I give unto you, That ye love one another; as I have loved you, that ye also love one another" (John 13:34). He set an example of how each of us can love his neighbor as himself. This commandment is referred to elsewhere in the New Testament as the *law of Christ* (see Gal. 5:14; 6:2; 1 John 2:7-11).

It is interesting in this connection to take note of the fact that each of the Ten Commandments (Exod. 20:3-17) deals, with some violation of a relationship. The first four commandments regulate our relationship with God. The last six regulate our relationships with people. "Thou shalt not commit adultery, Thou shalt not kill, Thou shalt not steal, Thou shalt not bear false witness, Thou shalt not covet, and if there by any other commandment, it is briefly comprehended in this saying, namely, Thou shalt love thy neighbour as thyself. Love worketh no ill to his neighbour: therefore love is the fulfilling of the law" (Rom. 13:9,10). Thus the two great commandments embody all others, for the law regulates relationships.

These two commandments and the law of Christ point to the timeless truth that loving relationship is the most important commodity in life. God is love. He is relationship of perfect harmony between Father, Son, and Holy Spirit. He has relationship with angels (Heb. 1:6). He seeks relationship with mankind whom He created in His own image: "The Spirit and the bride say, Come. . . . And let him that is athirst come. And whosoever will, let him take of the water of life freely" (Rev. 22:17).

We also take note of the fact that sin is breaking the law: "Sin is the transgression of the law" (1 John 3:4). Sin is essentially not having a loving relationship. Since law regulates relationships, we sin against God when we disregard Him, and we sin when we cause unloving relationships with each other. We might consider anything sinful which injures loving relationships. This is a very serious consideration of the importance of relationships and difficult to accept. But the greatest sin logically is breaking the greatest commandment.

When we think of sinning, we think of being condemned and punished. "So then every one of us shall give account of himself to God" (Rom. 14:12). But God takes no pleasure in condemning or punishing offenders. "Have I any pleasure at all that the wicked should die? saith the Lord God: and not that he should return from his ways, and live?" (Ezek. 18:23). "I have no pleasure in the death of the wicked; but that the wicked turn from his way and live" (Ezek. 33:11). "The Lord is . . . not willing that any should perish, but that all should come to repentance" (2 Peter 3:9).

There is a prevalent misconception about God and sin and punishment. God is holy and just and He has appointed a day in which He will judge mankind. Some assume they will somehow escape: "Thinkest thou this, O man, . . . that thou shalt escape the judgment of God?" (Rom. 2:3). But the New Testament as well as the Old Testament describes a God of mercy who justly holds the possibility of judgment and condemnation over our heads — but only to emphasize His gracious goodness in forgiveness. "The goodness of God leadeth thee to repentance" (Rom. 2:4).

God never tries to scare people into obedience or into loving Him; that would be utter folly. God reveals to us the extent of our evil so that we can appreciate His love and provision for our forgiveness; then this becomes the foundation for a new life, a new sense of identity, a new experience of love. "God sent not his Son into the world to condemn the world; but that the world through him might be saved" (John 3:17).

When we as children have been used to obeying our parents out of fear of being punished, it is hard to grasp the idea of being motivated to obedience to God by love. It is difficult to see God as a heavenly Parent who motivates by love and not by fear. God commands us to be perfect, but He readily forgives our imperfections as we confess them to Him. In the admission of our sins, we are able to face the reality of where we are wrong and overcome it. Because Christ has died for our sins, we do not have to make amends to God; we merely confess and apply ourselves to correcting the problem.

God's Design for Relationships

Obeying the first great commandment redeems us from the bondage of self-verification. We do not relate to God by our works of righteousness, but by His grace through faith. We do not seek, in other words, to verify ourselves with God; we simply believe His promises. Obedience changes the polarity of our relationships with people. We are delivered from seeking self-verification with them. We can love them because we feel interested and concerned; we are free to enjoy others for what they really are.

Having discovered that we are somebody to God, we automatically regard others as somebody also. Instead of loving others because we need to be loved by them, we find ourselves loving others because we know God loves them, because we are loved by God, and most of all, because we feel loving.

What a change this can make in personal relationships! Instead of maneuvering to make ourselves feel acceptable by some aspect of our appearance, performance, or status, or by avoiding some criticism, we are able to be more open and forthright; we are less defensive. We gladly affirm others, but we do not play the game of transactional self-verification, trading love for love or hate for hate. "The love of God is shed abroad in our hearts by the Holy Ghost which is given to us" (Rom. 5:5).

It is common for people to exclaim shortly after their spiritual conversion, as though they were surprised by their own attitude, "I feel a love for everyone! I don't understand it, but I love people I once hated. I feel all new inside." They are experiencing a new equation for their self-identity: *God + Me = a Whole Person*. From that new sense of being somebody, they are able to relate to others in the glow of the love of God.

The problem lies in our habit of relating to others in the framework of self-verification. This habit of identifying with and modeling after people who continually use self-verification as their only means of self-identity causes us to drift away from the joy of relying upon the Lord for our self-identity. We also have not grown sufficiently into the "liberty wherewith Christ hath made us free" (Gal. 5:1) to withstand antagonistic situations which threaten our sense of being somebody. We unwittingly begin to feel like a nobody and turn again to the "weak and beggarly elements" (Gal. 4:9) of self-verification for our sense of self-esteem.

This is why it is important to read God's Word daily, trust God in prayer, and meet together (Heb. 10:25) for worship and Christian fellowship. We must work to overcome the undertow of habit, or, as the Bible puts it, "Put ye on the Lord Jesus Christ, and make not provision for the flesh, to fulfill the lusts thereof" (Rom. 13:14).

During the moments we are loving God with this total devotion, all our separation anxiety is quieted; we know we are never alone. He is with us, and He is near. In such exchange of love with

God we experience the peace of God which surpasses all our under-standing (Phil. 4:7). The notion that we were a nobody, a nonentity, is erased in the overwhelming joy of being close to God and loved by Him.

There is an innate aggravation with life's rejections, its frustrations, its humiliations, and this aggravation reactivates our old sense of being separated from God. We are continually confronted with the tangible, and He is intangible. We must relate to Him by faith, but faith is a trust we will to exercise. This aggravation and its associated sense of aloneness revives in our minds the sense of being a nobody.

It is a challenge in Christian living to be able to recognize that this sense of being a nobody, the aggravating sense of separation, is actually an opportunity to return to God for reassurance of our self-identity. We need to overcome the tendency to try to relate to others for self-verification for our sense of self-identity. It requires vigilance to walk in the Spirit and not to walk after the flesh (Rom. 8:1).

I believe there is a great difference in the quality of fellow-ship between Christians using self-verification and Christians relying on God's grace for their sense of being somebody. Those who are "walking after the flesh" in this matter are relating transactionally and are subject to all the defensive ploys and ingratiating flatteries. Those who are "walking after the Spirit" in this matter relate with a genuine caring for the welfare and happiness of one another.

Relationships Can Be Peer in Quality

"Love thy neighbour as thyself" implies a truly peer re-lationship. Another wording for this commandment could be "Love thy neighbour as another person like yourself." In other words, if we love our neighbor, we want to favor him and be concerned for his welfare as much as we wish him to favor us. "As ye would that men should do to you, do ye also to them likewise" (Luke 6:31). This is the Golden Rule for peer relationship and for fulfillment in living with people.

Self-verification principles forward idealistic and parental components upon others so that we can feel better about ourselves when they give us their approval or attention. In Christ we recognize the humanity of other people, for they are like us, susceptible to making mistakes, meaning well but not always living up to expecta-tions. We do not expect more from them than we would objectively expect from ourselves. We are admonished "not to think . . . more highly than he ought to think; but to think soberly, according as God hath dealt to every man the measure of faith'' (Rom. 12:3). We are all responsible to God. We are all brothers and sisters in the Lord and have no right to regard ourselves above or below others: "That they may be one, as we are" (John 17:11,21,22,23). "There is neither Jew nor Greek, there is neither bond nor free, there is neither male nor female: for ye are all one in Christ Jesus" (Gal. 3:28).

The Bible clearly indicates that people are to be respected for the offices they hold. Whether kings or pastors or elders or deacons or teachers, it is only the office that gives the mark of distinction, because of the responsibility associated with it. The person himself is just as responsible to God as someone who does not hold an office. Each of us answers to God for the discharge of the responsibilities given to him by God: "Unto whomsoever much is given, of him shall be much required" (Luke 12:48).

Each adult is directly responsible to God as the primary Authority, the heavenly Parent. We are all brothers and sisters under God in His family. God reveals His will in His Word. While we cannot point to some divine decree that applies to a specific direction of God in the matter of an appointment or an election of someone to an office, yet in God's sovereign control of circumstances, all earthly authority figures are ordained of God (see Rom. 13:1).

We are to respect those in civil authority and in ecclesiastical position, but only as servants of God. We are not to regard them as though they possessed some superior virtues, though they may possess special abilities that qualify them for their position. Parents are appointed by God to govern their children until they reach an adult age. Children are to honor and obey their parents. But parents, because they are adults and responsible equally to God, have a possibility of peer relationship. We honor certain persons but this need not mean that we think of them as possessing greater intrinsic value than other persons.

It is easy to criticize others when we notice their faults. If we are obeying the second commandment, we will be interested in directing the other person's attention to his mistakes without depreciating his sense of being somebody. We appreciate it when others help us to overcome our faults by graciously protecting our sense of self-esteem while they make their criticism. Therefore when we make a criticism, we try not to attack the other person as though we considered him inferior or as though he intended to do wrong.

Basic Fear of People Abated by Love

We read, "He that feareth is not made perfect in love" (1 John 4:18). Here is an interesting contrast between love and fear. We usually tend to think of fear and faith as being antithetical, and they are. But faith is the foundational emotion to an expression of love. We tend not to trust people and relate to them lovingly because from infancy certain people in whom we have put confidence have seriously disappointed us. After a few such experiences, we tend to generalize so that by the time we reach adulthood, we are afraid of getting too close to people or of being too dependent on them. We also fear self-revelation beyond a certain point; we have vowed to ourselves never to let anyone pass that point. When certain friends become so familiar with us that they seem to approach that cut-off point, we begin to feel anxious. We are afraid they will hurt us in some way if they pass that imaginary mark.

This scheme of getting "close but not too close" is derived from patterns of self-verification. Actually, if we had insight enough to understand ourselves realistically, we would realize we are not so fearful of others as we are of ourselves. In ordinary social interaction we have been able to keep the idea of being a nobody out of awareness quite satisfactorily up to the cut-off point we have vowed to hold. Beyond that point we have been hurt in our childhood. We have no confidence in our ability to keep the idea of being a nobody out of awareness. We are terrified at the possibility of facing the repressed idea of being a nonentity. Instead of dealing with the matter as our personal problem, we project the idea onto other people and believe we are afraid of them. Yet when we try to think of just what we fear about *them*, we usually do not know.

We may have legitimate reason to protect ourselves from being hurt physically by certain cruel people, but our defensiveness with most people has nothing to do with the possibility of physical injury. Our anxiety is related to being hurt emotionally. The great emotional injury is the reawakening of the primitive idea that we are a nobody, a nonentity. So our fears of people are mostly related to our fear of being rejected, which indicates we are not wanted, not worth being accepted. Or, our fear of people may be that they will frustrate us, get in our way, disappoint us, lead us on, deceive us, or regard us as no good and not worth their cooperation and consideration. Furthermore, our fear of people may be that they will humiliate us, scorn us, mock us, or think us foolish. They might awaken the idea that we are inferior and inadequate and not worth their honor or respect.

As long as we need self-verification, we can be hurt by people. They have the power, which we have granted them, to remind us that we are nobody by their self-centered needs and antagonism. We will fear their criticism and sometimes fear their praise. We will fear being obligated and yet at times will want to be dependent. We may fear being too close and we may fear being too distant. We usually learn to manage our fear of people, but certain fears seem to persist in varying degress. We enjoy people, but we are alert to the dangers of being totally unguarded with them.

When we relate to God for our sense of being somebody, we find we are not so afraid of people. "The Lord is my helper, and I will not fear what man shall do unto me" (Heb. 13:6). Fear is an emotion that grips us when we feel alone, separated, and over-whelmed with our problems. When we are loving God, feeling aware of His presence with us, we feel like somebody to Him. In this frame of mind our fear of others and of life situations dissipates. We find ourselves more unguarded with people as if we have nothing to hide. We can speak freely of our faults and take responsibility for working to overcome them. Having a more settled sense of being somebody, we do not need to be defensive with others; they cannot hurt us by their attitude.

In Christ we have a better attitude about ourselves, and we do not need people for self-verification; therefore we are not so vulnerable. We are more objective in our relationships and will honestly desire to minister to anyone in need.

The Bible does not indicate that the Christian is to be promiscuous or careless in his openness with others. He is selective (Matt. 7:6). We are more inclined to be unguarded with others, and especially with those who are of "the household of faith" (Gal. 6:10).

When we relate lovingly to others who are resting in the assurance of being somebody to God, we can trust God to minister correctively to them as He does to us. We do not have to be militant in pointing out the faults of others, and they do not feel the compulsion to point out our faults. Love is shared mutually. We each feel responsible to God for the attitude we hold toward each other, and we know it is the will of God that we develop a spirit of oneness between us and our fellow Christians. We tend to feel we can trust others who also trust in God and are walking with Him.

Relationships Are Triangular, But Seem Linear

Relationships are not linear as they seem, but triangular. We pray to God and communicate with Him privately. God speaks to us in our quiet time with Him. Even in public worship we meet the Lord intuitively and privately in our thoughts. God also speaks to others in the same way He speaks to us. We genuinely seek to represent God to one another because we love God; our love for God inspires our love for them. We want to be Christlike in our behavior.

This inclusion of God in our thinking makes God a part of all our relationships; thus relationships are basically triangular, not linear.

His love is genuinely represented in the sincerity of our love. As our love is unconditional, we represent His love to each other, though as far as our awareness is concerned, we may be conscious only of an "I-thou" experience. One scarcely feels loved when someone explains, "I love you only because Jesus loves you."

We love God, and this liberates us to love others and relate to them as peers. Thus God is represented in our love for each other. As we respond to His unconditional love, our own self-identity is validated, and this liberates us to be unconditional in our feelings of love for others. But when other Christians minister to us with unconditional love, our mutual love validates our sense of being somebody.

We are not seeking self-verification, but in a mutual unconditional love we find validation for what we experience subjectively in our love relationship with God and faith in His Word.

As we sense the love of God in the attitudes of others, we feel validated in our belongingness, worthiness, and competence. We are assured by tangible evidence that God cares. As we sense the triangular aspects in our relationships with other Christians, we experience an increased dimension of being equal to and peers with them. "If we walk in the light, as he is in the light, we have fellowship one with another, and the blood of Jesus Christ his Son cleanseth us from all sin" (1 John 1:7).

Thus there is a way in which the bond of Christian fellowship validates our sense of being cleansed from our sins, and this validates our sense of worthiness. Because we can be more fearlessly open with our fellow Christians, experiencing an unusual acceptance with one another, we feel more capable of facing the parts of ourselves that we ordinarily might hide. Thus we validate our sense of personal worth to God for each other.

As we relate with other Christians in unconditional love, we are able to be more unguarded and self-disclosing. We may pray for each other and encourage each other. Thus we share in supporting one another with love and concern. This validates a sense of being special to each other, and in this special relationship we sense a tangible assurance of our own sense of competence.

We may not be trying to verify our sense of competence, for we have found it in our relationship with the Holy Spirit, who is with us in daily life situations. But we do find a tangible validation of our sense of competence in our Christian fellowship. As we share what God seems to be doing in our lives — answering prayers, leading in difficulties, giving opportunities to share His grace with others — we are reaffirmed in our obedience to the will of God. We validate one another as we share our blessings, trials, and feelings.

Relationships Provide an Island of Security

In our relationships with each other that occur within the framework of unconditional love, we not only validate each other's sense of being somebody, but also provide each other an island of emotional security as a beachhead from which we can deal with our own faults more courageously.

The reason we are defensive with each other, when we are under the jurisdiction of self-verification, is that we have no island of emotional security from which we can launch an attack upon our own problems. All our efforts are dedicated to keeping the idea of being a nobody out of awareness. To work on a weakness or a fault for the sake of being a better somebody is not the focus of our attention. The work we do to correct our deficiencies is dedicated to self-verification, that is, maintaining the image that we are a somebody.

Having once accepted our being a nobody before God — and accepting that He loves us and has taken our condition of being a sinful nobody into Himself (2 Cor. 5:21) so that now we are some-body to Him — we can work toward improvement as one of His very own children. Then, being validated in our Christian fellowship, we are encouraged to grow in grace and in knowledge of Jesus Christ and become a more mature person emotionally and spiritually. We can face our faults and deficiencies without threatening our own sense of self-identity.

This is why God admonishes us to "bear ye one another's burdens, and so fulfill the law of Christ" (Gal. 6:2). He also tells us, "Confess your faults one to another, and pray one for another, that ye may be healed" (James 5:16). In our triangular relationship with one another and with God, we can promote unity between believers and assist each other in growing. In our loving acceptance of one another, not being judgmental, we provide a beachhead of security for each other in coping with our own deficiencies before the Lord.

We have a no-condemnation plane of reference for our thinking (Rom. 8:1). In our loving, nonjudgmental attitude toward each other, we minister the grace of God in affirming that we do not have to measure up by some degree of perfection in order to be acceptable. This validates the no-condemnation plane of reference we know theoretically and liberates us to apply ourselves diligently to overcoming whatever faults we are aware of having. Not only do we strengthen relationships, but we are free to be more objective with ourselves. There is a real sense in which we become models for each other of God's gracious leading. Paul referred to this when he encouraged the Corinthians, "Be ye followers of me, even as I am of Christ" (1 Cor. 11:1).

When we speak of the ideal relationship with God and the ideals of relating to others with unconditional love, we need to see these ideals as goals of life. We have a resolution for our emotional problems in our faith in God and His Word, and this solution is validated in our Christian fellowship with others who also trust in God. But no one is fully matured spiritually or emotionally in this life; we still cope with imperfections in people and in ourselves.

We need to bear in mind, however, that we do grow emotionally and spiritually as we apply the Word of God to daily life situations — as indicated in 1 Peter 2:1,2: "Wherefore laying aside all malice, and all guile, and hypocrisies, and envies, and all evil speakings, as newborn babes, desire the sincere milk of the word, that ye may grow thereby."

As Christians we are not growing in our ability to keep a sense of being a nobody out of awareness as we tried to do before spiritual conversion. We are growing in our ability to accept ourselves as actually being somebody because we are somebody to God.

16

Attend to Your Negative Tendencies

"Man is born unto trouble, as the sparks fly upward" (Job 5:7). Life's troubles always seem difficult and often insurmountable. Impossibilities and hardships pound against us the way breakers at the seashore beat upon the rocks.

From the beginning, man has philosophized about his difficulties and trials. We do not wish to add to the confusion. Rather, it is our purpose to indicate how our love relationship with God as commanded in the first great commandment changes our point of view regarding our hardships. Also, how our love relationship with others as commanded in the second great commandment removes the sense of aloneness we tend to feel while enduring our miseries.

Having a positive sense of being somebody who is related to God — the mighty Sovereign over all that happens from the distant galaxy to the infinitesimal atom — changes the polarity of our thinking so that everything, whether pleasant or painful, has a good purpose. The Christian who anchors his sense of being somebody in the grace of God, and not in his own self-verification, has a persistent sense of destiny in every life situation.

At times the Christian may become a victim of his usual anxieties. But having tasted of the abundant life because he has been liberated from the need to verify himself, he will want to be led by the Holy Spirit to return to his optimistic moorings of having a vital part in God's omniscient scheme of things. He doesn't have to know all things to be able to trust in the goodness of life, for he trusts in God, who is good.

If this sounds like an extravagant, idealistic daydream about how Christians think in times of trouble because you have never experienced such a polarity of thought, then this chapter is probably written just for you.

The apostles Paul, Peter, James, and John and all the believers mentioned in Hebrews 11 achieved this stability by their faith in God. The Bible does not claim they were any different from us. They found their true sense of self-identity in the grace of God, and we are impressed with how invincible they were, even to suffering horrible martyrdom.

We have already emphasized the self-verification we seek from others in their acceptance of our appearance or performance or status. We have noticed how we use these assets to keep ourselves from thinking about being a nobody. In this chapter we take particular notice of the situational factors that tend either to verify our sense of being somebody or threaten to reawaken the idea that we are nobody.

Even though we may love the Lord with our total selves and love our neighbors as ourselves, we are at times also readily capable of reverting to our former ways of thinking. We can regress to godless ways of coping with a situation and scarcely realize we have done it. After a while, however, we may begin to realize we have drifted from our firm moorings in Christ. This is the reason why we need daily to refresh ourselves in God's Word and relate to Him continually in prayer.

And this is what spiritual growth is all about. The situations of life lade us with pressures that reveal our weaknesses. As we exercise our faith in God, we become stronger and more stable in our Christian walk.

We all manifest tendencies in coping with life situations which, if not dealt with correctively, prevent us from growing up spiritually to the full stature of a mature Christian. We now consider several of these tendencies that seem instinctively to affect us under certain circumstances to drift away from our sense of self-identity in Christ.

The Tendency to Treat People As Things

People play a major role in the situations that either gratify or distress us. There is often an impersonal element that deteriorates personal relationships: It is perceiving people as things — things that either assist us in accomplishing our goals, or things that get in our way and interfere with our realizing our dreams.

This tendency perhaps derives from the time of childhood when things were exceedingly important. The child is small, perhaps less than four years old, and not developed sufficiently to appreciate his parents as persons to a significant degree. He identifies with them as they relate to him, but he does not value them as he will be able to a little later.

When an unloving atmosphere prevails in the home, the child is not taught or encouraged to appreciate people. His deep resentment toward people for the way they treat him and his fear of them cause him to turn away from people to things. People are changeable and unpredictable; things are more stable, and they do gratify him to some extent. If the child can gather enough things to himself, he will not need to be dependent upon people who might hurt him. Thus things become love-substitutes. Some people are more affected by this than others.

Knowing this, we easily understand how love-starvation in childhood can cause a person to grow up to be heavily dependent upon things and his control of the elements of his circumstances for a sense of self-verification. He has never felt secure in his relationships with people, so he tends to treat people as things to be manipulated and used and discarded when they have lost their usefulness. He tends to be insensitive to the feelings of others.

Let us note how 1 John 2:15 instructs us to drop our love for things: "Love not the world, neither the things that are in the world." Love for things, as well as love for the three other values mentioned in the next verse, prevents us from doing the will of God. It is stated clearly that His will is that we love Him and love others; when love is diverted to things or to our personal gratifications, we cannot do the will of God. The Bible states we are to love God and others and use things responsibly. Things are to be kept in respect only to their utility value. We are to use things to share with others who are in need (see Matt. 6:19-21, 30-33; Luke 6:29,30,38; 2 Cor. 9:5-11; 1 Tim. 4:4; Heb. 13:5).

When we love someone, we idealize that person and iden-tify with him. This gives us a sense of being equal to and one with that person. When we love things, we depersonalize ourselves, for we cannot identify or interact with an inanimate object. We increase our love starvation.

Sherwin was accused by his wife of being a cold, unfeeling person, a materialistic husband, impossible to live with. She was most disappointed in her marriage. As Sherwin and I talked over his marriage problem, it was obvious his wife was right. He did not relate to her as a person; his total relationship with her seemed to be in terms of how much everything cost and how the family were abusing their possessions. Sherwin had depersonalized himself by loving things.

The Bible gives us a crucial insight about love. Love is commanded, and we are responsible for whom or what we love. Therefore love is under the control of the will; we are not victims of our love-emotion as some people assume. When the Bible says "Love not the world, neither the things that are in the world" or "Husbands, love your wives" (Eph. 5:25) or "Set your affection on things above, not on things on the earth" (Col. 3:2) or "Let us not love in word, neither in tongue; but in deed and in truth" (1 John 3:18), God is telling us that we do love and can love what we *choose* to love. We can also improve the quality of our love if we determine to do so.

Whenever you think of improving your love for God, begin by considering His love for you at Calvary: "We love him, because he first loved us" (1 John 4:19). Remember the suffering that paid for your willfulness in sinning against God; remember with gratitude, and love will no doubt begin to surge in your heart.

Whenever you think of improving your love for people, begin by reminding yourself of your standing with God: your belongingness in the Father's love, your worthiness in the Son's atonement, your competence in the Holy Spirit's strengthening presence. As your sense of being somebody to God firms up in your mind, you will very likely begin to want to love people more and to resolve the hostilities that separate you from them and defile your relationships. This should inspire you to seek ways of improving your communication with them and of being forgiving.

People belong to our hearts as our love objects, not things. The more people we love, the more we identify with a variety of different personalities, and the more mature we will become. Everyone we love becomes part of us, and we become part of everyone who loves us. These values are permanent, for love "never faileth" (1 Cor. 13:8).

The Tendency to Resent Unpleasant Circumstances

Most of us on occasion reveal some childhood tendency remaining within us to want situations to be made pleasant for us. We may hear ourselves say accusingly to someone we hold dear, "You know what I like that would make me happy; why don't you do it for me?"

Ordinarily we probably think we can withstand almost anything that might occur, but when something unpleasant happens, we show a tattletale to our unresolved infantile demand by the anger we express. If we were mature, we would be concerned about what actually caused the problem and wonder how to fix it. But our first thought seems to be, *Why does this have to happen to me?* or we start acting out our rage against the nearest object that can't strike back.

There seems to be a child in everyone at times that wants to be pampered. When we feel resentful over unpleasant circumstances instead of an interest in what is actually wrong, we are acting under the illusion that the situation is somehow rejecting us. This, of course, is ridiculous, but if we don't see it for what it is, we are not likely to correct it.

To resolve the problem, we need to face our infantile rage about waiting or being made to feel uncomfortable or rejected because "it" didn't provide everything just the way we wanted it. Having done this, we can reaffirm our faith in God's providential care of us and renew our sense of being somebody to God because He cares. It does little or no good to blame oneself for acting like a child; it is better to act like an adult and deal with the problem responsibly.

The Tendency to Resent Loss of Control

Frustration is a reaction we feel when we lose control of a situation. We expect one thing to happen, and something else occurs. Usually we need to be in control of the details of a situation because of our own anxieties. If we are driving along the road and start skidding on ice, we immediately reaffirm our control of the situation. We probably watch our driving more closely, slow down, and maintain a keen alertness. An excessive need to be in control of a situation is a manifestation of anxiety.

We probably assume we are ordinarily easygoing and quite capable of standing disappointment or a sudden change of schedule. When it happens, however, we may react with instant anger. For instance, we are delayed by traffic from getting to a destination on time, or when we are in a hurry, the car happens to be out of gas. On such occasions, do we patiently wait for the traffic to clear or take the blame for not thinking ahead to make sure the gas tank was filled? Our anger is a tattletale to our immaturity.

Being in control of a situation is often closely related to our sense of being somebody. There is an implied element of security in being the master in a situation. This is why some persons hope they will not weep under emotional stress, for they feel out of control. Many are self-conscious when giving a public address; their anxiety is related to a fear of not being able to control the situation so that they will be admired. Some people have such great need emotionally to maintain control that they speak first when meeting a friend so that they can manage the direction of the conversation.

The same is true of trying to avoid being controlled by others. We seek to avoid being obligated or indebted to someone. This can cause feelings of loss of control. A few people are so independent, they would be embarrassed to ask street directions from a nearby service station operator; instead they would try to look it up for themselves, as they feel a loss of dignity or loss of control if they did seek help.

The most common problem in this regard seems to be the trait of attempting to control those we love. When a person does this, he becomes possessive, jealous, and often demanding. This is commonly understood to be a mark of immaturity, and it is.

If we are to overcome this tendency to resent loss of control, we must deal with the resentment. We do not accomplish this by blaming ourselves for being too controlling. We need to reexperience the infantile rage of always having to have our own way, identify it by seeing it for what it is, and dissipate it by determining a more productive way of coping.

After we do this, we can reaffirm our faith in God's control of everything that happens to us, and try to accept what happens as being our responsibility under God to hold steady and try to resolve our frustrations without so much anger. When we don't get our own way in a situation, and we are concerned about our explosiveness, it might help to read again the Book of Jonah, and especially the fourth chapter. We can learn to accept what we don't like because God has allowed it.

We can lay aside our anger, wrath, and malice more easily when we return to our securities in Christ. As we return to a sense of His providential care and sovereign control of all things, we find great comfort in knowing that we are somebody to Him and He "worketh in you both to will and to do of His good pleasure" (Phil. 2:13).

The Tendency to Resent Humiliating Happenings

If our sense of competence was not firmly sustained in our home relationships when we were children, we may still be fighting with inferiority feelings as adults. Thus we may be sensitive to any slight implied in people's remarks or feel humiliated by their criticism. We may secretly want others to notice our achievements and give us credit for our sacrifices. We may want others to be cognizant of how hard we work or how much we suffer. Sometimes we get into the trap of trying to impress people with how hard life is for us by elaborating on the hazards we endure.

These tendencies act as tattletales to our immaturities. We are apparently not ready to accept the status values God has allowed us to have, and we employ self-verification strategies.

Some people are strongly competitive with everyone. They seem to need to prove themselves to be superior. Adults do not usually need to be competitive; they have a greater need to be cooperative. There is a smoldering anger that seems to be attached to the need to be competitive, and it takes little contradictory put-down to cause it to flare up into full flame.

Again, as we previously mentioned, it is important to deal with the infantile rage at being humiliated, put down, and made to feel inferior. After the anger has been externalized and identified, one needs to dissipate it by trying to find objectivity in the situation.

It is important to turn to God for a renewal of our sense of being somebody and reaffirm to ourselves that if God wanted us exalted, He would have allowed it to happen. The promise is "Humble yourselves therefore under the mighty hand of God, that he may exalt you in due time" (1 Peter 5:6). Our pride can greatly interfere with affirming ourselves in His grace.

The Tendency to Give Up When Proven Wrong

It takes faith to resolve true guilt. The Bible says, "The blood of Jesus Christ his Son cleanseth us from all sin. . . . If we confess our sins, he is faithful and just to forgive us our sins, and to cleanse us from all unrighteousness" (1 John 1:7,9). Romans 8:31-34 may also be helpful in resolving actual guilt.

It is easy to give up when proven wrong, for we can easily feel depressed over the matter. We may say to ourselves, *What's the use! I've spoiled everything.* This could be our anger at feeling guilty, but it is being expressed in a passive, I-don't-care manner.

We must face the fact: Either Christ died for our sins or He did not! If he died, we can be forgiven. He says He does forgive, and it is our responsibility to exercise the courage to believe what He says.

It takes courage to believe we are actually forgiven. In condemning ourselves for our sin, we have rated ourselves as bad and deserving of appropriate punishment. Unconsciously we do not expect ourselves to succeed in life or to do well, for we are essentially bad and do not deserve the joy of success or to feel good about ourselves. This attitude defeats the grace of God in forgiving us. It takes courage of faith to contradict this idea and to dare to accept the responsibility of being successful, expecting that our efforts will be blessed of God and produce good results.

If we have done someone else wrong and hurt them, we are instructed to make proper amends (see Matt. 5:23-26). This may be difficult to do, but when it is possible, we should certainly try.

Sometimes we have memories from childhood out of which we have terrible guilt over something that happened. We could never tell anyone; all our lives we have hoped that our secret would never become known. There may be times when we are filled with terror that our mate or someone else close to us will discover the vile person we think we are. Such harbored guilt can do great damage to one's peace of mind and mute one's successes. I have never seen it to fail that when such a person finds a trusted friend with whom he shares this burden of guilt, he gets wonderful relief. It may take a little time to work through the ramifications of the problem, but it is worth it. "Confess your faults one to another, and pray one for another, that ye may be healed" (James 5:16).

To give up when proven wrong is not only to punish oneself, but to avoid the responsibility for being right. This is not productive, and it cannot perform the will of God. We glorify God in our lives by acknowledging our guilt honestly, confessing it to God, then accepting His forgiveness and taking the courage of faith to live as though it never happened, being careful to learn how to avoid doing it again.

The Tendency to Be Paralyzed When Fearful

Fear paralyzes the mind, making us unable to think clearly. Fear of great magnitude disorganizes the mind temporarily so that confusion reigns. Fear also has a way of multiplying itself; we are so disabled when afraid that we become afraid of our fears. We cannot face problems when we are afraid of them.

For example, Arthur had a heart murmur accompanied by an occasional pain. When a spasm occurred, he became terrified he was going to die. This fear intensified the pain, so he became afraid of being frightened by the spasm.

It takes faith to master a fear problem. It is impossible to overcome fear by feeling guilty for the emotion. Nowhere in the Bible does God condemn a person for being afraid; instead He consistently encourages the fearful with such statements as, "Fear thou not; for I am with thee" (Isa. 41:10). When we are afraid, we feel all alone with our problem, and we feel overwhelmed. Faith accepts the fact that the problem is too much for us and also the fact that we are not alone in our problem; we have God with us.

When we feel guilty for our fear, we increase our problem. The guilt is debilitating, for it is a false guilt. "Love contains no fear

— indeed fully-developed love expels every particle of fear, for fear always contains some of the torture of feeling guilty. The man who lives in fear has not yet had his love perfected'' (1 John 4:18 Phillips). We are upheld by the ''right hand of his righteousness'' (Isa. 41:10), so in our fear we do not need to feel guilty. Feeling guilty means to feel disqualified for help; thus we return to our sense of being a nobody who is unworthy of help. Faith in God restores our sense of His forgiveness and our right to expect God to extend His grace to attend to our need. Feeling guilty for being afraid only makes us feel more alone and helpless.

We are not alone in our problem. We may feel alone because we do not sense that God will help us or can help us. When we are obsessed with feelings of such aloneness and unworthiness, it is good to turn to James 4:8 and obey God's invitation: ''Draw nigh to God, and he will draw nigh to you.'' Confess whatever we know is wrong in our lives, and read His Word to find a fresh sense of His loving care. God is able to quiet our fears. David said, ''I sought the Lord, and he heard me, and delivered me from all my fears'' (Ps. 34:4).

Some of our fears may be related to the fear of not getting our way about something we desire. If this is the case, the obvious answer is to make a fresh commitment to God of all desires, knowing He will allow and provide whatever is good according to His divine plan.

Other fears may be related to our fear of people. Intellectually we can cope with this because of Hebrews 13:6: ''The Lord is my helper, and I will not fear what man shall do unto me.'' But emotionally we may need to allow ourselves time to outgrow the tendency to be fearful of people by practicing and strengthening our relationship with God for our sense of self-identity. As we feel more secure in Him, we may tend less to be afraid of people.

The Tendency to Dread Problems

It is natural to dread problems the way we dread pain and any discomfort. Nevertheless, we must remember it is only as we face problems and difficulties that we grow to emotional and spiritual maturity. Growth does not take place without overcoming problems.

Wind blows some trees down, but for many others it strengthens the root system. Our problematic life situations can either destroy us or make us, depending on how well we are rooted in the truth of God's grace. We are all lazy at heart; we will not grow unless we have to in order to survive.

The Garden of Eden has been closed a long time, and when

the gates of that ancient land of tranquillity were closed, God said, "Because thou . . . hast eaten of the tree, of which I commanded thee, saying, Thou shalt not eat of it: cursed is the ground for thy sake; in sorrow shalt thou eat of it all the days of thy life; thorns also and thistles shall it bring forth to thee" (Gen. 3:17,18). Jesus said, "In this world ye shall have tribulation: but be of good cheer; I have overcome the world" (John 16:33). We may be searching and expecting to find a day when we will be relieved of all troubles, but in this life that cannot happen. It is in our troubles that we can find our God and relate to Him.

That we are alive means we have been overcoming the forces of death that are continually operating in us. No one should ever think of stopping growth, or arriving at a plateau where no more growth is appropriate, regardless of age. We do stop growing physically, but emotionally and spiritually there is no stopping place. James 1:2-4 says, "My brethren, count it all joy when ye fall into divers temptations; knowing this, that the trying of your faith worketh patience. But let patience have her perfect work, that ye may be perfect and entire, wanting nothing." Patience is a prime virtue of emotional maturity. But to be entire in actual maturity is hard to conceive of; yet it is a worthy ideal toward which to strive.

Faith in God of the quality that leads us to love God with our total selves and our neighbor as ourselves gives us the stamina to face our problematic situations without being overcome with pessimistic, critical, negative feelings.

"Therefore, my beloved brethren, be ye stedfast, unmoveable, always abounding in the work of the Lord, forasmuch as ye know that your labour is not in vain in the Lord" (1 Cor. 15:58).

The Tendency to Be Unforgiving

It is not our natural talent to be forgiving when someone offends, and there are some good reasons for this. Nevertheless, when we hold grudges, we actually injure ourselves far more than we hurt the offender. God has made it plain that the chief commodity in this world is loving relationship; harboring hard feelings directly violates His revealed will.

Some people seem more prone to harbor grudges than others. The makeup of their personalities is such that it is more difficult for them to release the offender and be reconciled to him. I am convinced, however, that one reason why Christians hold grudges is because they do not understand the true meaning of forgiveness or how to be forgiving. They say, "I can forgive, but I can't forget." They read about the need to be forgiving in the Bible, but do not know how to free themselves from their own grudges.

It is important to consider our grudges and release ourselves from them, for there are few emotions that bind us so tightly into self-verification strategies as does the unresolved memory of being offended. We may be able to move away from our enemies and forget them, or they may die, but the vengeful feelings we harbor toward them prevents us from developing an inner wholeness — and they block us from developing a meaningful relationship with God.

We are aware from our previous discussions how guilt feelings are actually feelings of being a nobody, a bad person. These feelings are devastating and impossible to live with. The mind immediately has to divert its attention from such feelings onto something else to maintain a desire to stay alive. Hence the denial and repression of the idea of being a nobody occur, and with them the defense reaction of trying to prove to ourselves we are not a nobody.

But hostility is the other side of guilt. When we feel hostile, we tend to want to strike out to punish and to restore our sense of well-being, but we can't. When we feel guilty, we usually cannot express our anger, so we find ways of punishing ourselves. We are inclined essentially to do to ourselves what we might like to do to someone else if we could express our anger.

In guilt we feel disqualified from relationship with others. This is why forgiveness is so vital in reconciling the sense of relationship. When we feel hostile or angry with someone, we want nothing to do with the offender. He is not worthy of our relating to him, and we want to make him feel guilty, punish him, or destroy him. We are able to wait for an appropriate time when this can be accomplished. This harbored hostility is called a *grudge*, and the desire to punish is called *vengeance*.

The problem with grudges for the one who holds them is that they cause him to be split emotionally, fragmented within. Part of him is dedicated to enforcing antirelationship, to keeping from any loving involvement; the rest of him is seeking loving relationship with others. He cannot be total in his love feelings for others, for a part of himself is committed to exercising vengeance, avoiding a personal involvement, any caring. The greater the number of grudges we hold, the greater is our fragmentation within.

We can only partially find an inner wholeness until we have resolved our fragmentation by being forgiving of others who have offended us. This includes all offenses that have occurred in our lifetime, because the unconscious aspect of our memory knows no time. Many of our present reactions to people are based upon childhood grudges or repressed hostility.

We cannot obey either of the two great commandments when we hold onto this frame of thinking about others. This is, no doubt, why the first great commandment delineates that we love God with our total self, heart, soul, and mind. Also, this is probably why Jesus emphasized forgivingness as conditioning our own forgiveness by God. "Forgive us our debts, as we forgive our debtors. . . . For if ye forgive men their trespasses, your heavenly Father will also forgive you: But if ye forgive not men their trespasses, neither will your Father forgive your trespasses" (Matt. 6:12,14,15).

The issue is just this: How can we be total in our relationship with God and find peace of God within, when a part of ourselves is opposed to relating to others and dedicated to hurting them? How can we have inner wholeness through loving relationship when a part of ourselves does not want relationship? How can we be sincerely accepting the sovereign government of God when by punishing others we are assuming the role of God in exercising a jurisdiction that belongs to God?

This is why it is so very important to deal with our grudges and be reconciled in our hearts to people as an act of faith in God and love for God. "Grieve not the holy Spirit of God, whereby ye are sealed unto the day of redemption. Let all bitterness, and wrath, and anger, and clamour, and evil speaking, be put away from you, with all malice: and be kind one to another, tenderhearted, forgiving one another, even as God for Christ's sake hath forgiven you" (Eph. 4:30-32).

Forgiveness is not excusing the offender; this is not what God has done for us. Forgiveness is also not forgetting the whole matter as though it never happened; God didn't do that either. He forgets *after* He forgives, not as a means of forgiveness. God forgives us because Christ loved us and died for us: "Who his own self bare our sins in his own body on the tree" (1 Peter 2:24). God forgives as a demonstration of His love and desire for oneness with us in a restored relationship, because the just demands of a broken law have been fully met in the death of Christ. "The wages of sin is death; but the gift of God is eternal life through Jesus Christ our Lord" (Rom. 6:23).

Without a relationship with God, it is impossible for us to forgive in any real sense of complete reconciliation. We hold the grudge because our sense of being somebody was injured by the offender. We assume a jurisdiction over that person because of our loss of self-identity related to him. We relate the pain we want the offender to suffer to the pain we have felt, but his pain is not related to our need for restoration.

Thus any true forgiveness must begin with acknowledging the sovereign ownership and government of God over all mankind. We must accept His love for others as well as for ourselves. If we do, we respect His jurisdiction in punishing all offenders. "Dearly beloved, avenge not yourselves, but rather give place unto wrath: for it is written, Vengeance is mine; I will repay, saith the Lord" (Rom. 12:19).

As we accept God's forgiveness of our sins and find our sense of being somebody to Him by His grace, we can do as God does: Forgive those who have offended us for Christ's sake; He died for them! We surrender to Him our desire to punish the one who has offended us. This is an act of faith and love.

It takes faith to be forgiving, for we trust God with one of our treasured possessions, our vengeance. There is a pleasure in "getting even" with those who have hurt us, but that pleasure belongs to God who can administer justice equitably. Surrendering the vengeance feelings means ridding ourselves of the desire not to relate lovingly. In doing this we are reconciled to the offender in our attitude toward him. God is glorified in us when we are forgiving, for we have accepted His love and government over our enemy and trusted Him to execute whatever is good for the one who offended us. This frees our minds to feel loving to the very ones we formerly were so bitter against.

A big part of holding a grudge is the fear that the one who hurt us once will do it again. We do not trust him, and to protect ourselves from this threat of being hurt, we erect this barricade in our emotional system against all relationship with him. Forgiveness removes this barricade and restores our openness to a relationship with him. We may know we will probably be hurt, but we trust God to work through us to change the heart of the offender. We conquer our fear of our enemy by our faith in God.

"Therefore if thine enemy hunger, feed him; if he thirst, give him drink: for in so doing thou shalt heap coals of fire on his head. Be not overcome with evil, but overcome evil with good" (Rom. 12:20,21). These verses teach that our surrender of vengeance will inspire an ability, if not a sincere desire, to do good to the ones who have offended us. Indeed, the good we may do him can be God's way of reaching to the offender and helping him to deal with his emotional problem that makes him our enemy.

When we have found our true sense of self-identity in our total love-commitment to God, we are able to relate differently to people. We do not need to protect ourselves from injury to our sense of being somebody, as we did with self-verification when we were not involved with God and His grace.

To forgive some old offense — perhaps one we have nearly forgotten — and remove the damaging effects it has upon our sense of inner wholeness and fulfillment in living, we need to treat the old grievances as though they were current. Reflect upon the past. When a memory of some incident is recalled, pause with that memory to reexperience the anger feelings; and allow time for those old hostilities to return so that you feel as if it just happened. Then prayerfully commit those vengeance feelings to God as something you have harbored that belongs to Him. Ask Him to take the vengeance and restore your desire for relationship with the offender, to fill you with love.

This transaction can be made with God, and when it is done, the relief will be so pronounced that other offenses will be recalled. It is a good exercise of faith and prayer to regurgitate these old, poisonous feelings and clean the basement of the mind so that the household of our thoughts will be filled with the sweetness of love.

When we harbor grudges, we break the triangular aspect of relationship. God cannot minister through us to others, and they cannot minister to us. When we forgive others and are again ready for relationship with them, we heal the broken triangle, and God can be glorified by communicating Himself to us in our relationships with others.

Forgiving others strengthens our own sense of being somebody to God; we are more than gratified for the sacrifice of vengeance by the peace of God that reigns in our hearts, for we know we are in His will.

We all tend to be idealistic and prefer to believe that somehow just trusting God and becoming a Christian will automatically cure our emotional problems and cure the ills of society. This is a gross oversimplification of God's scheme of things and more than a little misleading.

No one is perfect, we all know. When a person professes to be a Christian, we automatically expect a degree of perfection from him that is not ordinarily found in people. This is unfair, for after spiritual conversion we still have the problem of spiritual and emotional growth. There is no shortcut to growth on either a spiritual or an emotional level. No biblical miracles short-circuit the process of growth.

Growth is not easy, but it is rewarding. The Bible admonishes us to continue growing: "Every one that useth milk is unskilful in the word of righteousness: for he is a babe. But strong meat belongeth to them that are of full age, even those who by reason of use have their senses exercised to discern both good and evil. Therefore leaving the principles of the doctrine of Christ, let us go on unto perfection [full growth]'' (Heb. 5:13 - 6:1).

By attending to our negative tendencies as stated in this chapter, we can perfect our experience of being somebody to God by His grace. We can ''lay aside every weight, and the sin which doth so easily beset us,'' and we can ''run with patience the race that is set before us, looking unto Jesus the author and finisher of our faith'' (Heb. 12:1,2).

17

Revoke the Undertow of Selfism

Honest self-analysis surfaces convincing evidence that we all have a dominant tendency to be self-centered, practicing a selfism which is as strong as if we were capable of being self-existent. This tendency polarizes our thinking, making us impulsively defensive and self-centered instead of consistently objective in life situations. We are, as a result, far more prone to expect positive support from others than we are prepared to give to others the kindness and favorable consideration they deserve and need.

It is easy to comprehend how we became this way, for we started life in an inferior and dependent position, and we have had to defend against the devastation of unloving relationships. Because of this, some of us are more impulsive in our defensiveness, some are more needy of emotional support than others, and some are more fearful of people.

We often aspire to becoming more of a giving kind of person. We wish we were less defensive, less fearful of people and of life situations. We may succeed to some degree, for some people work harder at overcoming their emotional immaturities than others, and certain people seem to have a greater security factor built into their environment.

Unfortunately, however, many people see the problems they face as originating only in the environment; they seldom consider their part in the unpleasant situation they want to see changed. These people seldom introspect in order to develop a better means of coping, but instead devote their attention to trying to effect changes in others which would make life less annoying for themselves.

In whatever way we cope with this tendency toward self-centeredness, we find that our potential toward selfism is like a relentless undertow causing us to react more like children than adults in many situations. For instance, we find ourselves exploding in anger when we do not get our way, or slinking into a depression, or wanting to run away and hide. When we yield to this undertow, we usually expect people to be understanding of our good intentions and "pure" motives, but they seldom do. Our selfism injures relationships we desire, but we are apt to see the problem as the other person's fault. We may impulsively damage property of value, but again we reason that somehow the other person is responsible, perhaps because we feel he incited our anger. Sometimes we do things which injure our own health, but the compulsion to continue is so great we can't stop.

We only make matters worse for ourselves when we fail to cope with adult problems in mature, appropriate ways, taking the responsibility for our own conduct and for the feelings of hurt and antagonism we create in others. The undertow of selfism draws us away from an objective attitude and a good perspective in life situations.

Natural Origins of Selfism

Our habits of self-centeredness which developed into selfism were formed in early childhood. We began life in a totally helpless and inferior state and were entirely dependent upon others for survival. Our major concerns at that time were to enjoy, to investigate the unknown, and to avoid or to eliminate pain and discomfort.

As tiny infants we wanted immediate gratification when we were hungry or in any misery, and all our pleasures were essentially sensual in nature because of our immaturity. Our thoughts were all naturally self-centered.

As we grew a little, we began insisting on getting our own way, and we opposed parental government and circumvented it as much as we could. Our unrealized goal was to be in control of our environment to ensure self-gratification. Our pleasures in this early period were sensual and also somewhat acquisitional. We found a sense of security in having our own things. We also enjoyed the sense of power in being able to achieve and to do certain skills.

Continuing to grow and becoming a little older, we began to encounter intense feelings of inferiority as we occasionally lost in the competition with our peers. We tried to adjust to this humiliation. Entering our adolescence, we added to this struggle for superiority and recognition a need to develop into adequate men and women. Physical development was important along with other aspects of our growth. Our pleasures were not only sensual and acquisitional, but also recognitional. We sought desperately to be noticed and to be rewarded for excellence.

Our parents probably tried to teach us to be others-centered in our thoughts and behavior, to share and to be generous, but for the most part we must admit we retained a strong tendency toward self-centeredness. As we grew out of our adolescence into adulthood, this self-centeredness became socialized into a system of thinking I have chosen to call *selfism*.

Most of us have achieved clever disguises for our self-centered concerns and perhaps we believe ourselves at times to be quite interested in the welfare of others on a primary level. But if we lift the mask, we will probably be shocked to discover just how self-centered we actually are. We are all practitioners of selfism in a variety of ways.

A Few Telltales to Selfism

Perhaps the most obvious flimsiness in our altruistic mask is our impulsive reaction to praise or to criticism. Our selfism is revealed in our tendency to feel inflated with flattery when we are praised, or we have to cancel it by some negative remark like, "You like this dress? Why I've had it for years!" Self-adulation frequently extends beyond the appropriate reaction to receiving a simple compliment. On the other hand, if someone happens to be critical of our appearance or our performance or our status rating, we take personal offense and display defensiveness instead of being able to accept the value of the criticism or to see ourselves more objectively. We often fail to tolerate the overreaction of our critic or to make an allowance for his bad mood or unfortunate choice of words.

Instant anger at a disappointment is another evidence of selfism. Perhaps a delay occurs, or someone does not do as we expected, or an implement breaks down just when we need it, and we flash with rage. If we do not react with an open anger, we may invert the feelings and experience self-pity, saying, "I can never win!" "Nothing ever works for me." Pessimism, cynicism, sarcasm, moodiness, apathy, boredom, and even depression are all manifestations of selfism as well as overt anger and hasty defensiveness. Fears and phobias, compulsions and daydreaming all reveal selfism. The evidences of selfism are innumerable.

Dynamic Factor in Selfism

We have noted several behavioral evidences of selfism. Now we need to look a little deeper into the issue and consider a dynamic factor in it. This is the inner rage or hostile attitude we have against everything that opposes our wills. This is the potential for instant aggravation that seems to lie on the floor of our minds, needing to be subdued or overcome in order to deal with a disagreeable situation more objectively. We are usually out of touch with this negative reaction within us, for the ebb and flow of life situations doesn't usually stir us that deeply. But occasionally we find ourselves overreacting and bordering on being out of control with our anger. We may wonder where such a feeling came from or what originated such a reaction. The working of repressed hostilities are subtle and often elude our perception.

To understand this underlying level of hostility in our minds, we need to realize we are an accumulation of all the experiences we have ever had. In our memory bank, whether we can actually recall the details or not, are experiences dating back into early childhood. The unconscious aspects of our mind have no awareness of the passing of time; memories are filed more by category of feeling than by chronological dating.

In childhood, or at sometime since, we may have been furious over not getting something we expected — perhaps a promise was broken, or some injustice occurred, or we were rejected or humiliated. At that time we buried these feelings and tried to forget them, for there seemed to be no other resolution to our problem. Yet, though we repressed them, they are still with us, influencing our present behavior, and we have dedicated energy on an unconscious level to keeping those memories out of awareness. We do not usually sense those original feelings in a specific way, but more or less in a generalized manner. When they begin to erupt again into our thinking, we may become anxious, almost paralyzed with fear.

Gordon said, "At times I feel so full of rage I am afraid of my own feelings. I know I could destroy everything in sight if I let loose. I have to keep myself under control!"

Myrna explained a similar rage. "I'm always angry at something," she said. "I know I am not always feeling angry, for I have other feelings too, but as soon as the other feelings are quieted, I am angry. I keep wanting to fight something, but I don't know what it is."

Claude remarked, "The frustrations at work get me down. By the time I get home at six for dinner and an evening with my family, I am so filled with rage I have held in all day that I can hardly be civil to the ones I love. When I stop to think it over, I know that much bad didn't happen during the day. I shouldn't be so mad. I guess I am just an angry person deep inside."

Effie, a housewife, complained of yelling at her children over trivialities. "I can't get over how angry I get with my kids. They have a way of setting me off. I'm like a charge of dynamite inside, and they light my fuse quicker than anything."

Each person, whether he has experienced spiritual conversion or not, has some degree of hostile rage within. He has a potential for being angry, and this potential is more apparent on certain occasions than at other times.

We usually manage to keep such inner feelings of rage fairly well suppressed. Days may go by with scarcely an indication of our adverse, regressive disposition, but the potential is there from early childhood whether or not we are immediately aware. Those who seem to maintain a good control of this inner, negative antagonism are considered well adjusted. We tend to rate people who have weaker controls as immature or neurotic.

Selfism in the Christian's Thinking

As we have mentioned in earlier chapters, not only do we tend habitually to be enraged when things don't go our way, but we also resent deeply situations that make us feel rejected, frustrated, or humiliated. In these kinds of situations, we are threatened with the sensation of being nobody, and our instinctive reaction to such a loss of self-identity is anger.

After spiritual conversion, these godless, self-centered immaturities remain on the floor of the mind in forgotten memories. They emerge at times to find expression in our conduct as we act out the effects of them on our thinking. Our spiritual regeneration gives us a totally new sense of being somebody in the grace of God, but the experience does not automatically erase memories of a lifetime or immediately change a person's life style. Motivations are changed, but habits need to be overcome.

The Bible clearly indicates that spiritual growth is related to dealing with ungodly impulses. For instance, "Set your affection on things above, not on things on the earth. . . . Mortify your members which are upon the earth; fornication, uncleanness, . . . covetousness: . . . put off all these; anger, wrath, malice. . . .Lie not one to another, seeing that ye have put off the old man with his deeds; and have put on the new man, which is renewed in knowledge after the image of him that created him'' (Col. 3:1-10).

We naturally want to do the will of God after we are converted, for His Spirit is within, claiming and using the life committed to Him. But we all have an undertow toward our unconverted ways of thinking. ''For God, who commanded the light to shine out of darkness, hath shined in our hearts, to give the light of the knowledge of the glory of God in the face of Jesus Christ. But we have this treasure in earthen vessels, that the excellency of the power may be of God, and not of us'' (2 Cor. 4:6,7). We naturally desire to know God better and His Word more completely and to have the wisdom to apply divine truth in daily situations. We want to love people and to trust in the goodness of life. We want to be used of God in being helpful to others who do not know the good news of this wonderful new sense of self-identity in Christ.

Despite these noble aspirations, we find other desires and impulses still plaguing our minds at various times. These drives we know are ungodly and are derived from the unconscious stratum of hostility that sponsors our tendency toward selfism. This hostile stratum makes us rebel at authority and resist being in total submission to the governing control of God. This is the area in our minds that is vulnerable to satanic influence, for it is rebellious to God's sovereignty and fearful of His punishment.

Regardless of how strongly and sincerely we may endeavor to achieve the will of God in one set of circumstances, we are vulnerable to opposite desires under different circumstances. The polarity within us to do right at one time is neutralized or canceled by an opposite polarity within our minds at another time. We wonder why it is possible to have such a strong motivation and commitment to do the will of God and yet be tempted so easily to sin, when all that happens is a change of setting on the stage of life. The power of temptation to entice is related directly to the unresolved polarity toward rebelling against authority. This rebellion is sponsored by our hostile memories.

This problem puzzles many Christians, but the Bible speaks plainly of the conflict, and it is within the mind of Christians. ''For that which I do I allow not: for what I would, that do I not; but what I hate, that do I. If then I do that which I would not, I consent unto the law that it is good. Now then it is no more I that do it, but sin that dwelleth in me. . . . I find then a law, that, when I would do good, evil is present with me. For I delight in the law of God after the inward man: But I see another law in my members, warring against the law of my mind, and bringing me into captivity to the law of sin which is in my members'' (Rom. 7:15-17,21-23).

People who have not experienced spiritual conversion have inner conflicts, but they are not of this nature, for they have not made a commitment of themselves to God. This passage indicates the conflict between our sincere desire to obey the instruction of the Word of God and our habitual style of behaving according to patterns of self-determination where selfism dominates the mind. Theologically this conflict is regarded as the antagonism between the two natures of the Christian: the flesh and the Spirit.

The conflict is actually between the forces of good and the forces of evil that seek to dominate the will of the child of God. We identify with both. We yield to one side or to the other. ''Do not yield your members to sin as instruments of wickedness, but yield yourselves to God as men who have been brought from death to life, and your members to God as instruments of righteousness'' (Rom. 6:13 RSV; cf. 16,19).

The Christian has a choice between yielding to his old, unconverted ways of selfism, or he can yield to his spiritual resources in Christ-centered thinking.

The Undertow of Selfism Has Historical Roots

Before we experience spiritual conversion, we usually are conscious only of ourselves and others and the factors which help us gain our objectives. It is not until after we have experienced a personal relationship with God through Jesus Christ that we become aware that the gigantic conflict of the ages between Christ and Satan is staged in the drama of human lives and that we hold a deciding factor between the forces of righteousness and the forces of evil as we yield ourselves to do what is right or to do what is wrong. We find that our desires and insecurities, our struggles with circumstances, our inner conflicts form the arena for determining whether Christ or Satan shall have the victory in that moment of time.

We read, ''Be strong in the Lord and in the strength of his might. Put on the whole armor of God, that you may be able to stand against the wiles of the devil. For we are not contending against flesh and blood, but against principalities, against the powers, against the world rulers of this present darkness, against the spiritual hosts of wickedness in the heavenly places. Therefore take the whole armor of God, that you may be able to withstand in the evil day, and having done all, to stand'' (Eph. 6:10-12 RSV).

As we commit ourselves to God and arm ourselves with the awareness of spiritual virtues (see Eph. 6:13-18), we defeat the efforts of Satan to thwart the control of God in our lives. On the other hand, if we neglect to make ourselves aware of spiritual values from God's Word and return to the philosophies of selfism, we will be deceived into believing we are right when we are not. We will be likely to take the divine truth we know and twist it to support our grasping for immediate gratification of our desires. We will try to employ God in the service of our self-determinism instead of submitting to God even when it means waiting or deprivation. Paul said, "I feel a divine jealousy for you, for I betrothed you to Christ to present you as a pure bride to her one husband. But I am afraid that as the serpent deceived Eve by his cunning, your thoughts will be led astray from a sincere and pure devotion to Christ" (2 Cor. 11:3 RSV).

It is logical that Satan should choose to nullify the grace of God in the relationship between God and man in his efforts to overthrow God. God keeps drawing us to Himself because He loves us, and Satan keeps drawing us away by enticing us through self-determinism to do as we please regardless of the will of God.

We must realize that Satan's temptations usually relate to man's sense of self-identity. The ultimate in inner security is to rest in the equation *God + Me = a Whole Person*. Satan tempts us in various ways to return to self-verification as a means of feeling we are somebody. When we depend upon selfism and self-verification as our means of self-identity, God's grace is momentarily nullified in our thinking, and Satan has a victory. This is the undertow, and we revoke that undertow when we by faith return to our simple, childlike faith in God and His grace for our sense of being somebody. "I know who I am," we may tell ourselves. "I belong to Jesus. What others think of me does not make me a person; I am a person because God loves me and has accepted me."

The Exemplary Overcomer

Man was created in the image of God and designed to actualize the supreme attributes of God in a space-time context of life. Satan attacks God in the affairs of human life. God sent His Son to be born into this space-time context, "made of a woman" (Gal. 4:4), in order to nullify by His life, death, and resurrection the works of Satan. "We see Jesus, who was made a little lower than the angels for the suffering of death, crowned with glory and honor; that he by the grace of God should taste death for every man. . . . Forasmuch then as the children are partakers of flesh and blood, he also himself likewise took part of the same; that through death he might destroy him that had the power of death, that is, the devil; and deliver them who through fear of death were all their lifetime subject to bondage. . . . Wherefore in all things it behoved him to be made like unto his brethren, that he might be a merciful and faithful high priest in things pertaining to God, to make reconciliation for the sins of the people. For in that he himself hath suffered being tempted, he is able to succour them that are tempted'' (Heb. 2:9, 14-18).

Our inner conflicts have eternal implications. Our understanding of biblical truth reveals that we are intimately involved with far greater issues in our decisions than just our own immediate gratification and welfare. Paul the apostle was concerned that we know something about what we are doing in this conflict: ''Lest Satan should get an advantage of us: for we are not ignorant of his devices'' (2 Cor. 2:11). When we ignore the reality of Satan, we are obviously ignorant of his devices, and to be ignorant is to be vulnerable to his influence. We are taught by Jesus to pray, ''And deliver us from [the] evil [one]'' (Matt. 6:13). Jesus has overcome Satan, and He is our exemplary Overcomer. He is able to deliver us in times of temptation. ''Whatsoever is born of God overcometh the world: and this is the victory that overcometh the world, even our faith. Who is he that overcometh the world, but he that believeth that Jesus is the Son of God?'' (1 John 5:4,5).

We must bear in mind that the essential difference between godly and ungodly thinking is faith in God through Jesus Christ. Faith in God inspires obedience, and love for God motivates obedience. ''Faith without works is dead'' (James 2:20,26). ''If ye love me, keep my commandments'' (John 14:15). ''Whoso keepeth his word, in him verily is the love of God perfected'' (1 John 2:5). As we trust God and obey His Word in our hearts, our minds are polarized toward righteousness, and the Holy Spirit uses that polarization to give us the strength to resist temptation and to do what is right and good. ''Ye are of God, little children, and have overcome them: because greater is he that is in you, than he that is in the world'' (1 John 4:4). ''He that is in the world'' is Satan and all the forces of evil which are at work. Satan is called ''the prince of this world'' (John 12:31), ''the god of this world'' (2 Cor. 4:4), and ''the prince of the power of the air'' (Eph. 2:2).

Jesus has already conquered Satan and nullified his effectiveness. When we reckon ourselves to be dead to sinful temptation on the basis of His suffering for us on the cross, we identify with His suffering for the very evil we are tempted to commit. *This identification with Christ's death for us because of His love has a way of nullifying within us the influence of the rebellious, hostile stratum of our minds.* Having reckoned ourselves dead to sin (Rom. 6:11) by the crucifixion of Christ, we can identify with the resurrection victory of Christ and proceed to ''walk in newness of life'' (Rom. 6:4). We have overcome the temptation by identifying with the death and resurrection of Christ.

But let us remember that *the source of our temptation is the underlying rebellious hostile stratum within our own minds which makes the opportunity to sin appealing.* Thus in Christ, our exemplary Overcomer, we have submitted to a competent defense against the "wiles of the devil." By faith we have defeated the undertow toward selfism which continually works from the repressed memories to short-circuit our good intentions and noble ambitions to do the will of God. "I have been crucified with Christ; it is no longer I who live, but Christ who lives in me; and the life I now live in the flesh I live by faith in the Son of God, who loved me and gave himself for me" (Gal. 2:20 RSV).

Selfism Causes Many Emotional Insecurities

Since the underlying repressed hostile stratum in our minds inspires selfism, and since this stratum is the level on which Satan has access to our wills to lead us to sin against God and His sovereign authority, we who are Christian especially have a source of emotional insecurity that needs to be understood and overcome. We "delight in the law of God after the inward man," for we sincerely want to do the will of God. But as Paul explained, "I see another law in my members, warring against the law of my mind, and bringing me into captivity to the law of sin which is in my members" (Rom. 7:22,23). This internal warfare of the Christian is our continual struggle to overcome the undertow to selfism and the anxieties which this conflict creates within us.

Temptation seems to come toward us from two directions. One is the immediate opportunity to do something in violation of God's Word. The other is the desire to express or act out unacceptable feelings that bombard us from within, such as hostility or guilt or fear. Actually both are the same, but because of our tendency to project our inner conflicts onto our environment, we feel we are being tempted from without. "He makes me angry," we say, for example.

In reality, as the Bible explains in James 1:13-15, our temptations generate within our own desires. We have this rebellious stratum which influences our wills to act out in defiance of divine law to gain a certain immediate gratification. When we have an unacceptable feeling, we want to express it. When we have to restrain ourselves from either indulging in immediate gratification or expressing an unwanted feeling, we have an internal conflict and feel insecure.

Paul recognized the terrifying threat of this conflict: "O

wretched man that I am! who shall deliver me from the body of this death?'' Then he explained the source of relief from the insecurity. "I thank God through Jesus Christ our Lord. So then with the mind I myself serve the law of God; but with the flesh the law of sin. There is therefore now no condemnation to them which are in Christ Jesus, who walk not after the flesh [i.e., selfism] but after the Spirit'' (Rom. 7:24 - 8:1).

Trusting in Christ does several important things for us. It restores our sense of being somebody, our self-identity. It nullifies the appeal of temptation to sin, because we identify with His suffering for that sin before we indulge. It provides a ''no-condemnation'' plane of reference for our thinking so that we can concentrate our energies on overcoming the problems of life without being hindered by a sense of guilt or a need to compensate for past mistakes and sins. We have recognized that we are never strong in ourselves; we are strong only as we relate to Jesus Christ and His Word by faith. We are sinless only as we identify with the Sinless One.

While the potential to sin never leaves us in this life — because the underlying rebellious, hostile stratum in our minds is never resolved — yet by faith we reckon ourselves to be dead indeed to sin, and alive to God through our Lord Jesus Christ (Rom. 6:11). Sin is never dead to us, but by faith we can be dead to its appeal for the present moment. This is the ''shield of faith, wherewith ye shall be able to quench all the fiery darts of the wicked [one]'' (Eph. 6:16).

As we practice this dimension of reality in our Christian living, we affirm our sense of being somebody to God and live with a self-concept that is intimately involved with the Absolute. Truly our hearts rejoice in gratitude as we experience His power to overcome within us our own emotional insecurities. As we overcome, we ''grow in grace, and in the knowledge of our Lord and Saviour Jesus Christ'' (2 Peter 3:18).

When Temptation Becomes Sinful

One issue needs to be clarified. When does a temptation begin to become sinful? Temptations involve thoughts and fantasies. Ideas themselves are just thoughts and come to our minds from various sources. We are not responsible for having ideas or fantasies, but there is a point at which we begin to be responsible for the ideas and fantasies that are contrary to God's Word, and at that point they do become sinful.

Our Lord ''was in all points tempted like as we are, yet without sin'' (Heb. 4:15). The record of our Lord's temptations (Matt. 4:1-11; Luke 4:1-13) indicates that He had thoughts inspired of the devil and contrary to God's Word. Jesus took the responsibility to contradict each idea with a reference to the Scriptures. He reasserted a profound allegiance to God and His Word.

As we have indicated, the source of our temptation lies in our own desires (James 1:14,15), which are in rebellion to governing authority. We can take the responsibility to dismiss the idea or fantasy on the basis of God's Word, or we can accept the idea and proceed to act upon it. When we have accepted the idea and begin making plans for fulfilling the fantasy, we have "conceived" the sinful idea, made it a part of us. We might change our minds at this point and abort the idea, or we can continue until we have actually done the deed, delivered ourselves of the conception.

To illustrate, we need to draw an imaginary line to represent the flow of thought from the first tempting *impulse* to the final sinful act. At the beginning of the line is the idea, the impulse. Next, in a split second of time is a *realization* of that impulse of fantasy, what the idea is about, perhaps some associations. The third point on that line is an *evaluation* of the idea as to whether it is acceptable or not, whether it is right or wrong. If the idea is not discarded here as unacceptable, but pondered and savored, it begins to enter into a fourth level of thinking called *planning for action*. The final point is the deed itself, the *action*.

Obviously points one, two, and three are the actual temptation, and points four and five are the areas of sinful thought and action. If we discard the idea after we have evaluated it, or even if we begin to savor the idea and start planning for action, then realize our peril and abort the idea, we have not sinned. Planning for action indicates a yielding to the temptation and accepting the fantasy as a goal for fulfillment; planning has a negative value much the same as the action itself.

Let us see how this works in a life situation. Jerry comes home from school for lunch, and his mother sends him to the store for a loaf of bread. While waiting to pay for the bread, he notices some bulk candy in a bin nearby. Jerry thinks, I wish I had some of that candy (*the impulse*). That is good candy and no one is looking (*the realization*). It is wrong, but I don't care (*evaluation*). I'll quickly take some (*planning*). I have it and I'll eat it on my way home. And he does (*the action*).

Suppose Jerry has decided to take the candy, but just as he reaches for a piece, a lady appears from nowhere. He clears his throat and pretends to be adjusting the sign on the basket. On the way home, he is angry, because he is frustrated. He doesn't have the candy, but he is a thief in his heart. His anger over disappointment indicates this.

Again, let us suppose that Jerry has evaluated the tempting idea and reasons, "It isn't very much, but it would be stealing just the same. I won't do it." He will leave the store knowing he has done what is right. He will probably have a good feeling about himself, though he is still hungry for the candy. He was tempted, but he did not sin.

If we change the story a little more and presume that Jerry berates himself on the way home after resisting the temptation — saying, "Why would I want to steal? I must be a very wicked person! I want to be a good person, so I must never want to do wrong things" — we observe a very confused boy. He would be trying to stop a thought before it occurs by blaming himself for having a natural desire. Some people try to do this, and they become depressed, confused, and unproductive.

Christ has redeemed us from feeling responsible for having impulses to lie, to steal, to kill, to commit adultery, to covet, etc. "God was in Christ, reconciling the world unto himself" (2 Cor. 5:19). We are not sinful because we have sinful ideas; we are sinful when we *yield* ourselves to unrighteousness. This is one of the implications of the "no-condemnation" plane of reference for thinking. Being redeemed, we can concentrate on overcoming temptation as stated above.

Three Types of Pleasure Lure to Selfism

A striking passage in 1 John 2:15-17 describes three ways we are lured away from doing the will of God to function under the domination of selfism. Each of these three relates to a stage in our emotional development as children.

"Love not the world, neither the things that are in the world. If any man love the world, the love of the Father is not in him. For all that is in the world, the lust of the flesh, and the lust of the eyes, and the pride of life, is not of the Father, but is of the world. And the world passeth away, and the lust thereof: but he that doeth the will of God abideth for ever."

1. *"Lust of the flesh" is a desire for sensual pleasure.* When we love a desire, we make the fulfillment of that desire our goal in life. Sensual pleasure is a natural desire and ordained of God. It relates to some of our earliest experiences in childhood. It is sinful only when indulged in a way unauthorized by God. Eve, for example, could have eaten of any other tree in the garden, but she chose to eat the forbidden fruit because she saw that it was "good for food." Christ was tempted to make bread of stones because He was hungry, but He decided to endure His hunger until God authorized the pleasure of eating.

God does not condemn the natural sexual impulse, but He does say, "Thou shalt not commit adultery" (Exod. 20:14). Opportunity for sexual pleasure may be available in a variety of situations, but God has commanded that we limit our sexual pleasure to marriage, where there is a commitment and an appropriate sense of responsibility.

Like small children trying to circumvent our parents' government, we as adults tend to compromise with what we know to be right. "A little won't hurt," we often reason within ourselves. We do not want to be ignorant of what others are experiencing. We want the knowledge of good and evil as long as we do not hurt ourselves in obtaining it. The most damaging thing we might do to ourselves lies in the amount of sin we tolerate and excuse ourselves for enjoying. If we can swear a little, we soon find ourselves being profane. If we permit a little violation of a strict diet, we soon discover we are off our diet completely. If we excuse ourselves for a deliberate flirtation with the opposite sex, a little indulgence in erotic pleasure outside marriage, it very likely will not be long before we are involved in an affair. If we excuse a little dishonesty, we may discover soon we are lying or cheating almost without conviction.

"Be sober, be vigilant; because your adversary the devil, as a roaring lion, walketh about, seeking whom he may devour: whom resist stedfast in the faith" (1 Peter 5:8,9). Returning to selfism by way of yielding to the appeal of unauthorized sensual pleasure is a shortcut to emotional insecurity and an inadequate self-concept. We have fragmented ourselves within and lost our awareness of being somebody to God.

2. *"Lust of the eyes"* *is a desire for acquisitional pleasure.* We behold the environment with our eyes, and we want to possess many of the things we see. We love to possess things, and this makes the acquisition of possessions a goal in life.

There is also a pseudo-security factor in the ownership of wealth. We can devote our attention to objects and avoid being hurt by close relationships with people. We can more or less buy friendships and be able to make life easier for ourselves by employing others to do our work. Many don't stop to think, however, about the increased anxiety factor in the ownership of wealth; we have to protect ourselves from losing what we own. Material possessions are a stewardship awarded us by God, and our use of things must always be with relation to their utility value, not to their security potential.

Jesus warned us that the "deceitfulness of riches" would "choke the word" (Matt. 13:22), and God's Word would not become fruitful in our lives. There is a selfism which takes over the mind when we love things, and this creates many anxieties which cause us to redouble our efforts to gain more things and to protect what we have. Thus we spiral away from our love for God and the sense of being somebody to Him. We return to the inadequate self-concept of selfism. John the apostle warned, "Little children, keep yourself from idols" (1 John 5:21).

Acquisitional pleasure lured Eve in the Garden to eat the forbidden fruit. "It was pleasant to the eyes, . . . she took of the fruit . . . and did eat" (Gen. 3:6). It would be absurd for Satan to try to tempt Jesus with some earthly possession, for he knew that "by him were all things created" (Col. 1:16). He tempted Christ by suggesting He expose Himself to danger so that old friends from heaven, the angels, who before His incarnation served him night and day, might come to his rescue (Matt. 4:6). The luring power of acquisitional pleasure is most subtle, and often used by Satan to distract us from doing the will of God.

3. *"The pride of life" is a recognitional pleasure.* This is a desire to be important, to be admired by others as someone who is great. We enjoy feeling superior. This is the pride of life and a key to selfism.

Eve was tempted at this point by the suggestion that she would be as wise as God, knowing good and evil. Christ was tempted in His third temptation to a pride factor. Satan promised He would be ruler of all the kingdoms of the world if He would but bow down and worship him. Jesus remained in the will of God by skillfully using the Word of God.

To make status values a love object is to step out of the will of God, for God is basically our only source of a secure sense of being somebody. The pride of life is an attempt to feel like somebody without relying upon God or incorporating Him in our thinking.

If we do receive recognition for some excellency in this life, it is because God has allowed it. When we receive praise, we can overcome the pride factor by being truly thankful to God that He has been effective in our lives. When we do this, we can receive praise without selfism.

The pride of life also is subtle, for it is related directly to our tendency to defend against inferiority. It opens the way to greater insecurities and anxieties, for whatever excellence we might have achieved at one time must be maintained or surpassed. Someone else will remove us from our pinnacle of glory if we don't defend it by becoming greater.

Faith in God Revokes the Undertow of Selfism .

Faith in God erases the basic cause for the anxiety that is the dynamic force in selfism.

Since God created man in His image and for His glory, we can assume that God never intended for man to function without a constant awareness of a vital relationship with Himself. Remember, the image only has meaning because of the object; the two always go together. "Pray without ceasing" (1 Thess. 5:17).

Selfism, founded in self-centeredness, then, is the natural result of man's innate need to relate to God, though man may have no immediate awareness of that need. *Selfism is our adaptive compensation for the anxiety we feel in our sense of aloneness while coping with life without God.* In this aloneness we have no certain sense of being somebody, no secure self-concept; selfism is our natural reaction to that missing spiritual element in our thinking.

Faith in God restores the missing sense of being somebody and of being united to the sovereign, loving, absolute God. Faith in God gives us a perspective in life that is related to eternal processes and values. We are anchored into God's great scheme of things in the minute details of everyday happenings. At the same time we face the unrelenting demands in our circumstances from without and have to cope with the strong, unpredictable drives from within. Faith in God quiets anxieties about all these things; by faith we discover "peace with God" (Rom. 5:1), and this lays the foundation for the "peace of God" (Col. 3:15) to reign in our thinking.

Jesus said, "Peace I leave with you, my peace I give unto you: not as the world giveth, give I unto you. Let not your heart be troubled, neither let it be afraid" (John 14:27). As we rest in the biblical truths which reaffirm our sense of being somebody to God, we have a self-concept that not only is adequate for daily living, but is gilded with the ideal and the perfect. Our sense of perfection is only by identification with the Perfect One; we never attain a perfection in this life on which we can repose and stop growing. We defeat the undertow of selfism by faith in the Word of God, and we overcome all the insecurities and anxieties that the domination of selfism produces as we submit ourselves to God because He loves us.

The risen Christ said just before He ascended to heaven, "All power is given unto me in heaven and in earth. . . . And lo, I am with you alway, even unto the end of the world" (Matt. 28:18,20). In our walk of faith, our separation anxiety is fundamentally ended. He is with us at all times whether or not we are immediately aware of His presence. He says, "Have no anxiety about anything, but in everything by prayer and supplication with thanksgiving let your requests be made known to God. And the peace of God, which passes all understanding, will keep your hearts and minds in Christ Jesus" (Phil. 4:6,7 RSV).

We are reassured in our walk of faith by this timeless truth:

"Thou wilt keep him in perfect peace, whose mind is stayed on thee: because he trusteth in thee. Trust in the Lord for ever: for in the LORD JEHOVAH is everlasting strength" (Isa. 26:3,4).

18

Perfect Your New Self-Concept

To be alive means to grow. There is no zenith in Christian maturation. The more we grow, the more we are capable of growing; life is ever-expanding. Though with the passing of the years our physical energies plateau and decline, there is no point, regardless of how infirm we might be, at which we can think of being as spiritually or as emotionally mature as we need to be.

The Bible says God's Word is the source of spiritual growth. "Laying aside all malice, and all guile, and hypocrisies, and envies, and all evil speakings, as newborn babes, desire the sincere milk of the word, that ye may grow thereby: If so be that ye have tasted that the Lord is gracious" (1 Peter 2:1-3). Indeed, we who are "in Christ" have tasted of the kindness of the Lord. Now we need to feed on the Word and grow to become more mature emotionally and spiritually.

There is a sense in which we work diligently to achieve a more perfect self-concept. We are responsible to God for how we implement His Word in our lives. Yet there is another sense in which God works in us who are His children to motivate us to accept this responsibility and to yield to His will in all things. On the one hand, we are told to "grow in grace, and in the knowledge of our Lord and Saviour Jesus Christ" (2 Peter 3:18). On the other hand, we are told that "we are his workmanship, created in Christ Jesus unto good works'' (Eph. 2:10), and ''it is God which worketh in you both to will and to do of his good pleasure'' (Phil. 2:13). The growth of the Christian is a mutual working together between God and man, allowing Him to work in and through us and at the same time doing our best to work with Him and for Him.

In John 15 God uses the analogy of the farmer and his vineyard. He prunes and dresses His vineyard that it might bear more and more fruit. Our part as His vineyard is to abide in Him as the branch abides in the vine; His part is to prune and care for us so that He can manifest Himself through us in the effectiveness of our lives.

An analogy I frequently use in describing emotional and spiritual growth is climbing a ladder. Climbing is a process of taking hold and of letting go. As we ascend, we must release as many steps as we take hold of; for every step we climb, we leave a step we once depended upon.

In emotional and spiritual growth, we seize new understanding of truth and gain insight regarding its application. On the other hand, new truth implies that the old has outlived its usefulness; we must release old ways of thinking in which we found a measure of security. This involves voluntary effort on our part, for we have to trust the new step we are about to take.

Frequently Review the Basic Identity Equation

When we begin to feel uncertain while climbing a ladder, we look down at the base and up to the top to reaffirm that we are secure. In the same way, we are instructed to reaffirm our spiritual securities (2 Peter 1:10) to remind ourselves of our base and our destiny. ''As ye have therefore received Christ Jesus the Lord, so walk ye in him: rooted and built up in him, and stablished in the faith'' (Col. 2:6,7). Baptism, administered once, symbolizes our entrance into the ''body of Christ'' (1 Cor. 12:13; Eph. 4:5). The Lord's Supper, which is repeated often, symbolizes our continual dependence upon Christ's atonement for relationship with God and for an eternal destiny. ''As often as ye eat this bread, and drink of this cup, ye do shew the Lord's death till he come'' (1 Cor. 11:26). In partaking of the Lord's Supper we symbolize our continual need to assimilate Christ into our ways of living, ''partakers of the divine nature'' (2 Peter 1:4).

So it is with the growth of our new self-concept. We need to return repeatedly to the basic identity equation: *God + Me = a Whole Person*. In doing this we associate each element of our self-concept — belongingness, worthiness, and competence — with one member of the blessed Trinity.

We remind ourselves that we are somebody to the Father, for He has accepted us in His Family as one of His own children (Rom. 8:14-16). We are reminded of our absolute sense of belongingness in our relationship with the Father (Eph. 1:6).

We are somebody to the Son because He died for us personally. No one took His life; He laid it down for us because He wanted to (John 10:18). "Looking unto Jesus the author and finisher of our faith; who for the joy set before him endured the cross, despising the shame, and is set down at the right hand of the throne of God" (Heb. 12:2). "Who his own self bare our sins in his own body on the tree, that we, being dead to sins, should live unto righteousness: by whose stripes ye were healed" (1 Peter 2:24). We can reckon ourselves dead to our selfism, our sin which makes us feel like a nobody, because He bore it on the cross! We are healed of our identity deficiency. We simply have to accept the new identity we have in Him.

We have an absolute sense of worthiness in Christ. He provides us a no-condemnation plane of reference for thinking.

We are somebody to the Holy Spirit because He is with us and in us, managing our life situations. "No temptation has overtaken you that is not common to man. God is faithful, and he will not let you be tempted beyond your strength, but with the temptation will also provide the way of escape, that you may be able to endure it" (1 Cor. 10:13 RSV). The Holy Spirit is God ministering to us in our daily life problems and relationships. "We are more than conquerors through him that loved us" (Rom. 8:37). We have an absolute sense of competence in our relationship with God the Holy Spirit.

Spiritual growth occurs as we work through our tendency to seek self-verification from human relationships and develop the ability to rely upon divine acceptance for our self-identity. This is "abiding in Christ" and it is the dynamic of Christian living (1 John 2:27,28).

Enlarge Your Capacity for Belongingness by Forgiving Others

In 1 Peter 2:1,2, we are told plainly to lay aside our hostilities if we are to grow as Christians. God's method of erasing hostility is forgiveness, dying to the need to avenge. It is easy to hold a grudge against someone who has offended, but God expects us to rid our minds of our anger feelings before they have a chance to be repressed (Eph.4:26).

Hostilities are anti-relationship feelings of antagonism. Such feelings interfere with our sensing belongingness or a wholesome concern for the welfare of others. Hostility polarizes the mind to be indifferent and to spurn others regardless of their needs. Such an attitude is negative and contradictory to the love of God. According to 1 John 4:20,21, if we truly loved God, we would love others also.

Harbored hostilities tend to fragment our thinking and quickly return us to the domination of selfism. Feelings are always a part of ourselves, regardless of whether they are love or hate feelings. When we have certain desires for vengeance committed to a variety of offenders, we are split internally as many times as we have been offended. Eventually we can become so divided internally in our antagonism toward people that we have little or no energy left for a positive, constructive attitude about anything, even ourselves. The whole world turns sour and we become cynical.

Furthermore, we not only fragment ourselves by our conflicts with others that we do not resolve, but we deprive ourselves of relationships we need. We depend increasingly upon negative interactions in which we have the illusion of putting others down for a sense of self-identity. Love is missing. When I was chaplain in a mental hospital, I observed unresolved hostility underlying most forms of mental illness.

The only way to erase these hostilities is by being forgiving of the offenders. The subject of what true forgiveness is was discussed at some length in Chapter 16. The emphasis we make here is that forgiving others opens the way for a new sense of inner wholeness and of growing in one's sense of belongingness. Being forgiving revitalizes our sense of being somebody to God, it lessens our fear of people, and it enlarges our capacity for belongingness.

"Forgiving one another, if any man have a quarrel against any: even as Christ forgave you, so also do ye" (Col. 3:13). We cannot presume to obey the first great commandment to love God with our total selves while we are at the same time violating the second great commandment to love our neighbor. On the other hand, we demonstrate our love for God in our readiness to forgive.

Hostility is a projective emotion; we project blame onto others with whom we are angry. When we project blame, we are not assuming our share of the responsibility for whatever happened that was wrong. This keeps us from introspecting and prevents our changing.

When God forgives us, He expects us to change. "Go and sin no more" is His injunction (John 5:14; 8:11). It is logical for Jesus to say, "If ye forgive not men their trespasses, neither will your heavenly Father forgive your trespasses" (Matt. 6:15). If we continue holding grudges after God has forgiven us, we will not change in our spirit toward others. It is the law of Christ that we love one another (John 15:12). God wants a loving relationship with us, and He wants us to have loving relationships with others.

If we have a grudge against someone, and he treats us with kindness instead of reacting with hostility, the anger we feel soon turns to guilt. God's Word admonishes, "Dearly beloved, avenge not yourselves, but rather give place unto wrath: for it is written, Vengeance is mine; I will repay, saith the Lord. Therefore if thine enemy hunger, feed him; if he thirst, give him drink: for in so doing thou shalt heap coals of fire on his head. Be not overcome of evil, but overcome evil with good" (Rom. 12:19-21).

Thus we see that the exercise of forgiving others is an essential element in our Christian growth and maturation. We enlarge our ability to sense belongingness with others as we cleanse our hearts from our desire to avenge ourselves and to punish offenders.

Enhance Your Capacity for Worthiness by Being Generous With Others

True generosity is hard to find in this mercenary world. Harboring grudges encourages one to be guarded and stingy with others. Forgiving others opens the way to being generous, for we begin to care for people when we cease to resent them. In being helpful, we increase our own sense of self-respect, which enhances our sense of worthiness.

You will recall that restored belongingness becomes the basis for a sense of worthiness. As the child feels forgiven by his loving parents and is restored in their good will, he senses a value and a feeling of virtue within himself. So it is with our heavenly Parent. We are united to Him by His grace in forgiving us our sins. In our daily walk we confess our sins and find a relief from guilt in His continued forgiveness (1 John 1:9). Jesus once told Peter, "He who has bathed does not need to wash, except for his feet, but he is clean all over" (John 13:10 RSV). As we experience daily cleansing from sin — having our feet washed, as it were, from the contamination of contact with the world — we sense a restored sense of belongingness as worthiness.

Jesus expects us to be forgiving of others "as God for Christ's sake hath forgiven you" (Eph. 4:32). In this way we share in the sufferings of Christ: "Ye are partakers of Christ's sufferings" (1 Peter 4:13). We not only partake of Christ's sufferings when we are persecuted for righteousness' sake, but also share by identifying with the other person's faults and forgiving him.

Forgiving others helps us to identify with Christ and His

love for us. Paul expressed a desire to share with Christ that might be our desire also: "That I may know him, and the power of his resurrection, and the fellowship of his sufferings, being made conformable unto his death" (Phil. 3:10).

As we are forgiving, we are filled with gratitude to Christ for forgiving us. A natural feeling of generosity results in which we want to share with those who are in need. When we love others, we are affectionately interested in their welfare, and this love is reinforced by the fact that Christ loves them as much as He loves us.

We consider ourselves His agents in sharing the goods He has entrusted to us with those who are in particular need. "Pure religion and undefiled before God and the Father is this, To visit the fatherless and widows in their affliction, and to keep himself unspotted from the world. . . . If a brother or a sister be naked, and destitute of daily food, and one of you say unto them, Depart in peace, be ye warmed and filled; notwithstanding ye give them not those things which are needful to the body; what doth it profit?" (James 1:27; 2:15,16). In our sharing generously because we are impressed with God's generosity with us and are inspired by His love to do so, "the love of God is shed abroad in our hearts by the Holy Ghost which is given unto us" (Rom. 5:5).

In an earlier chapter we mentioned greed as a form of hostility in which a person wants to extract all the good from another. Greed wants to contain enough so that he will never want again. The envious person hates anyone who possesses something he wants for himself. Both greed and envy are antagonistic to relationship. True generosity can occur only when a person has rid himself of these two negative feelings toward others.

Covetousness is the result of greed and envy working together. Covetousness is renounced in the Bible as a form of idolatry. "Mortify . . . covetousness, which is idolatry" (Col. 3:5). This means we are to reckon ourselves dead to the inclination to covet; put the feelings to death.

"Let your conversation [manner of living] be without covetousness; and be content with such things as ye have: for he hath said, I will never leave thee, nor forsake thee" (Heb. 13:5). Covetousness is related to acquisitional pleasure, which lures us to selfism. Refusing to allow these covetous feelings to possess us opens the way for true generosity in our relationships with others.

Further, when we forgive others, we disown the right to judge, punish, and reject them. The offender belongs to God, is loved by God, and is governed by God, even as we. In being generous with others, we disown our assumed right to control them by making them obligated to us. We give without expecting to receive something in return. Because we have found our sense of being special to Christ in His love, we are able to believe Him for the provision of our needs. We can sense the will of God in behalf of sharing what we have with others who are in need. This experience of caring for others and sharing with them according to the will of God enhances our sense of worthiness.

In experiencing true generosity, we have ceased loving things, and have restored our respect for others; they are elevated to the dignity of being persons with feelings like our own (cf. Luke 6:38; Acts 20:35; 2 Cor. 9:7).

Strengthen Your Sense of Competence by Honoring Others

We have noted how harboring grudges strangles our sense of belongingness, and how being tight and stingy inhibits our sense of worthiness. We will now turn our attention to noting how being critical of others limits our own ability to sense competence and how honoring others strengthens our sense of competence.

There are two ways of criticizing others: One way respects the person's sense of being somebody who has good intentions and capabilities and is constructive; the other way disregards the other person's feelings and is destructive of his self-esteem. It is this latter, destructive type we are concerned about. In being critical we are projecting our own sense of inferiority, telling others to change instead of dealing with our own sense of deficiency.

Envy and jealousy have subtle ways of motivating destructive criticism. These emotions express antagonism and hate. The one who has a desired object — skill, appearance, performance, or status — is envied by the less fortunate person. The one who seems loved by others is resented with jealousy by persons who do not feel so loved. When the envious or jealous person does not feel like attacking directly, he does so indirectly by being critical, sarcastic, and cynical. He seems to find a virtue for himself in being capable of discovering the faults of others, and he takes a peculiar pride in publicizing them. "Scorners delight in their scorning" (Prov. 1:22).

Constructive criticism usually offers a solution to the problem it points out. Destructive criticism never concerns itself with a solution, but leaves the person under attack with the feeling of being a bad, inferior nobody.

Pride or conceit is on the other side of feeling inferior. A person who seems conceited is trying unconsciously to divert his own attention from his feelings of inferiority. The practice of one is the denial of the other.

When we find ourselves critical of others, it is time to do some introspective thinking. A critical, impatient attitude with others is evidence that we are functioning in selfism and have drifted away from our self-identity in Christ. We may be harboring a grudge, or we may be resenting the inconveniences of our present circumstances, or we may be anxious about being a failure, or something else, but this indicates that we are in need of returning to our basic sense of being somebody in our relationship with God.

"Be clothed with humility: for God resisteth the proud, and giveth grace to the humble" (1 Peter 5:5). "Be kindly affectioned one to another with brotherly love; in honour preferring one another" (Rom. 12:10). Return to a sense of being peers with others by refreshing your sense of self-identity in God's grace.

Another subtle influence infests us at times. It is the competitive spirit in which others have to be defeated or put down to an inferior position for us to feel important. We may be asking God, like Peter, "What about this man?" (John 21:21 RSV). Jesus' reply is full of meaning: "If it is my will that he remain until I come, what is that to you? Follow me!" (John 21:22 RSV). We may feel at times as if God has favorites, that He does not care as much for us as for others. We also may feel we have to make a showing, become great, create a name for ourselves as someone who has achieved great things. This competitive drive can be insidious and self-deceiving.

When we have accepted the role in life God has seemingly designed for us, and we have determined to do our best to fulfill that role until He shall indicate clearly any changes, we will discover a contentment within that is premised upon faith in God and a loving relationship with Him. We will be free of selfism and truly able to take our place among others as one of them. We will be glad to honor others as we would like to be honored if we were in their situation. The fellowship with God that makes this attitude possible will expand our sense of competence.

Safeguard Against Selfism by Being Grateful

The Bible says, "In every thing give thanks: for this is the will of God in Christ concerning you" (1 Thess. 5:18). A grateful heart is always in the will of God if the feeling of gratitude is not in any way manipulative. This means that we truly feel grateful; we are not just trying to be thankful because we are supposed to be. We are not just trying to impress God by our attitude in order that He not withhold future blessings from us.

In every situation we can give thanks when we sense His love and care in it. We may not feel grateful *for* the experience, but we can indeed be grateful *in* the situation. We know He has permitted the happening, and He will lead us to glorify His name in the experience.

The key to being thankful *in* everything is to be thankful for Jesus Christ: "Thanks be unto God for his unspeakable gift" (2 Cor. 9:15). When we think of His love and His gift of salvation and what that means to our eternal destiny, and we identify with His suffering for us by sensing His abiding presence and patience with us in our instabilities, we will be very thankful.

When we feel truly thankful, we have given God all the importance we usually reserve for ourselves. He is honored as God in our hearts, and we are accepting with a sense of being responsible to Him the place of dependency in our relationship with Him. We cannot be self-centered and grateful at the same time. True gratitude arises from a commitment to Christ and at the same time realizes that He loves and cares.

False gratitude is manipulative and forced. When we find ourselves trying to be grateful, we are trying to force an emotion we do not actually feel. A few authorities have suggested that we should be grateful whether we feel that way or not, and after a while the gratitude will be felt. This might work, but I believe the best way to rediscover one's lost sense of thanksgiving is to return to the reality of our indebtedness to God's grace for everything we enjoy, even for life iself. When we think of His love and grace, His mercy and longsuffering, His gentleness and patience, we are usually over-whelmed with a sense of gratitude for our blessings.

Unresolved resentments keep us from the spirit of thanksgiving. Such hostilities sponsor a complaining, disgruntled, pessimistic, unhappy attitude. These negative feelings negate the sense of gratitude.

Guilt feelings rob us of gratitude. Self-condemnation, self-pity, and other negative feelings stifle a sense of thanksgiving.

In other words, we can be truly thankful only if we have overcome our selfism. "Let the peace of God rule in your hearts, to the which also ye are called in one body; and be ye thankful" (Col. 3:15).

True gratitude is the universal vitamin of spiritual and emotional growth and maturation. It glorifies God and is pleasing to Him. A thankful heart motivates a person to keep on growing and trying to improve in every way. It maintains an objective attitude in life.

True gratitude results from an all-out effort to obey the first great commandment to love the Lord our God with one's total self.

19

Manifest an Adequate Self-Concept

The question "What is the will of God?" has puzzled many persons on various occasions. God has taught me by His Word and by experience that it is impossible to do the will of God with our hands until we are in the will of God in our hearts.

The two great commandments — love God with your total self and love your neighbor as yourself — constitute in a capsule the will of God for our hearts. God wants relationships to be prime in our thinking, first our relationship with Him and then with others; then we will be able to discern the will of God for a specific situation. Our tendency has been, and always will be in this life, to begin with the situation to try to discern the will of God before trying to relate to God and others properly in our hearts. We tend to try to live by sight before we stop to make the effort to live by faith. Life's total reality begins with spiritual values. We confuse ourselves when we attempt to discern an appropriate course of action only from tangible factors.

When we function under the domination of selfism to any degree, we are not in a frame of mind to discern or appreciate realistically the attitudes, actions, and motives of others. We tend to desire approval, or we are already biased against the other's attitude. We may be defensive or antagonistic, or we may be manipulative and insensitive instead of realizing just what the situation actually is. To the degree we are controlled by selfism, we can expect to be confused and insensitive in our relationships.

When we rely on the equation *God* + *Me* = *a Whole Person* for our sense of being somebody, we manifest an adequate self-concept by our sensitivity to other's feelings and by our awareness of what is actually happening. We are able to function relatively free of hindering biases. We are able to think with our best faculties. Instead of wondering how we are going to cope with whatever is happening, we consider how God may be leading us to cope with the situation He has allowed us to experience.

We must keep in mind that the most important commodity in life is personal, loving relationships. The tangible aspects of the situation are ephemeral, lasting only a short time. The intangible feelings between people are more permanent, having lasting influence for good or evil.

The important consideration for us now is just this: Having determined our sense of self-identity in the grace of God which is entirely subjective, will we take the step of faith necessary to manifest that self-concept objectively in our relationships with people? Will we dare to act out the love we feel and get involved with people? "Love thy neighbor as thyself." The testimony of the Christian life is basically the quality of the self-concept a person has lived in his relationships. The testimony will only be glorifying to God if self-concept is derived from a relationship with God; it will tend to be superficial if derived from values of self-verification from people.

Two centers of concern are fundamental to any and all forms of Christian service if we are to do the will of God from the heart. One is this: Knowing you are somebody to God, manifest that adequate self-concept by loving others in ways that convince them they are truly loved. The other is: Knowing you are somebody to God, manifest that adequate self-concept by maintaining a healthy, biblical self-love. In other words, *our objective relationships with people give us a chance to live out the love we feel for God in our subjective relationship with Him.*

Three Ways to Love So That Love Is Felt

1. *Respect the other person's conscience.* Every person has a conscience, and he usually does what he believes is right. No one can stand feelings of guilt — they are equal to feeling like being a nobody. Regardless of how wrong or evil a person might be in his behavior, he has rationalized with his own conscience so that he does not really feel wrong. He somehow tries to justify his behavior, or he is ignorant of what is actually right.

To respect the other person's conscience means that we are

not critical or judgmental in our attitude. We may feel rightly constrained to point out his error, but our love for him as a person will motivate us to respect his need to feel like somebody to us even though he has done wrong. He will sense our love in our concern for his feelings about himself while we are informing him about something that could make him feel unacceptable to us. This concern, or respect, for his self-esteem gives him an island of inner security from which he can accept our criticism on the same level as if he had been his own critic. He does not have to be defensive to protect his sense of being somebody to us, so he is more likely to consider his fault more objectively and probably do something to correct it.

This is consistent with the way God deals with our sinful conduct. He reproves sinful behavior, but He loves the sinner and wants him to change. He does not condemn the sinner by disapproving him with insulting, demoralizing judgments about his person; He simply indicates the unacceptable conduct and holds the sinner responsible as a person to change. God does not condemn the sinner because of his sinful deeds, but because he did not exercise faith in God. "He that believeth on him is not condemned: but he that believeth not is condemned already, because he hath not believed in the name of the only begotten Son of God" (John 3:18). Sinful conduct reveals the lack of faith in God. "Faith without works is dead" (James 2:20). In other words, the only evidence of genuine faith in God is right conduct.

In our emotional and spiritual immaturity, we manifest a confusion in our roles with each other. Like children who make comparisons when they are corrected by their parents and complain that their siblings are also wrong and need punishment, we adults tend to take special notice of the faults of others we know and complain about how they are getting by with their evil. We project our own guilt, which we have repressed, onto others and criticize them the way we might feel we deserve criticism if we were in the mood to be self-critical.

God says that we are ambassadors (2 Cor. 5:20) for Him and not judges (Matt. 7:1-5). He consistently says, "Vengeance is mine; I will repay, saith the Lord" (Rom. 12:19). One of our functions as ambassadors is to seek people to be reconciled to God, which means our role in society is to incite people to believe in God and to be united to Him in a love relationship. We may feel led of God to point out their faults, but we are to do so in a way that does not violate God's love for the sinner. We always are to respect the other person's autonomy and personal responsibility to God, whether or not he is a Christian (Rom. 14:7-13).

When we love people, it is a challenge to our creative imagination to design ways of informing others of their need to change without doing a disservice to their conscience. The general principle in doing so is to assume the position of being *with* them empathically in their fault, not coming *at* or *against* them as though we were not just as capable of doing the same thing.

Jesus exemplifies this principle in the story of the woman at the well in Samaria (John 4:5-26). This was a sensitive, social situation in which Jesus was talking to an adulteress and He knew it, but He never talked down to her with disrespect. His request for a drink of water, His discussion of where men ought to worship and the instruction He gave her, His admission to being the Messiah were all done with respect for her dignity as a person. He respected her questions, though they revealed gross ignorance and incorrect knowledge. He knew she was a sinner, but he did not deny her sincerity in the knowledge she possessed.

When He pointed out her adultery, He did so in a way that did not belittle her. "Go, call thy husband and come hither," Jesus said. "The woman answered and said, I have no husband. Jesus said unto her, Thou hast well said, I have no husband: for thou hast had five husbands; and he whom thou now hast is not thy husband: in that saidst thou truly" (vv. 16-18).

By the time Jesus pointed to her adultery, He had already communicated a friendliness that gave her an island of inner security from which she could look at her own sinfulness objectively. He won her heart, and this incited her faith. The result was that a whole village was brought into personal encounter with the loving Son of God!

Jesus said, "A new commandment I give unto you, That ye love one another; as I have loved you, that ye also love one another" (John 13:34). Showing a friendly respect for the person who is wrong helps the person to face his responsibility to God for the wrong of which he is guilty. It is not our role to take the place of the other person's conscience and accuse him, but by obeying the law of Christ we are able to awaken his conscience so that he deals with his guilt before God. "If a man be overtaken in a fault, ye which are spiritual, restore such an one in the spirit of meekness; considering thyself, lest thou also be tempted. Bear ye one another's burdens, and so fulfil the law of Christ" (Gal. 6:1,2).

Our love for the person with a fault causes us to identify with him and his guilt. In that attitude of mind, we communicate a friendliness toward him as a person. This interest in his welfare helps him to be more objective in coping with his faults and overcoming them. We are God's ambassadors to help people to be reconciled to God.

2. *Respect the other person's volition.* Every person is autonomous and responsible for his own decisions. As autonomous individuals we must maintain a peer relationship with each other, for each person is responsible to God for his own self (Rom. 14:7-12).

True love for others respects their autonomous right of being decisive, even if they decide to oppose us. When we relate to others from this sense of peer value for others, they feel our love.

A common form of emotional immaturity is to be inappropriately dependent upon others to help us make decisions. We may use this dependency as a way of promoting relationships, for there is an aspect of forwarding honor to others by asking their advice. Another form of emotional immaturity is to be inappropriately inclined to give advice and to be directive with others. We may want to solve their problems and to protect them from hurting themselves by a bad decision; we presume we are doing it because we love them, but usually the person does not feel the love we intend. There are many ways people play the role of a dependent child or the authoritative parent in social relationships. These elements destroy the ideal peer values and create feelings of rejection, frustration, humiliation, and a great deal of hostility.

We evidence a lack of love for others when we become offended or slighted if they do not accept our attempt at telling them what we believe is right or best for them. We also display an unloving attitude when we reject a person as wrong if he does not agree with our point of view on a subject. Most of our convictions are based upon certain premises, and those premises are conditioned by our understanding of truth or facts. Often a slight change in understanding leads one to alter his conclusions considerably.

Each person must function from a set of values he is persuaded is correct, but he may not have understood the truth (as we believe we do) upon which those values are premised. If we are relying upon our relationship with Christ as our source of feeling like somebody, we are more inclined to hold a steady sense of accepting the person who contradicts us while attempting to discuss his point of view. We might be able to reconsider with him the truths, basic to his values and decisions, that cause the present difference. We will have contradicted our natural tendency to reject anyone who does not agree with us. We may also be helpful to the other person and to ourselves by reconsidering basic issues. We will have demonstrated our love for him and maintained a relationship in spite of our differences.

In Romans 14:3-23 we are told not to assume any authority over others to judge them or to exercise an administrative responsibility for them. When we do, we interfere with their basic autonomy and responsibility to God. We are told to respect one another as autonomous and responsible individuals even though our sense of what is right or wrong may differ slightly about matters of expedience. Each person is responsible to abide by his own conscience in his decisions.

3. *Respect the other person's feelings.* Everyone has natural emotions and should be able to express his feelings without feeling guilty or embarrassed for having the feelings. Everyone is more or less sensitive about how others think of his expression of emotion. We show love as we allow others to sense their natural feelings without being scolded, mocked, or punished. Others feel loved and accepted when they feel free to express emotions.

The story of Mary and Martha and Jesus after the death of Lazarus (John 11:19-35) is an example of accepting the feelings of others even when those feelings are not altogether appropriate. Martha and Mary both were blaming Jesus' delay for the death of their brother. "If thou hadst been here, my brother had not died," they each said (vv. 21,32). They were apparently disappointed and angry with Jesus for waiting so long after He was notified of Lazarus's illness. They had trusted Him, and He seemed to have failed them.

It is important to note that Jesus' love did not stifle the expression of their angry feelings even though they were directed at Him, the Son of God; neither did He make them feel guilty for being angry with their Lord. To Martha, He simply emphasized that He was the resurrection and the life and "he that believeth in me, though he were dead, yet shall he live" (v. 25). He asked Martha, "Believest thou this?" and Martha reaffirmed her faith in Him as the Christ the Son of God.

With Mary, Jesus did not contradict her feelings, but identified with them. "When Jesus therefore saw her weeping, and the Jews also weeping which came with her, he groaned in the spirit, and was troubled, and said, Where have ye laid him? They said unto him, Lord, come and see. Jesus wept" (vv. 33-35). He shares their grief and no doubt was troubled by their unbelief in Him. He expressed His own emotions openly and freely.

We learn much about showing love from this story. Feelings are an emotional reaction to an experience, to a way of understanding a situation. Jesus helped Martha by giving her a renewed faith in the nature of God, His goodness and power. This helped her to resolve her hostility. Jesus helped Mary by identifying with her feelings so that she did not feel so deserted and alone. Jesus either said something or did something which would give a reason for having different feelings. Feelings are like symptoms; Jesus dealt with the roots, or causes, of the feelings.

With some Christians, it is unthinkable to be angry with God. The anger emotion is a taboo. Yet they know they are actually angry because God seems to enjoy making them wait until the zero moment before answering their prayers, and occasionally He seems not to answer at all. Have we forgotten the story of Jonah? He was angry with God (Jonah 4:4) and all God said or did was ask a simple question, "Doest thou well to be angry?" God did not say, "Don't you be angry with me, I am your heavenly Father. You must show me proper respect!" No, God simply asked, "Is that really the way to cope with the situation?"

We show love to people by accepting whatever feelings they are having. In some cases we can direct their thinking to some timeless truth that may help them to obtain a better perspective. At other times we may feel it best to identify with their feelings so they will not feel so alone. And in a few cases we may need to expose the inappropriateness of their reaction. This may help them to grasp a better perspective and cope in a better way than to be throwing a temper tantrum like Jonah.

Again, in another situation, Jesus' disciples were fearful and grieving over the prediction that He was soon to die and leave them (John 13:31-33). Jesus told them not to be overcome by their feelings but to keep a great truth in mind, and this truth would help them to cope with their feelings and feel differently. "Let not your heart be troubled: ye believe in God, believe also in me" (John 14:1).

"Let not your heart be troubled" is very different from saying, "You should not be troubled." "Let not" means when the emotion comes, overcome it. "You should not" means you are wrong for having. No one can stop a feeling before it occurs or a thought before it happens. God never indicates that we should, but He does clearly tell us to deal with the emotions and ideas *after* they do occur.

Some Christians believe they should never be angry. They try to stifle the emotion. God's Word says, "Be ye angry, and sin not: let not the sun go down upon your wrath" (Eph. 4:26). "Put off all these; anger, wrath, malice . . . " (Col. 3:8). Deal with the emotion *after* if occurs; don't try to stop it from happening.

Hilda, for example, came into my counseling room seeking help for her depression. In her initial interview she expressed an intense sense of defeat: "I should not be here. If I were the kind of a Christian I should be, I would not be coming to a counselor. I am ashamed of myself."

"Why are you ashamed of being here?" I inquired.

"Christians are not supposed to be depressed," she replied. "It's an admission that you are not much of a Christian if you can't be happy and thankful, but I just can't anymore."

"You're supposed to be happy all the time if you're a good Christian?" I asked.

"Yes, of course. I used to be a good Christian, but lately I feel so dead inside. It doesn't do any good to pray. God doesn't seem to care. I guess I'm just a terrible person. I give up trying. I've decided to come to you for help, and if that doesn't work, I'm going to kill myself. I'm bad any way I go!"

Hilda got help, and God taught her an important lesson. It is no sin to be depressed, or to seek help when you are depressed. In fact, after she found relief, she concluded that God allowed her to come to the end of herself to teach her that her natural emotions must not be denied but accepted and dealt with.

Being Christians does not mean we have arrived at a state of perfection in which we will never again be disturbed or overcome or feel defeated. It is heresy to believe that Christians ever reach a state in this life in which they are always feeling victorious and never downhearted. The Bible teaches a very different message. We are imperfect, though Christians, and we are growing toward a more complete realization of the joy of the Lord within.

Everyone responds to love unless he has some reason not to. People are happy unless something is making them sad. Love tries to find the reason why a person is having unwanted emotions. In a nonjudgmental way, love helps a person find a reason to feel differently.

We usually consider 1 Corinthians 13 as the great love chapter in the Bible, and it is. But 1 John 4 is also a great love chapter. As 1 Corinthians 13 describes the nature and importance of love, 1 John 4 discusses the motivation and working of love.

1 John 4:12 ties the two great commandments together in a circular fashion to explain how love begets love and causes love to increase. "If we love one another, God dwelleth in us, and his love is perfected in us." The idea in this verse and in verse 20 is that as we love God whom we do not see, we love others more unconditionally whom we do see, and this experience reflects a growth of love for God which in turn perfects our love for others and for God.

Three Ways to Increase a Healthy Self-Love

"Love thy neighbor as thyself" implies that we show a

regard for others that is conditioned by the feelings we have for ourselves. This commandment not only tells us to practice the Golden Rule of loving others the way we would like to be loved, but strongly implies that we love others because we regard ourselves with positive self-esteem.

Many verses in the Scriptures imply self-love, but Ephesians 5:28,29 clearly states it as a normal and acceptable feeling: "He that loveth his wife loveth himself. For no man ever yet hated his own flesh; but nourisheth and cherisheth it, even as the Lord the church." There is a healthy self-love; we instinctively take care of ourselves and attend to our own welfare. The caution is, "I bid every one among you not to think of himself more highly than he ought to think, but to think with sober judgment" (Rom. 12:3 RSV). There is a legitimate self-esteem which we "ought to think."

With the mention of self-love, the Christian mind usually flashes a warning signal: pride is approaching! But we must have self-esteem in order to love others. Pride is one of our reactions when under the domination of selfism. There is a self-love that is not proud, but humble.

The fact of the matter is just this: Until we have overcome the idea that we are a nobody in the discovery that we are somebody to God and have stopped our need for self-verification, we are unable to love others with unconditional love. We cannot love others when we need them for self-verification. We can only *act* loving toward them — we cannot accept them apart from a transactional element in the relationship. A good self-concept is a result of a healthy self-love; when we have the new Christian self-concept, we are able to love others in an unconditional way that represents the love of God.

Knowing this fact, let us speak of three ways to improve our attitude toward ourselves.

1. *Keep our consciences clean.* We tend habitually to rationalize away our guilt feelings instead of confessing our sins to God and refreshing our dependence upon His grace for our sense of being somebody. Because we rationalize, we compromise with our own better judgment in a variety of situations, and this nullifies our sense of wholeness, which in turn causes us to return to the domination of selfism.

A clean conscience is necessary for a healthy prayer-life. "Hereby we know that we are of the truth, and shall assure our hearts before him. For if our heart condemn us, God is greater than our heart, and knoweth all things. Beloved, if our heart condemn us not, then have we confidence toward God. And whatsoever we ask, we receive of him, because we keep his commandments, and do those things that are pleasing in his sight'' (1 John 3:19-22).

When we compromise with our conscience by excusing ourselves for doing something we know is not right before God, we create a split within ourselves, and this split is a source of anxiety. We insult our own integrity when we tolerate known evil in our conduct, and we interfere with our sense of being somebody to God. He "that knoweth to do good, and doeth it not, to him it is sin" (James 4:17).

2. *Assume responsibility for our decisions.* An adult is a person able to be decisive and responsible for his decisions. We block our own emotional growth if we project our responsibilities to others. Children do this, and we are quick to correct them for it. "He made me do it" or "I can't help it" or "I didn't understand" are common ways of passing the blame or responsibility to others. Paul said, "When I was a child, I spake as a child, I understood as a child, I thought as a child: but when I became a man, I put away childish things" (1 Cor. 13:11).

It is not always easy to assume responsibility. The immature child in us often wants to dominate our attitude. For instance, we have an automobile accident. It is easy to retell the incident so as to exonerate ourselves from all blame. We commit a social blunder, and we quickly excuse ourselves by projecting blame instead of stating, "I am sorry" or "I meant no harm" or "I am not thinking clearly today."

It is a mark of emotional maturity for a person to be honest in his admission of responsibility for whatever he has done wrong. Honest admission is usually the easiest way out of the problem, for being deceitful always causes others to lose confidence in our reliability. Knowing we have been truthful and honest enhances our self-respect.

We enhance our self-love and sense of integrity by being responsible for our decisions regardless of the immediate consequences.

3. *Don't force our feelings to be acceptable.* Some people are so concerned about "What will they think?" that they hardly know what their true responses actually are in a given situation. When we force our feelings to conform to some assumed standard, we are in a sense being hypocritical. We are not true to ourselves.

"But," some people react by saying, "no one will like me if I let my feelings go." What they lack is knowledge of how to cope with their feelings when they do erupt. Many people are not aware that they can talk about their feelings without acting them out. For example, we can say, "This makes me angry" or "I am feeling moody today and depressed" or "I'm so high I feel a little out of control.'' In any of these three moods, the feelings are well contained, yet they are felt and acknowledged.

It is important to become aware of elementary feelings and to acknowledge them. This can strengthen one's sense of inner wholeness. If these feelings are anger, guilt, or fear, they need to be sensed as they really are. Sometimes this is difficult to do, for we are so accustomed to concealing certain of our feelings that we may not be able at first thought to recognize just how we do feel. Some of these feelings seem exceedingly infantile, and we are embarrassed to acknowledge them even to ourselves. With a little practice, almost anyone can get in touch with how he really feels in any situation. This helps release certain inhibitions and make a person more aware of himself.

From childhood, many people have felt throttled and subdued in the expression of feelings, especially certain feelings. For instance, some children receive little or no affection when small. They may want to be affectionate when older, but feel as though they never could be. A little specific practice being affectionate can be very helpful. Some people have been so overpowered by their childhood environment that they have withdrawn to themselves and do not dare have many feelings in response to what is happening. Psychotherapy is usually involved with rediscovering lost feeling responses to situations.

In acknowledging our true feelings, we are acknowledging an aspect of our true selves, and this makes us more aware of ourselves, more alive. In trying to recall certain unfamiliar feelings, there is a tendency to feel guilty — such as, we are bad if we feel certain ways. One should avoid making value judgments on his feelings. After all, they are only feelings.

Love itself is an emotion, and as we rediscover our true feelings, we can be more sure of our love for others. We will know if our love is only a pretense or if we truly mean it. We can also be more certain of ourselves in our decisions.

When we acknowledge our gamut of feelings, both bad and good, we become more sure of ourselves in our sense of being somebody to God. We are more aware of being a whole person.

20

Hope for Experiencing Your Ultimate Self

Man has an eternal destiny. What he is now he has ever been becoming, and where he is going he has always been headed.

We know we were created in the image of God. An image has no particular meaning in and of itself; its true meaning is found in the object it represents. God's identity is clearly stated, I AM THAT I AM (Exod. 3:14). Man's identity is, "I am because God is. I am made a living person" (cf. Gen. 2:7).

When our time comes to leave this body, we do not cease to exist. We who have received spiritual regeneration in Christ have a hope of a new body like His glorious body. "As we have borne the image of the earthy, we shall also bear the image of the heavenly" (1 Cor. 15:49). "Eye hath not seen, nor ear heard, neither have entered into the heart of man, the things which God hath prepared for them that love him. But God hath revealed them unto us by his Spirit" (1 Cor. 2:9,10).

By faith we received a new self-concept, a sense of being somebody to God in this life. By faith we will receive a new sense of being somebody to God when we enter the next life and see Him face to face (1 Cor. 13:12). Again and again in Scripture we are admonished to rely upon this living hope (Rom. 8:24; Eph. 1:18; Col. 1:5,27; Titus 2:13).

Our great problem is that we, an image, are determined to

235

establish our own sense of identity apart from the Object we repre-sent. Logically we should be confused about our self-identity, and we will continue to be until we are willing to recognize our spiritual relationship to God and live in His love and grace.

"Dust thou art"

Dust has no particular meaning or identity. But God moves in strange ways. "O the depth of the riches both of the wisdom and knowledge of God! how unsearchable are his judgments, and his ways past finding out! . . . For of him, and through him, and to him, are all things: to whom be glory for ever" (Rom. 11:33,36). "Base things of the world, and the things which are despised, hath God chosen, yea, and things which are not, to bring to nought things that are" (1 Cor. 1:28).

God took of the dust of the ground and formed man, then God breathed into man the breath of life and created man in His own image, a person. God gave man, by the very nature of his creation, an identity in a loving relationship with Himself. *God + Man = a Whole Person. God is the Person in the absolute and intangible; God plus man equals a whole person in the finite and tangible.*

When man sinned, he broke his relationship with God, so logically he lost his sense of identity. "In the sweat of thy face shalt thou eat bread, till thou return unto the ground" was God's pro-nouncement. "For out of it wast thou taken: for dust thou art, and unto dust shalt thou return" (Gen. 3:19). Having been taken from the dust and given an identity in a relationship with God, then having lost that fundamental relationship by disobedience, man naturally returns to the dust from which he was taken, a condition of no identity.

Dust symbolizes having no identity. Man comes from no identity and without God returns to no identity. "As by one man sin entered into the world, and death by sin; and so death passed upon all men, for that all have sinned" (Rom. 5:12). But God did not stop there; He sent His Son to be our Savior.

"As by the offence of one judgment came upon all men to condemnation; even so by the righteousness of one the free gift came upon all men unto justification of life. For as by one man's disobedi-ence many were made sinners, so by the obedience of one shall many be made righteous" (Rom. 5:18,19). The Bible consistently speaks of persons who are unbelievers as being "dead" (Eph. 2:1; 1 Tim. 5:6), and this is while they are physically alive. The Bible also consistently speaks of persons who believe in Jesus as being made "alive" with everlasting life (John 3:36; Rom. 6:13).

From this contrast we conclude that to be dead has three

applications, and to be alive also has three applications. Being either dead or alive applies to us physically or emotionally or spiritually.

Whether we are alive or dead physically is easily verified by vital life signs. To be alive or dead emotionally relates to whether one has a sense of self-identity; he is either somebody or a nobody in the way he feels about himself. To be alive or dead spiritually has to do with one's relationship with God. If a person believes in Jesus Christ as his personal Savior, he is declared by the Scriptures to be alive; if not, he is declared dead. "The wages of sin is death; but the gift of God is eternal life through Jesus Christ our Lord" (Rom. 6:23).

In Christ, that which is nothing becomes something. We are His new creation: "If any one is in Christ, he is a new creation; the old has passed away, behold the new has come. All this is from God, who through Christ reconciled us to himself" (2 Cor. 5:17,18 RSV).

We have an identity in Christ, and for that reason we are something and shall be raised from the dead. Our bodies will return to the dust, but will be called out of the grave and be renewed, resurrected into a body like Christ's, the first to return from the dead (see John 5:25,28,29; 1 Cor. 15:35-57; 2 Cor. 5:1-10; 1 Thess. 4:13-18). "And so shall we ever be with the Lord" (1 Thess. 4:17) is most comforting, for we will never be separated from Him again. Our identity is secure for eternity!

We Are His Workmanship

Not only are we His new creation; we are His workmanship. The purpose of God's working in us, molding us in our circumstances as we submit to Him, is to make us like Jesus Christ. "My little children, of whom I travail in birth again until Christ be formed in you . . . " (Gal. 4:19). God is supervising the circumstances of His children in order to develop their character. It is clearly stated that He is determined to make us Christlike. "We know that all things work together for good to them that love God, to them who are the called according to his purpose. For whom he did foreknow, he also did predestinate to be conformed to the image of his Son, that he might be the firstborn among many brethren" (Rom. 8:28,29).

Christ is our model Person. "Put on the new man, which is renewed in knowledge after the image of him that created him" (Col. 3:10). He had the perfect self-concept, and as we find our sense of being somebody in our relationship with Him, we tend to become more and more Christlike in our attitudes and behavior.

When We Become Complete

In our present life we aspire to being complete someday. Our imagination cannot fathom what our new life in Christ really is all about.

When we accepted Christ by faith, His atonement applied to us on a spiritual and emotional level. We became a new creation spiritually; we were quickened, made alive. We were raised spiritually with Him to walk in newness of life (Rom. 6:3,4). We have a new spiritual self-concept.

But life is only beginning for the Christian, regardless of how long he lives. The best is yet to come. Like the wine that was made from water at the wedding feast, we will declare when we get to heaven, "Lord, you've saved the best until now" (cf. John 2:10). In this life we have temporal fulfillment; in the next life we will enjoy eternal fulfillment.

The apostle John exclaimed, "Behold, what manner of love the Father hath bestowed upon us, that we should be called the sons of God. . . . Beloved, now are we the sons of God, and it doth not yet appear what we shall be: but we know that, when he shall appear, we shall be like him; for we shall see him as he is" (1 John 3:1,2). In other words, regardless of how joyful it is to be assured we are somebody to God now, it is not to be compared with the joys we will experience when Christ comes for His own, His church. We will be like Him, for we shall see Him as He is. What a fulfillment that will be!

It is important that this hope never die in our thinking. It helps to make all else worthwhile, and it inspires us to continue to improve. "And every man that hath this hope in him purifieth himself, even as he is pure" (1 John 3:3). This blessed hope inspires us to continue, to persevere, and to become more Christlike in the process.

Indeed, we can face life with a secure sense of being somebody because we are somebody to God. Indeed, the sensation of being somebody has only begun! We can live always and forever with an adequate self-concept.

notes

1. English, Horace B., and English, Ava C., *A Comprehensive Dictionary of Psychological and Psychoanalytical Terms* (New York: Longmans Green and Co., 1958), p. 299.

2. Sadler, William S., *Mental Mischief and Emotional Conflicts* (St. Louis: The C. V. Mosby Co., 1947), pp. 29,30.

3. Arieti, Silvano, ed., *American Handbook of Psychiatry* (New York: Basic Books, Inc., Publishers, 1959), p. 817.

4. Hinsie, Leland E., and Campbell, Robert J., *Psychiatric Dictionary,* 3rd ed. (New York: Oxford University Press, 1960), p. 392.

5. Segal, Hanna, *Introduction to the Word of Melanie Klein* (New York: Basic Books, Inc., Publishers, 1964).

6. Horney, Karen, *The Neurotic Personality of Our Time,* (New York: W.W. Norton and Co., Inc., 1964).

Those desiring to contact the author may write him at the following address:

Dr. Maurice Wagner
P.O. Box 88
Santa Margarita, CA 93453

subject index

scripture index